The U.S. War Crimes
Trial Program
in Germany, 1946-1955

Recent Titles in
Contributions in Military Studies

THE U.S. WAR CRIMES TRIAL PROGRAM IN GERMANY, 1946-1955

FRANK M. BUSCHER

CONTRIBUTIONS IN MILITARY STUDIES, NUMBER 86

Greenwood Press

New York • Westport, Connecticut • London

Library of Congress Cataloging-in-Publication Data

Buscher, Frank M.
 The U.S. war crimes trial program in Germany, 1946-1955 / Frank M.
Buscher.
    p.   cm. -- (Contributions in military studies, ISSN 0883-6884
; no. 86)
  Bibliography: p.
  Includes index.
  ISBN 0-313-26471-6 (lib. bdg. : alk. paper)
  1. War crime trials--Germany. 2. War crime trials--United States.
3. War criminals--Germany. I. Title. II. Series.
JX5434.B87   1989
341.6′9′0943--dc19   88-24706

British Library Cataloguing in Publication Data is available.

Library of Congress Catalog Card Number: 88-24706
ISBN: 0-313-26471-6
ISSN: 0883-6884

First published in 1989

Greenwood Press, Inc.
88 Post Road West, Westport, Connecticut 06881

Printed in the United States of America

The paper used in this book complies with the
Permanent Paper Standard issued by the National
Information Standards Organization (Z39.48-1984).

10 9 8 7 6 5 4 3 2 1

For my parents

Contents

Acknowledgments

This study would not have been possible without financial support and the help of many individuals. I am particularly grateful to the Smith family and the Arthur J. Schmitt Foundation whose generous fellowships enabled me to conduct research in both the United States and the Federal Republic of Germany and to spend many months writing this manuscript. I also wish to thank the Harry S. Truman Library Institute and Milwaukee German Fest Inc., for their research grants, which allowed me to work at the Harry S. Truman and Dwight D. Eisenhower presidential libraries. In addition, I am deeply indebted to Marquette University's Department of History for its continuous support over many years.

Many American and German archivists provided valuable research assistance. I am grateful to Amy Schmidt and David Pheipher at the Washington National Record Center; Erwin Mueller at the Harry S. Truman Library; Frau Ludden, Claus Wiedey and Dr. Pretsch at the *Politisches Archiv des Auswärtigen Amtes* in Bonn; Herrn Bauer, Dr. Henke and Dr. Werner at the *Bundesarchiv* in Koblenz; Herrn Gabriel at the *Bundeszwischenarchiv* in St. Augustin/Hangelar; and Frau Nelles at the *Parlamentarisches Archiv* in Bonn. I also wish to thank Kathryn Schiess and Ron Lutz of Marquette University's Computer Services Division as well as the staffs of Marquette University's Memorial Library and the Milwaukee Public Library.

My sincere gratitude goes out to Professors Athan G. Theoharis, Julius R. Ruff, Thomas E. Hachey, John W. Rooney and doctoral student Larry O. Woods, Jr., for the many hours they spent reading this study. Their suggestions have greatly improved the manuscript. I owe a particular debt to Professor J. Michael Phayer for his friendship, guidance, and encouragement during the entire project.

Finally, I would like to thank my parents, Irmgard and Günter Büscher, and my wife Terese for their love and their continuous support throughout the years.

Introduction

Although more than forty years have passed since the end of the Second World War, several recent events have shown that the topics of Nazi war crimes and Allied policy toward war criminals are still timely and of great interest to historians and the general public. Thus, in 1985 the Majdanek concentration camp trial before the *Landgericht* Düsseldorf ended after a duration of five and a half years. Perhaps the last large-scale proceeding against Nazi war criminals by a German court, this trial received much worldwide attention, particularly due to tasteless defense strategies and the fact that none of the defendants was positively identified after almost 300 witnesses had been questioned. A year later, after persistent efforts by Senator William Proxmire (D-Wisconsin), the United States Senate finally ratified the United Nations convention making genocide a violation of international law. During the same year, the Reagan administration extradited two suspected war criminals, Karl Linnas and John Demjanjuk, to the Soviet Union and Israel respectively so that they could stand trial for their wartime offenses. Most recently, the controversy surrounding the shady past of former U.N. Secretary General and current Austrian President Kurt Waldheim proved that war crimes remain a highly emotional issue. Last, the Vatican's decision to extend a formal state reception caused widespread controversy, even though Waldheim has never been formally charged with war crimes. These incidents underscore the continued strong interest in the Holocaust and other Nazi crimes as well as the punishment of the perpetrators.

For obvious reasons, the Trial of the Major War Criminals before the International Military Tribunal (IMT) in 1945 and 1946, usually referred to as the Nuremberg Trial, has drawn the most attention and has been the topic of numerous books and articles. Nuremberg featured the top Nazi leadership and included individuals like Hermann Goering and Joachim von Ribbentrop, almost household names in the immediate aftermath of the German surrender. For historians and legal scholars, the IMT proceedings were significant because of their precedent setting nature. The Nuremberg Trial was also the last time that the four major Allies jointly tried and sentenced Nazi war criminals. Already during the IMT, the Truman administration decided to conduct twelve additional war crimes trials in its zone of occupation before American military tribunals, without interference from the other Allies. During this part of the operation, appropriately named the "subsequent Nuremberg tribunals," a total of 185 defendants who had held important positions in the German High Command, the government ministries, industry, the *SS*, the *Gestapo* and other organizations stood trial at Nuremberg.

However, it was the United States Army which was most active in bringing war criminals to justice. Between 1944 and 1947, the Army prosecuted 1,672 individuals for violations of the laws of war before military courts under the jurisdiction of the theater commander. If one adds the Army's figures to those of the subsequent Nuremberg trials, the American war crimes trial program appears impressive. With two exceptions, it should be noted that most of the Army's trials remained obscure and little noticed, even though they dealt with almost 90 percent of all defendants in the American zone. They have also suffered from neglect on the part of historians and the public. The same is true regarding another aspect of the American war crimes program, the post-trial treatment of war criminals as a judicial and political problem, which is a focus of this study.

The American war crimes program served several purposes. The most obvious one is the punishment of the perpetrators. Second, U.S. officials intended to use the trials of war criminals as well as their post-trial treatment as an integral part of a policy to reorient the Germans. The proceedings, U.S. authorities thought, offered a great opportunity to demonstrate to the German public the evils of totalitarianism and the virtues of democracy since under the latter system even the worst defendants were granted the right to a fair trial and to sentence reviews. Third, U.S. officials hoped that the trials would result in a future code of conduct for governments and armies. Violators would have to fear prosecution and sentencing for their offenses by the international community. We already know that this last point was never accomplished. In the wars since World War II we have neither observed a marked improvement in the conduct of governments and armies nor have we noticed a decrease in the brutality of warfare, especially regarding its impact on civilian populations. In addition, since the 1940s there have been no trials of war criminals based on the Nuremberg precedent, although there have undoubtedly been a number of well-qualified candidates for prosecution in the recent past. I argue here that the U.S. program also failed to achieve its two other goals: to punish war criminals adequately and to democratize the Germans.

Why did the war crimes program fail? To answer this question, both the American and the German sides of the issue must be considered. The American commitment to the operation faded rather quickly due to constitutional questions and controversies surrounding the Malmédy and Buchenwald trials. These trials put those in charge of carrying out the program on the defensive. Consequently, between 1946 and early 1951 the Theater Judge Advocate Division of the Army's European Command and, beginning in 1949, the U.S. High Commission mainly concentrated on ensuring the program's integrity to avoid additional charges of misconduct and becoming the targets of attacks from critics. Starting in 1951, the focus of the U.S. effort was no longer on punishing war criminals and reeducating the German public but rather on preventing the war criminals problem from causing further criticism in both the United States and Germany of the American occupation. During this period American officials instituted clemency and sentence modification procedures which eventually allowed the complete dismantling of the war crimes operation without strong public opposition within the United States. This latter phase was closely connected to the 1950 decision to rearm the Federal Republic and the inception of negotiations to establish the European Defense Community.

Examining the German response is equally important to explain the program's failure. Education is a two-way process and it was certainly that way in occupied Germany.[1] If the war crimes program as an educational tool was to succeed, it required that the Germans be willing to learn about what had gone wrong in their recent past. Kurt P. Tauber has shown that German nationalism was by no means dead in the immediate post-war era.[2] Already in the fall of 1947 Hajo Holborn reported to the U.S. Department of State that the Germans tended to shrug off Nazi war crimes as an evil that was inherent in every foreign occupation of another country.[3] Thus, from the beginning it appeared questionable that the war crimes program as an educational device would lead to the democratization of the Germans and thus the destruction of their authoritarian and militaristic tendencies. Here, the historian faces a significant problem. With the exception of several U.S. High Commission surveys, we have little evidence as to what the average German thought. There are, nonetheless, numerous documents from the leaders of both the Catholic and Protestant churches, the government of Konrad Adenauer after 1949, almost all political parties, veterans and refugee organizations and groups of legal experts, which express strong opposition to the trials of war criminals. We must assume that sooner or later the opinions of these groups had a considerable impact. If Germany's political and moral leadership did not think that the German people were in need of reorientation, why should the average man in the street think otherwise?

Furthermore, few authors have studied what became of the convicted war criminals in the late 1940s and the 1950s.[4] Owing to the lack of publications on this historical problem and inspired by a chart in Adalbert Rückerl's *NS— Verbrechen vor Gericht*, I was prompted to undertake this study.[5] The latter lists the defendants of the *Einsatzgruppen* (mobile killing squads) trial, their original sentences and the years of their release. The American tribunal gave fourteen of the twenty-one mobile killing squad leaders on trial the death penalty for their involvement in the murder of approximately two million victims. However, only four were actually executed. U.S. High Commissioner John J. McCloy commuted the sentences of the remaining condemned to life or term sentences. By the fall of 1958 all these defendants had been released from prison. The rather radical reduction of the sentences attracted my interest in exploring the history of the war crimes program in the U.S. zone. I have chosen, however, to limit the study to the period from 1946 to 1955. The former marks the end of the Nuremberg trial and the beginning of the subsequent proceedings, while the latter is the year when the Federal Republic of Germany became sovereign and an equal partner in NATO. By May 1955, only fifty prisoners remained at Landsberg, the American prison for German war criminals, a number too small to prevent the completion of West Germany's rehabilitation. In the late summer of 1958 the warden of Landsberg released the last inmate. The war crimes operation had come to an end after the United States had spent millions of tax dollars and employed hundreds in the program. For fairness' sake, one must emphasize that the British and French closed their prisons even a year earlier.

I have used German and American records for this study. Most of the McCloy papers are now declassified, with the exception of some documents in the *Eyes-Only* and *Top Secret* files. To understand the policy of the Army, which often collided with the interests of the United States High Commission for Germany, I have consulted the files of the Judge Advocate Division of the European Command, United States Army. The holdings of the Harry S. Truman and Dwight D. Eisenhower libraries provided solid background concerning the political priorities of these administrations and the German question. The National Security Council minutes in both archives were most helpful. The Truman Library also holds the State Department Briefs for the president, which were rather useful. In the Federal Republic of Germany I studied the documents of the federal, parliamentary, justice ministry and foreign office archives. Generally, access to the German files was granted liberally. There was one exception, however. The documents of the *Bundestag* Committee for the Occupation Statute and Foreign Affairs remain classified. The committee had a subcommittee with the name "Prisoners of War," although it dealt almost exclusively with war criminals and not regular POWs. Thus, the subcommittee's records would have been helpful in providing an even more complete picture. Fortunately, I found sufficient references in the foreign office and justice ministry archives relating to the activities and interests of the subcommittee.

Finally, I apologize for using the term "war crimes program," which makes it appear that the United States had its own program to commit war crimes. Regrettably, almost all documents from the High Commission and the Army's Theater Judge Advocate Division refer to the operation in this manner instead of the more appropriate term "war crimes trial program."

NOTES

1. See Edward N. Peterson, *The American Occupation of Germany: Retreat to Victory* (Detroit: Wayne State University Press, 1977); and James F. Tent, *Mission on the Rhine: Reeducation and Denazification in American-Occupied Germany* (Chicago: University of Chicago Press, 1982).

2. Kurt P. Tauber, *Beyond Eagle and Swastika: German Nationalism since 1945*, 2 vols. (Middletown, Conn.: Wesleyan University Press, 1967).

3. Erich J.C. Hahn, "Hajo Holborn: Bericht zur deutschen Frage. Beobachtungen und Empfehlungen vom Herbst 1947," *Vierteljahrshefte für Zeitgeschichte* 35 (1987), 135-166.

4. British Broadcasting Corporation reporter Tom Bower and Berlin publicist Jörg Friedrich have examined the fate of convicted German war criminals in the post-war era. However, their works are of limited use to the historian due to a lack of historiographic integration, and, in Friedrich's case, an overreliance on published primary and secondary sources with little evidence of original research. See Tom Bower, *The Pledge Betrayed: America and Britain and the Denazification of Germany* (New York: Doubleday, 1982); and Jörg Friedrich, *Die kalte Amnestie* (Frankfurt: Fischer, 1984). National Archives archivist John Mendelsohn discusses U.S. sentence review and clemency programs in both Germany and Japan in Robert Wolfe's *Americans as Proconsuls*. Mendelsohn's article provides the reader with a solid overview of U.S. war crimes policy. See John Mendelsohn, "War Crimes Trials and Clemency in Germany and Japan," in Robert Wolfe, ed., *Americans as Proconsuls: United States Military Government in Germany and Japan, 1944-1952* (Carbondale: Southern Illinois University Press, 1984), 226-259.

5. Adalbert Rückerl, *NS—Verbrechen vor Gericht* (Heidelburg: Müller, 1982), 131.

1

The Search for a Punishment Policy

An old saying has it that too many cooks spoil the broth. This age-old truism is particularly relevant for students of America's planning and actual implementation of policies for the occupation of Germany after World War II. For much of the war, United States officials were not particularly concerned about formulating policy for the future treatment of Germany and consequently paid little attention to the issue. In 1944 military reality finally caught up with the administration of President Franklin D. Roosevelt and during the last two years of World War II a maze of governmental agencies and committees became involved in drafting their own plans, leading to considerable interdepartmental rivalries. The most prominent antagonists were the Departments of State, War and the Treasury. These agencies based their positions regarding the treatment of post-war Germany on their different interpretations of the nature of Nazism and recent German history as well as future U.S. interests in Europe. The State Department believed that Germany could again be integrated into a peaceful, democratic community of nations, once it had been denazified, demilitarized and democratized during a lengthy Allied occupation. In contrast, the Department of War was not interested in preparing for a military occupation spanning several decades. Instead, the War Department's main concern was to formulate a short-term general policy, which did not interfere with the decision-making of U.S. Army commanders in Germany. The Treasury Department, convinced that National Socialism and World War II had been the results of Germany's long authoritarian and militaristic tradition, proposed the harshest measures. Since these perceived flaws in the German character, combined with Germany's industrial might, would continue to threaten world peace, the Treasury Department felt that the enemy should suffer deindustrialization in addition to strict social reform measures. While Washington was engaged in bureaucratic in-fighting, the Allied armies were advancing in the field. Lacking specific directives, military commanders, now faced with the responsibility of physically occupying Germany, added to the confusion and formulated their own policy. In addition, all four Allies still had to come to terms as to how Germany should be treated once defeated.[1]

Scholars writing about U.S. goals in post-surrender Germany are sharply divided over the purpose and the objectives of this policy. John Gimbel points out that American occupation authorities had a variety of goals. In addition to fulfilling official policy directives calling for denazification, decartelization, demilitarization and democratization, U.S. officials also had numerous unstated, but at times equally significant, objectives ranging from reviving the German and European economies to reducing the cost of the occupation for the American taxpayer to containing communism.[2] Earl F. Ziemke also argues that the United States intended to achieve several objectives in Germany, including democratizing the Germans and reintegrating the former enemy into the world community. In Ziemke's opinion, however, economic unification to ease the financial burden of the occupation on Great Britain and the United States took precedence over all other occupation programs.[3] In contrast to Gimbel and Ziemke, several authors are much more critical of U.S. actions in Germany. Paul Y. Hammond and Harold Zink have charged that the initial goals of the occupation were essentially negative and vindictive. Zink is particularly critical of American attempts at democratizing the German people, a position shared by other scholars.[4] Indeed, Edward N. Peterson claims that U.S. military government officials had only a negligible impact on the establishment of German democracy. In contrast to the opinions of U.S. policy planners, Peterson emphasizes, the Germans did not need to be taught democratic values.[5] Even those who favor the concept of democratization are uncomfortable with the way in which it was applied in post-war Germany. John D. Montgomery describes the introduction of democracy in Germany as an "artificial revolution" based on an Allied, not a domestic, initiative.[6] Montgomery also laments that this revolution relied largely on negative purge programs, particularly denazification.[7]

The decision to hold trials of war criminals in Germany was clearly the result of the desire to reeducate the German people. To many influential Americans, particularly President Roosevelt and Treasury Secretary Henry Morgenthau, Jr., the Germans' apparent preference for militarism and authoritarianism had already led to two world wars and the murder of millions of innocent civilians. To avert a recurrence, they had concluded, the Germans needed to be democratized. As part of this program, these officials decided to use the trials of war criminals to not merely bring the perpetrators to justice, but to demonstrate the evils of totalitarianism. The evidence which was to be presented at the trials would, the Americans hoped, convince the Germans that their society was in dire need of reform and that the goals of the occupation were noble in this respect. However, like the search for an overall policy, the planning for the war crimes operation was also confused.[8] This chapter will focus on the development of a war crimes policy for occupied Germany by the U.S. government and the Allies. I argue here that the planners made important mistakes which eventually required modifications and readjustments with respect to the war crimes program. The results were extensive sentence review and clemency processes in the 1940s, only to be followed with the complete dismantling of the operation during the following decade.

In the Moscow Declaration of October 30, 1943, the three major Allies issued a tough warning that the Nazis would be held responsible for their war crimes once the Second World War had ended. The result of a tripartite conference between British Foreign Secretary Anthony Eden, Soviet Foreign Minister Vyacheslav Molotov and United States Secretary of State Cordell Hull, the Declaration divided German war criminals into two groups. One consisted of those whose crimes had "no particular geographic localization" and the Allies only stated that this group would be punished in accordance with a joint policy of the United Nations which would be determined in the future. The other group of perpetrators, whose crimes occurred in a specific geographic location, would be returned to individual countries where their offenses would fall under national jurisdiction. The question of how the Allies would treat war crimes and the future punishment of the offenders was a relatively minor issue at the conference. At the time, the three foreign ministers were far more concerned with the political and military problems of the alliance. Thus, in the absence of a coherent punishment policy on the part of the Allies, the promise that the "recoiling Hitlerite Huns" would soon find themselves facing retribution for their atrocities was indeed a hollow one.[9]

British Prime Minister Winston Churchill himself did not attach too much importance to the Moscow Declaration and preferred to view it as a preventive measure rather than a blueprint for the punishment of Nazi war crimes. "I am not particular about the phraseology," Churchill wrote to President Roosevelt and Soviet Premier Joseph Stalin, "but if this, or something like this, were issued over our three signatures, I believe it would make some of these villains reluctant to be mixed up in butcheries now they realize they are going to be defeated."[10] Churchill, who liked the idea of prosecuting German war criminals locally, believed that the Nazis might show "moral scruples" once they were aware of the fate that was in store for them.[11]

Roosevelt backed Churchill's position, although it contradicted a vaguely defined punishment policy which the president had announced a year earlier on October 7, 1942. FDR wanted the perpetrators judged and sentenced in courts of law. That in itself did not preclude local and national tribunals from assuming responsibility over war crimes matters. However, other aspects of Roosevelt's statement had little in common with the language of the Moscow Declaration or its localization of jurisdiction provision. The president made it clear that the United States did not want to retaliate on a massive scale and thereby lower itself to Nazi Germany's standards. Instead, FDR's interest was "that just and sure punishment shall be meted out to the ringleaders responsible for the organized murder of thousands of innocent persons and the commission of atrocities."[12] If the strength of the Moscow Declaration was the threat of vigilante justice,[13] FDR's plan to pursue only the policy-makers of the horrors which were occurring in the German-occupied Eastern territories would have greatly weakened what the Allies wanted to accomplish at Moscow.

Such considerations, however, did not play a role in the U.S. administration's decision to endorse the Moscow Declaration. Roosevelt was concerned that public opinion in the United Nations would unfavorably interpret the foreign ministers' conference. Therefore, the administration viewed the document as an opportunity to let the world know "that the fate of these unhappy people under German control has not been overlooked at this Tripartite meeting."[14] Clearly, the U.S. government, with the exception of Treasury Secretary Morgenthau, did not yet consider the future treatment of German war criminals a crucial issue and thus lacked a well-defined policy of its own. The Moscow Declaration thus marked the completion of a year which offered much in the way of rhetoric but little in the way of substance.[15]

Roosevelt himself was only partially responsible for the lack of action during this period in matters relating to German atrocities. For example, Jewish immigration into the United States during the war years had been hampered by the government's unwillingness to relax immigration restrictions and to admit larger numbers of Europeans into the country. The exaggerated security consciousness of the Justice Department, now in charge of the Immigration and Naturalization Service, and Assistant Secretary of State Breckenridge Long, who controlled immigration for his agency, had significantly slowed the influx of Europeans into the United States since the beginning of the war. In addition, FDR needed congressional support for his foreign policy goals and he did not want to jeopardize his relationship with the legislature over the question of increased immigration. During talks with Vice President Henry Wallace and Speaker of the House Sam Rayburn in November 1942, the president touched on the problem. Rayburn's prediction of resistance in the Congress quickly laid the issue to rest.[16] If opposed to increased Jewish immigration, the Senate and the House of Representatives nonetheless did pass Senate Concurrent Resolution 9 condemning Nazi atrocities and threatening retribution.[17] The problem of Jewish refugees and immigration never was resolved in 1943, despite the Roosevelt administration's participation in the Bermuda conference on refugees. The results of the conference were essentially meaningless and "a façade for inaction," as British delegate Richard Law later recalled the event.[18]

Only a few weeks after the United States had agreed to the Moscow Declaration, leading administration officials began to have doubts about its application. In November and December 1943 Soviet authorities, armed with the spirit of the Declaration and evidence prepared by the Extraordinary State Commission,[19] began to prosecute and try several Germans and their Russian accomplices as war criminals. These trials took place before military tribunals in Kiev and Kharkov. The Soviet Union evidently wanted to demonstrate its intent to enforce the tripartite agreement. The court proceedings and subsequent public hangings received wide publicity in the Soviet press. To ensure that the United States and Great Britain would support their legitimacy, the Soviets invited American and British news correspondents to attend the trials.[20]

Washington's reaction to the Kiev and Kharkov trials provided a preview of the Roosevelt administration's internal division concerning Germany's future treatment and U.S. relations with the Soviet Union. Soviet propaganda claimed that a direct link existed between the Moscow Declaration and the first war crimes trials inside Soviet territory. The U.S. State Department, however, denied that this agreement covered the question of jurisdiction in the Kharkov and Kiev cases. On December 31, 1943, Hull informed the counselor of the U.S. embassy in Britain, Howard Bucknell, Jr., and Ambassador John G. Winant that the United States did not agree with the Soviet point of view on this issue. But the Secretary of State did not want the differences of interpretation between the Americans and the Soviets to become a matter of public record. Hull was afraid German propaganda would exploit the incident as a sign that the Allies were experiencing problems. Consequently, he instructed Bucknell and Winant to keep a low profile on questions relating to the Soviet trials.[21]

The Department of War also desired as little publicity as possible, but for reasons different from those of Hull and the State Department. Secretary of War Henry L. Stimson feared that the Germans might retaliate against American prisoners of war if U.S. propaganda endorsed the outcome of the Soviet war crimes trials. Aside from this practical consideration, the Secretary of War was troubled by yet another issue. Stimson apparently saw the Soviet trials not only as being outside the sphere of the Moscow Declaration, but, more importantly, as violating the Geneva Convention of 1929 on the treatment of prisoners of war. To Stimson it seemed highly suspect that the Soviets had not seen fit to adhere to the convention. Thus, in an obvious attempt to discredit the Soviet trials the War Department informed Hull that it "considers it most important that efforts should at all times be made to preserve the humanitarian concepts so arduously built up under this Convention."[22]

By the beginning of the last full year of the war the Allies had completed remarkably little planning with regard to the treatment of post-war Germany, including the problem of war criminals. The victory of the United Nations in Europe was certain and the only remaining question was the timing of the Axis defeat. The planners in the individual departments of the U.S. government finally caught up with military reality during 1944, and most of the year witnessed a flurry of activity as well as an abundance of proposed plans to deal with post-war Germany. Unfortunately, no unified approach to the problem emerged, leading to suspicions and struggles for supremacy between the Treasury, State, and War departments. With the surrender of Nazi Germany almost in sight, disputes erupted on the bureaucratic home front. The result was what the historian Bradley F. Smith aptly describes as "The Great German War on the Potomac."[23]

At the tripartite conference of October 1943 the United States, Britain and the Soviet Union also agreed to form the European Advisory Commission (EAC). During their meeting at Tehran a month later the Big Three instructed the EAC to work out a program for the dismemberment of Germany. Stalin, afraid that a unified Germany would continue to be a threat to the Soviet Union, had the strongest interest in rendering the soon to be defeated enemy incapable of launching future attacks against his country. The Soviet leader received strong support from Roosevelt on this issue, although Churchill was rather skeptical about the proposal's practicality. The U.S. senior representative on the EAC, Ambassador Winant, had as his principal assistants George F. Kennan, Philip E. Moseley and E.F. Penrose. All three were ardent anti-Communists and favored a softer policy toward Germany owing to their distrust of the Soviet Union.[24]

On July 12, 1944, the EAC submitted a draft directive for the post-surrender period to the three Allied commanders in chief. The document gave the Allied military commanders control over almost every aspect of life in a defeated Germany. However, the EAC did not propose a harsh peace and Winant saw it only as a temporary measure. The draft directive called for a unified Germany and encouraged the Allied commanders "to permit those elements among the German people who desire German participation in a peaceful international life to lay the foundations for such participation by the establishment of responsible democratic government."[25] Winant and his assistants had moved light years away from the earlier wartime agreements of Moscow and Tehran. Instead, the American EAC members desired that the occupation result in the creation of a politically stable, democratic, prosperous and unified Germany. Only the proposed disarmament of Germany in the EAC program resembled a punitive measure.[26]

At the State Department in Washington the future of Germany and the long-term interests of the United States in that country were the responsibility of the Committee on Postwar Programs.[27] In an August 5, 1944, memorandum titled "The Treatment of Germany" the committee did not even mention war criminals and German war crimes. Instead, the committee's main interest was to find a formula for a peace which would deprive Germany of its potential to conduct wars without coming across as another *Diktat*. The memorandum, which reached the president on August 26, proposed an occupation program more intent on ensuring Germany's economic survival and political revival than on punishing the Germans for their country's past aggression. The committee was convinced that "an indefinitely continued coercion of more than sixty million technically advanced people . . . would at best be an expensive undertaking that would afford the world little sense of security and, more important still, there exists no convincing reason to anticipate that the victor powers would be willing and able indefinitely to apply coercion." The State Department evidently doubted already that the wartime alliance between the Big Three, a marriage of convenience at best, would last until long after V-E Day. In addition, the occupation might come under fire in Congress for its price tag. To avoid future disappointments of that nature, the State Department committee proposed that the most effective means to ensure world security required that the Germans repudiate any designs for future conquests and let themselves be assimilated "into a cooperative world society" as "equal partners."[28]

To add to the confusion concerning the post-war treatment of Germany, the staff of Gen. Dwight D. Eisenhower at the Supreme Headquarters, Allied Expeditionary Forces (SHAEF), began in the summer of 1944 to draw up its own plans. On June 6, 1944, the Allies launched the D-Day invasion across the English Channel and established several beachheads in Normandy. With the American policy-makers unable to make a final decision, the Allied armies seemed to be the only ones moving forward that summer. The European Advisory Commission was stalled over questions relating to the zones of occupation into which Germany would be divided. Similar delays existed over the question of the duration of Allied military government in Germany and what type of governmental structure would eventually replace it. Eisenhower felt that the war in Europe would end sooner than Washington expected, and he instructed SHAEF to formulate its own policy for the post-surrender period. The most important document prepared by Eisenhower's staff was the *Handbook for Military Government in Germany*, whose first draft SHAEF submitted to Eisenhower in June. The *Handbook* as well as some of the other manuals and directives were sent to the War Department in Washington for authorization. But the lack of agreement among the Allies and the absence of a unified approach on the part of the U.S. government finally prompted SHAEF, still operating without specific instructions, to proceed with its own plans.[29]

The *Handbook* called for the maintenance of a highly centralized administration in Germany to make the military's job of governing easier, as well as the restoration of the German economy to ensure self-sufficiency and a somewhat comfortable standard of living. SHAEF, primarily interested in the military aspects of the occupation, listed the ranks and positions of those Nazi officials who might pose a threat to the security of the occupation forces. For that reason the *Handbook* ordered the automatic arrest and detention of almost 250,000 high-ranking Nazis. Furthermore, it prescribed mandatory arrest for all members of the *Gestapo* and the *Sicherheitsdienst (SD)*, but not the lower ranks of the *Sturmabteilung (SA)*, the *Schutzstaffel (SS)*, and the regular army.[30]

Henry Morgenthau learned about the State Department's Committee on Postwar Programs memorandum and SHAEF's *Handbook* on his trip to Europe in August 1944. The treasury secretary regarded the proposed measures as wholly inadequate. His foremost goals were the complete restructuring of Germany's economy so that it would forever lose its ability to launch another war and the reeducation of the German people to convince them to adopt democratic values. Morgenthau thus used the trip to meet with those who now appeared to represent a soft policy toward Germany. The first person whom Morgenthau asked for an explanation was Eisenhower. The general admitted to the secretary that he had not concerned himself with economic planning for Germany. The only issues which Eisenhower had seriously considered thus far were the destruction of the country's capacity to manufacture armaments and post-war reparations payments by Germany. On other issues the general gave the impression that he was a hardliner. He told Morgenthau that the German people as a whole should suffer "a sense of guilt, of complicity in the tragedy that has engulfed the world." With regard to the leading Nazi party members and German industrialists, Eisenhower suggested that they be tried and punished.[31]

Satisfied with Eisenhower's response, Morgenthau moved on to London. There, the secretary had two rather unpleasant experiences. During a conversation with Ambassador Winant and his assistants Penrose and Moseley, in which he repeated his plan to destroy the industrial basis of Germany's war machine forever, Morgenthau discovered that the American EAC staffers were working to accomplish entirely different goals. Moseley was not at all impressed with Morgenthau's post-war scenario and argued that the destruction of Germany's economy would make that country dependent on Russia. Such an arrangement might lead to Soviet dominance over all of Europe. To Morgenthau's astonishment the pro-German and anti-Soviet biases of the American EAC staff constituted only part of the problem. During a meeting with Eden, the Secretary also learned that the EAC had not been following its instructions from Roosevelt, Churchill and Stalin, and was planning for a unified Germany, not the dismemberment of the enemy. Since the Big Three had ordered the partitioning of Germany at Tehran, the EAC was clearly working without authorization.[32]

Morgenthau feared that Assistant Secretary of War John J. McCloy, temporarily replacing Stimson for a few days in August, would let the *Handbook* become official U.S. occupation policy. To avoid a potential disaster of that kind, Morgenthau, after returning to Washington, took his discoveries straight to the president. FDR was furious that certain sections within his government were planning the future of Germany without proper authorization and against the Big Three's instructions. Stimson bore the brunt of the president's anger. In a letter to the Secretary of War on August 26, 1944, Roosevelt strongly criticized SHAEF's *Handbook*, which Morgenthau had of course forwarded to the White House. "It gives me the impression that Germany is to be restored just as much as The Netherlands or Belgium, and the people of Germany brought back as quickly as possible to their pre-war estate,'' FDR complained. Roosevelt reminded Stimson that he favored strict punishment for the entire German people, not just a few Nazi leaders. The *Handbook's* section on the German economy particularly disturbed the president. Using language spiced with a good dose of sarcasm, FDR informed Stimson that he did not intend to extend the policies of the New Deal to the enemy because he saw ''no reason for starting a WPA, PWA or a CCC for Germany when we go in with our Army of Occupation.''[33]

Roosevelt's outrage, directed at the proponents of a soft peace, resulted from more than the mere realization that his subordinates had acted without his authorization. In August news about the discovery of the Majdanek concentration camp near Lublin, Poland, by the Red Army removed any remaining doubts which the president might still have had that Nazi Germany was a scourge to civilization.[34] Majdanek, a combination labor/extermination camp, was one of the pillars of the economic empire which the *SS* had planned to build for itself. Due to the speed of the Soviet advance in the Lublin area, the *SS* at Majdanek had not been able to destroy the camp. A mixed Soviet-Polish commission immediately launched an investigation into Majdanek and invited thirty foreign journalists to tour the site in late August. The results of that tour appeared on America's breakfast tables only a few days later. Reporting from what he described as the ''most terrible place on the face of the earth,'' *New York Times* correspondent W.H. Lawrence provided a detailed account of the camp and its victims. More importantly, Lawrence, who admitted that he had entertained doubts about the manner in which the Soviets had presented evidence of German crimes in the past, now claimed that he was ''prepared to believe any story of German atrocities, no matter how savage, cruel and depraved.'' The evidence—including gas chambers, ovens to burn the victims, mass graves, unused cans of Zyklon B gas and a warehouse containing the shoes of an estimated 400,000 victims—was indeed overwhelming. Such news accounts, now appearing in American papers demonstrated to the president and the badly divided administration the urgency of soon formulating a punishment policy for post-war Germany.[35]

In early September the Treasury Department completed its plan for post-war Germany. Morgenthau, who had very closely supervised the work on his agency's proposal, presented it to Stimson and McCloy on September 4. The *Morgenthau Plan*, as the Treasury's policy later became known, had little in common with any of the other plans dealing with the United States' future objectives in Germany. The most controversial section of the *Morgenthau Plan* centered around the de-industrialization of Germany. Convinced that Germany would continue to have the willingness and the means to go to war, if the Allies treated it mildly, Morgenthau recommended the destruction of the country's heavy industry as the most important part of his program. The secretary sought to moderate ''Germany's lust for armed conquest'' by annihilating its capacity to produce military hardware. To achieve this purpose, the Treasury Secretary felt that the Allies should convert the German economy from an industrial to a pastoral one.[36]

According to the *Morgenthau Plan*, other dramatic changes would accompany the complete restructuring of the German economy. Morgenthau proposed the decentralization of Germany's administrative and political system, in stark contrast to SHAEF's *Handbook*, and the creation of a democratic government. The secretary also wanted to impress upon the German populace the reasons for the harsh policies so that the realization of why Germany was being punished would linger for a while. To accomplish that feat, Morgenthau urged that Germany pay heavy reparations to the countries it had victimized and suffer a prolonged military occupation by Allied troops.[37]

Morgenthau's proposal for the punishment of German war criminals was equally uncompromising. For the group Morgenthau termed the "arch-criminals," the plan called for the simplest of procedures. These perpetrators were to be captured, identified and shot before a United Nations firing squad.[38] Lesser war criminals, in contrast, would have the right to a trial. To administer the program, Morgenthau envisaged the creation of military commissions consisting of representatives of the Allied Military Government and the liberated countries. These commissions would have jurisdiction in cases involving homicide. If convicted, the accused would receive the death penalty unless mitigating circumstances existed. In that case the individual would face either deportation to a penal colony outside Germany or suffer alternative appropriate punishment. To ensure that the execution of a sentence would not be delayed in an appellate process, Morgenthau's plan called for immediate enforcement.[39]

Stimson regarded the *Morgenthau Plan*, particularly the sections on the destruction of German industry and the handling of war criminals, as a big mistake. The Secretary of War felt that Morgenthau was entirely wrong on these two "fundamental points." The arch-criminals should not be shot without a trial, he wrote Roosevelt on September 9, 1944, suggesting that the United States observe "at least rudimentary aspects of the Bill of Rights." Stimson had no interest in providing the villains with the privilege of full due process, but he recommended that the defendants receive notification of the charges, have the opportunity to speak out for themselves and call in defense witnesses. Such a procedure would not simply be more appropriate; the experienced Republican politician had another practical reason in mind. Trials of war criminals, Stimson emphasized to Roosevelt, would show the world the brutal nature of Nazism and, at the same time, portray the Allies as the ones who defeated this menace and were now protecting mankind from a Nazi revival. Thus, Stimson recommended the creation of an international tribunal with U.S. participation[40] to try the members of Morgenthau's arch-criminal category. The secretary also questioned the jurisdiction of the military commissions, which the *Morgenthau Plan* had proposed for the second group of perpetrators. Such courts should lack jurisdiction for crimes committed by Nazi authorities against German citizens. With a painful reminder of an issue which had caused friction between Roosevelt and Southern members of Congress in the mid-1930s, Stimson argued that the military commissions would have no authority to hear these types of cases, just as no foreign court could "try those who were guilty of, or condoned, lynching in our own country."[41]

Stimson, described as a "social anti-Semite" at worst,[42] knew that Morgenthau had a special interest in punishing Germany. As a Jew, the Treasury Secretary was particularly affected by the news about the plight of Europe's Jewry and Nazi atrocities. Stimson certainly shared Morgenthau's disgust for Nazi Germany's deeds, but did not sympathize with the latter's desire for revenge. The two cabinet officers disagreed on the underlying assumptions of the *Morgenthau Plan*. The Treasury Secretary's vision of a peaceful and democratic post-war world underlay his approach to the German problem. Morgenthau desired continued cooperation among all nations and the restoration of Britain's prosperity after the war. Good relations between the United States and the Soviet Union, as well as the complete reorganization and reeducation of German society, were essential to Morgenthau's design.[43] To Stimson, in contrast, the Second World War was more the result of pure power politics than flaws in the structure of German society. Thus, although also favoring the disarmament of Germany and other punishment measures, the War Department was mainly interested in an occupation that would not result in resentment and anti-Allied sentiment among the Germans.

In early September 1944, FDR appeared to prefer the *Morgenthau Plan* to the proposals of the State and War departments. Roosevelt viewed the plan, at least temporarily, as a means to cement the alliance with the Soviet Union since it demonstrated the United States' willingness to treat Germany harshly. As a result, it would help eliminate Soviet fears that the United States was seeking a soft peace, only to rebuild Germany against the Soviet Union some time in the future. The president tried to convince Churchill of the *Morgenthau Plan's* benefits at the Quebec conference later that month. The prime minister accepted the proposal after some hesitation.[44] However, within a few days, Roosevelt had changed his mind about Morgenthau's prescription for the treatment of post-surrender Germany. The Quebec talks seemed to show the impracticality of Morgenthau's approach, which had been Hull's position from the beginning. The *Morgenthau Plan* was bound to interfere with Soviet plans to extract reparations from Germany. In addition, British support, already lukewarm, might disappear in the future. But there were also concerns by the Army and the War Department that the publicity surrounding Morgenthau and his proposal would strengthen Germany's resolve to resist and thus delay the Allied victory.[45] That was not a good prospect for the president, who was now campaigning for his fourth term.[46]

Despite these counterarguments, the *Morgenthau Plan* was nonetheless incorporated into the Quebec agreement signed by Churchill and FDR, as Stimson discovered after the meeting.[47] When Stimson later showed Roosevelt the final conference document, the president expressed his shock about the secretary's discovery. FDR told Stimson he was astounded that he had in fact initialed the Quebec agreement.[48]

Although FDR's comment to Stimson appeared to indicate that the *Morgenthau Plan*, or at least portions of it, was no longer a viable policy, the influence of the Treasury in the decision-making process for post-surrender Germany did by no means disappear entirely. Morgenthau's chance to put his ideas into effect arose when the War Department, after Roosevelt had rejected its *Handbook*, began to work on a new directive for Eisenhower. The new instructions, which the War Department saw as a temporary measure, became known as *Joint Chiefs of Staff (JCS) 1067* due to its cable reference number.

When Churchill, Roosevelt and Stalin met at Yalta in February 1945 the future of the *Morgenthau Plan* was clearly in doubt. The Big Three expressed a stronger interest in controlling the affairs of Germany for an extended period, instead of forcing the Germans to face their own problems. But control over Germany also implied the assumption of responsibility for the defeated enemy. The *Morgenthau Plan* proposed to have the Germans, as Eisenhower put it so eloquently, "stew in their own juice."[49] That concept, which Roosevelt had earlier endorsed, fell prey to "the general tendency of the Yalta talks towards increased Allied control over (and hence responsibility for) Germany."[50] Rather than calling for the dismemberment of Germany, Yalta proposed the formation of separate zones of occupation. In addition, Morgenthau's vision of a purely agrarian German state was also not incorporated into the Yalta agreement. Of all the measures the Treasury had suggested, only the denazification proposal remained from the original plan.[51]

The competing Washington bureaucracies rushed to incorporate the result of Yalta into *JCS 1067*. This time, unlike previous episodes, the Departments of Treasury, State, and War were able to formulate a unified approach. These agencies' willingness to cooperate resulted in part from personnel changes. Former Undersecretary of State Edward R. Stettinius had replaced the ailing Hull, and McCloy led the War Department for Stimson, who, although he officially stayed on as Secretary of War, had decided to remove himself from the continuous in-fighting. McCloy was in charge of most of the work on *JCS 1067* and proved to be a skillful diplomat, who commanded the trust of the other officials. In addition, Morgenthau, with his two old adversaries out of the way, also showed a greater willingness to compromise. Advised by McCloy that Roosevelt actually only wanted to change German industry and not preside over its destruction, Morgenthau backed off on a number of issues. In a joint memorandum, which the president approved on March 23,

1945, the three departments stated that certain basic industries would have to be maintained. On the other hand, the memorandum recommended other stern economic measures, which apparently satisfied Morgenthau.[52]

FDR did not live to see the final refinement of *JCS 1067* and it was left to his successor Harry S. Truman to sign the directive. Morgenthau made further concessions after his long-time friend died on April 12, 1945. Thus, when *JCS 1067* became official U.S. occupation policy on May 11, three days after the Allied victory in Europe, the final directive contained instructions which stood in stark contrast to Morgenthau's earlier thinking. *JCS 1067* authorized the commander of the American zone of occupation (the later official title was United States Military Governor) to "permit the production of synthetic rubber and oil, aluminum, and magnesium."[53] The directive also relaxed the provision governing the detention of war criminals by U.S. occupation authorities, ordering the zonal commanders to arrest Adolf Hitler, "his chief Nazi associates, other war criminals and all persons who have participated in planning or carrying out Nazi enterprises involving or resulting in atrocities or war crimes." But in cases where the U.S. military governor recommended different treatment for a suspected war criminal, arrest could be delayed. *JCS 1067* offered a great loophole in that respect. The zonal commander could choose alternative action if an individual, whose rank fit one of the categories on the detention list, might be useful "for intelligence or other military reasons."[54] Such language had little in common with the original Treasury plan.

Morgenthau's apparent abandonment of some aspects contained in his September 1944 memorandum to Roosevelt was only part of the failure to ensure that *JCS 1067* would severely punish a nation which had terrorized much of the world for six years. In contrast to its initial purpose as an interim measure, the directive remained U.S. occupation policy until July 27, 1947. *JCS 1067*, moreover, left the details of the occupation to the military authorities in the American zone by providing for a number of "escape clauses."[55] The Army's main interest in Germany was to govern and administer as smoothly as possible. For that reason, the loopholes in *JCS 1067* ensured that "the future of Germany began to rest in German hands,"[56] which was precisely what Morgenthau had feared.

The signing of *JCS 1067* ended, at least temporarily, the interdepartmental feuding over general policies for post-war Germany. However, the Allies still had to agree on the much-heralded punishment of German war criminals. Between May and August 1945 the United States assumed the leading role in that area, persuading its principal partners in the war against Germany to share the American government's eagerness to hold war crimes trials. On May 2, 1945, Truman appointed Supreme Court Justice Robert H. Jackson as the chief prosecutor for the United States. Since the Allies had not yet come to a definite agreement on the issue of trials, Jackson's marching orders were to evaluate the evidence with regard to German atrocities and war crimes, and to formulate the charges against "the leaders of the European Axis powers and their principal agents and accessories."[57]

The Congress used the joyous occasion of VE-Day for a rare display of agreement with the executive branch. House Concurrent Resolution 39 called on the U.S. and Allied governments to cooperate in the prosecution and punishment of war criminals. Similar to the language of Executive Order 9547 appointing Jackson, the House also expressed its desire to prosecute the Nazi policy-makers or, as Morgenthau described that group, the arch-criminals.[58] Truman's executive order and the House resolution signaled the abandonment of yet another important aspect of the *Morgenthau Plan*. The mere shooting, without trial and fanfare, of the top Nazi officials was now out of the question. Stimson's scheme to boost Allied, and ultimately American, prestige by means of war crimes trials had triumphed over the cruder, but probably more effective and perhaps less controversial, measures suggested by the Treasury Secretary.

Just how much the United States had dominated the process of trial planning became evident during a meeting between Stettinius, Eden and Molotov on May 3, 1945, during the San Francisco Conference. Judge Samuel I. Rosenman, special counsel to the president, presented the British and Soviet delegations with U.S. proposals for the establishment of an international military tribunal consisting of four members, one from each country on the Allied Control Council for Germany. Rosenman pointed out to the British and the Soviets the difficulty of prosecuting individuals since, to the disappointment of the Allies, Hitler, Goebbels and Mussolini were no longer available for trial. The U.S. plan had a remedy for this calamity: Rosenman proposed to try the "Nazi organizations themselves rather than individuals and to convict them and all their members of engaging in a criminal conspiracy to control the world, to persecute minorities, to break treaties, to invade other nations and to commit war crimes." The idea was simple enough. If the organizations were found guilty, the tribunal would not have to go through the trouble of prosecuting individual defendants. Voluntary membership in any Nazi organization would translate into an automatic guilty verdict.[59]

While the United States was able to present a clear strategy for the prosecution of war crimes, the foreign ministers conference indicated how little thought the British and the Soviets had given to the eventual practical application of the Moscow Declaration. The British War Cabinet still sought to deal with the worst category of perpetrators, those whose crimes could not be pinpointed to a specific location, the Morgenthau way. But London's preference for *Realpolitik* allowed for a good deal of flexibility in this area. If "their two great Allies" absolutely wanted to try the top Nazi villains, Britain would go along. The stoic Molotov provided no indication as to how the Soviet Union intended to deal with the problem. The Soviet foreign minister only asked that his government be given the time to study Rosenman's proposals and the right to comment on them.[60]

Only a month after his appointment Justice Jackson filed his first report with Truman. The document featured most of Rosenman's report to the foreign ministers. But aside from seeking the indictment of such Nazi organizations as the *SS* and *Gestapo*, Jackson's other goal was to try a "large number of individuals and officials." Jackson outlined three types of crimes for which the international court should prosecute major war criminals: offenses involving infractions of international law and the rules of war, crimes against racial and religious minorities, and aggressive warfare in violation of international law and existing treaties. In addition to the most notorious Nazi war criminals, Jackson identified three classes of lesser offenders. The first group consisted of perpetrators who had killed American soldiers, particularly airmen. Defendants accused of such crimes were eventually prosecuted by the Theater Judge Advocate Division as part of the Army's war crimes trial program at Dachau. The remaining two categories, those with localized crimes, as defined by the Moscow Declaration, as well as "Quislings, Lavals, 'Lord Haw-Haws,' and the like" would fall under the jurisdiction of the local and national courts in the individual countries. The U.S. chief prosecutor also sensed that British and Soviet enthusiasm for the holding of war crimes trials did not match that of the United States. Therefore, feeling a "deep sense of urgency," Jackson emphasized the necessity of continuing to formulate the United States case against the Axis war criminals, despite the lack of an Allied agreement regarding the shape and the competence of the international tribunal.[61]

On August 8, 1945, during the first post-war conference of the three powers' foreign ministers in London, the Allies finally established the International Military Tribunal (IMT) to deal with the major war criminals. The IMT's charter gave the court jurisdiction over the categories of crimes which Jackson had pointed out to Truman.[62] The actual indictment of the twenty-one defendants at the Nuremberg Trial, which opened on October 18, 1945, contained four counts: Count One, conspiracy; Count Two, crimes against the peace; Count Three, war crimes; and Count Four, crimes against humanity.[63] The London Agreement specifically called for a fair trial and incorporated Stimson's "rudimentary aspects of the Bill of Rights" into the Nuremberg procedure. But the Agreement which became the legal basis for subsequent war crimes proceedings after the conclusion of the Trial of the Major War Criminals, also included Article 26, stating that the judgment and the sentences of the court would be "final and not subject to review."[64] The United States alone followed up Nuremberg by appointing twelve subsequent military tribunals for high-ranking Nazi officials and the Army's own Dachau war crimes program, totaling more than 1,500 convictions in the U.S. zone of occupation. Thus, the lack of an appellate instance was bound to become a procedural headache in the long run.[65]

The United States initially had good reason to be proud of its achievements in formulating a policy to prosecute Axis war criminals and playing a key role in designing the Nuremberg System.[66] However, this system was without a foundation due to the absence of a more general long-range punishment policy encompassing all aspects of the occupation. *JCS 1067*, although viewed by some as too punitive and negative, was essentially a compromise measure, lacking or modifying many of Morgenthau's proposals for the "strict treatment" of Germany.[67] This had important consequences for convicted war criminals in the U.S. zone. As economic and eventually political unification emerged as the occupation's priorities, the long-term future of the war crimes program became increasingly doubtful. In addition to changes in the general occupation objectives, U.S. war crimes policy soon encountered additional obstacles. The war crimes program could not rely on a consensus at home. Its operation highlighted significant problems with regard to defendants' rights and often a lack of consistency. Once wartime emotions had cooled off, the treatment of war criminals came under attack in many circles, and not all of them were pro-German.

A second important shortcoming was the lack of any planning for an appellate court. Although the London Agreement included some aspects of American procedure and did not deny the defendants important rights, it was nonetheless foreign to those Americans charged with carrying out the program. The fact that the accused could not appeal the judgments and the verdicts which the war crimes courts handed down made U.S. war crimes authorities uncomfortable. It also left the impression that the Allies were really not interested in justice. American authorities finally began to address these questions in 1946. Executive clemency and regular administrative sentence reviews became substitutes for an appellate court. This procedure allowed U.S. officials to ensure that equal offenses had been punished evenly, which had not always been the case, particularly during the early years of the functioning of this judicial system.

Third, the war crimes program did little to change German attitudes. Cries of foul play and "victors' justice" accompanied the proceedings of the Trial of the Major War Criminals and the subsequent tribunals. Already during the occupation, German legal scholars questioned the legality of the Nuremberg trials under international law. The constant attacks against the Allies, especially the United States as the main instigator of these proceedings, in the late 1940s by Germany's church leaders, politicians, veterans and refugee organizations demonstrated that the war crimes program had not reeducated and democratized the Germans. Ironically, the War Department, not wanting the occupation to result in anti-Allied sentiment, achieved exactly the opposite on the problem of war criminals.

NOTES

1. For information on U.S. planning for the occupation of Germany and the disagreements between government agencies, see Paul Y. Hammond, "Directives for the Occupation of Germany: The Washington Controversy," in Harold Stein, ed.,

American Civil-Military Decisions (Birmingham: University of Alabama Press, 1963), 311-464; Peterson, *The American Occupation of Germany*, 19-44; Warren F. Kimball, *Swords or Ploughshares? The Morgenthau Plan for a Defeated Germany, 1943-1945* (New York: Lippincott, 1976); Walter L. Dorn, "Die Debatte über die amerikanische Besatzungspolitik für Deutschland (1944-1945)," *Vierteljahrshefte für Zeitgeschichte* 6 (1958), 60-77; and Günter Moltmann, "Zur Formulierung der amerikanischen Besatzungspolitik in Deutschland am Ende des Zweiten Weltkrieges," *Vierteljahrschefte für Zeitgeschichte* 15 (1967), 299-322.

2. John Gimbel, *The American Occupation of Germany: Politics and the Military, 1945-1949* (Palo Alto: Stanford University Press, 1968), xiii.

3. Earl F. Ziemke, "The Formulation and Initial Implementation of U.S. Occupation Policy in Germany," in Hans A. Schmitt, ed., *U.S. Occupation of Europe after World War II* (Lawrence: Regents Press of Kansas, 1978), 27-44.

4. Hammond, "Directives for the Occupation of Germany: The Washington Controversy," in Stein, ed., *American Civil-Military Decisions*, 427; and Harold Zink, *The United States in Germany, 1944-1955* (Princeton: Nostrand, 1957), 94. Zink charges that U.S. calls for the democratization of the Germans were "of the sort penal institutions are supposed to furnish in the making of good citizens."

5. Peterson, *The American Occupation of Germany*, 342.

6. John D. Montgomery, *Forced To Be Free: The Artificial Revolution in Germany and Japan* (Chicago: University of Chicago Press, 1957), 3.

7. Ibid., 5-7.

8. For example, see Earl F. Ziemke, *The U.S. Army in the Occupation of Germany, 1944-1946* (Washington, D.C.: Government Printing Office, 1975), 169-173.

9. Leland M. Goodrich and Marie J. Carroll, eds., *Documents on American Foreign Relations, 1943-1944* (Boston: World Peace Foundation, 1945), VI, 231-232.

10. Churchill to Roosevelt and Stalin, October 12, 1943, United States Department of State, *Foreign Relations of the United States, 1943*, 6 vols. (Washington, D.C.: Government Printing Office, 1964), I, 556-557.

11. Ibid.

12. *Documents on American Foreign Relations, 1942-1943*, V, 177-178.

13. Vigilantism appeared to be one option if one considers the following sentence from the Declaration: "Thus, the Germans who take part in wholesale shootings of Italian officers or in the execution of French, Dutch, Belgian or Norwegian hostages or of Cretan peasants, or who have shared in the slaughters inflicted on the people of Poland or in the territories of the Soviet Union which are now being swept clear of the enemy, will know that they will be brought back to the scene of their crimes and judged on the spot by the peoples whom they have outraged." *Documents on American Foreign Relations, 1943-1944*, 232.

14. Undersecretary of State Edward R. Stettinius to the American delegation in Moscow, *Foreign Relations of the United States, 1943*, I, 566.

15. Other public warnings directed at Germany regarding war crimes between October 1942 and October 1943 included a statement of the Allied governments of December 17, 1942; the concurrent resolution of the U.S. Congress of March 18, 1943; and Roosevelt's "Declaration on German Crimes in Poland" of August 30, 1943.

16. Robert Dallek, *Franklin D. Roosevelt and American Foreign Policy, 1932-1945* (New York: Oxford University Press, 1979), 445-446.

17. Senate Report No. 252, March 9, 1943, *Congressional Record*, 78th Congress, 1st Session, 1723.

18. Henry L. Feingold, *The Politics of Rescue: The Roosevelt Administration and the Holocaust, 1938-1945* (New Brunswick: Rutgers University Press, 1970), 206. For additional information on Allied refugee policy and the decision not to bomb the extermination camps in the East, see Martin Gilbert, *Auschwitz and the Allies* (New York: Holt, Rinehart, and Winston, 1981). The American administration firmly believed that the victims of Nazi Germany would benefit more from a German surrender at the earliest possible moment than individual rescue missions. Assistant Secretary of War John J. McCloy to the Executive Director of the War Refugee Board, John W. Pehle, in John Mendelsohn, ed., *The Holocaust*, 18 vols. (New York: Garland, 1982), XIV, 118.

19. The Soviet government created the Extraordinary State Commission in November 1942 to investigate German war crimes.

20. *Foreign Relations of the United States, 1943*, III, 845-848.

21. Hull to the U.S. Ambassador to Great Britain John G. Winant, December 31, 1943, *Foreign Relations of the United States, 1943*, III, 853-854.

22. Hull to the U.S. Ambassador to the Soviet Union W. Averell Harriman, January 1, 1944, United States Department of State, *Foreign Relations of the United States, 1944*, 7 vols. (Washington, D.C.: Government Printing Office, 1966), IV, 1198.

23. Bradley F. Smith, *The Road to Nuremberg* (New York: Basic Books, 1981), 12-47. Also, see Hammond, "Directives for the Occupation of Germany: The Washington Controversy," in Stein, ed., *American Civil-Military Decisions*, 311-464. In his foreword Hammond argues that the "disputes within the American administration were even more acrimonious than the disputes with our Allies."

24. John Morton Blum, *From the Morgenthau Diaries*, 3 vols. (Boston: Houghton Mifflin, 1967), III, 329.

25. Winant to Hull, July 11, 1944, *Foreign Relations of the United States, 1944*, I, 244-246.

26. Blum, *From the Morgenthau Diaries*, III, 330.

27. The Committee consisted of Hull, Undersecretary Stettinius, the vice chairman of the Advisory Council, assistant secretaries, and directors of offices, *ex officio*.

28. *Foreign Relations of the United States, 1944*, I, 302-325.

29. Forrest C. Pogue, *The Supreme Command*, in the official Army history, *The United States Army in World War II: The European Theater of Operations* (Washington, D.C.: Government Printing Office, 1954), 353-354.

30. Blum, *From the Morgenthau Diaries*, III, 331; Smith, *the Road to Nuremberg*, 16-17. Also, see Document I/3 in Bradley F. Smith, ed., *The American Road to Nuremberg: A Documentary Record* (Palo Alto: Hoover Institution Press, 1982), 15-16.

31. Dwight D. Eisenhower, *Crusade in Europe* (New York: Doubleday, 1948), 287.

32. Blum, *From the Morgenthau Diaries*, III, 338-339. For information on the authority of the EAC, see United States Department of State, *Foreign Relations of the United States, 1943. The Conferences at Cairo and Tehran* (Washington, D.C.: Government Printing Office, 1966).

33. *Foreign Relations of the United States, 1944*, I, 544-546. Stimson must have been surprised about the sharply worded letter. One day earlier FDR had formed the Cabinet Committee to formulate a Germany policy. Stimson claims credit for talking

the president into setting up the committee, consisting of Hull, Morgenthau, the Secretary of War, and presidential advisor Harry Hopkins. See Henry L. Stimson and McGeorge Bundy, *On Active Service in Peace and War* (New York: Harper, 1947), 569.

34. Harriman to Hull, August 19, 1944, *Foreign Relations of the United States, 1944*, IV, 1208.

35. "Nazi Mass Killing Laid Bare in Camp," *New York Times*, August 30, 1944, 1. The evidence found at Majdanek is included in Central Commission for the Investigation of German War Crimes in Poland, *German Crimes in Poland* (New York: Fertig, 1982).

36. Henry Morgenthau, Jr., *Germany Is Our Problem* (New York: Harper, 1945), 16-17, 48-49.

37. Ibid.

38. This particular idea was not exactly new. The British and the Soviets were in favor of a similar measure before they agreed to the holding of war crimes trials. Smith, *The Road to Nuremberg*, 34.

39. Morgenthau to Roosevelt, September 5, 1944, United States Department of State, *Foreign Relations of the United States: The Conference at Quebec 1944* (Washington, D.C.: Government Printing Office, 1972), 105-106. Morgenthau identified three types of homicide for which the military tribunals should try lesser war criminals: "a. the crime involved a violation of the rules of war; b. the victim was killed as a hostage; c. the victim was killed because of his 'nationality, race, color, creed, or political conviction.' "

40. Stimson felt the United States should participate despite his doubts that the United States was truly a victim of Nazism. Stimson to Roosevelt, September 9, 1944, ibid., 123-125.

41. Ibid.

42. Smith, *The Road to Nuremberg*, 31.

43. Blum, *From the Morgenthau Diaries*, III, 327.

44. The majority of historians on the subject agree that Churchill supported the *Morgenthau Plan* due to his realization that he would need the secretary of the treasury in order to obtain financial assistance for Great Britain. Hull and Stimson had similar suspicions when they received word that Morgenthau had also brought to Quebec a memorandum proposing $6.5 billion in credits for Britain. Cordell Hull, *The Memoirs of Cordell Hull*, 2 vols. (New York: Macmillan, 1948), II, 1613-1615.

45. "A Good Example of Value of Publicity," *New York Times*, September 24, 1944, 1.

46. Dallek, *Franklin D. Roosevelt and American Foreign Policy, 1932-1945*, 473-475.

47. In addition to policy differences, there existed a great deal of personal resentment within the State and War departments against Morgenthau and the fact that the Treasury was meddling with the planning for post-war Germany. FDR and Churchill's adoption of the *Morgenthau Plan* aggravated this situation. Thomas M. Campbell and George C. Herring, *The Diaries of Edward R. Stettinius, 1943-1946* (New York: New Viewpoints, 1975), 153.

48. Stimson and Bundy, *On Active Service in Peace and War*, 581. According to Warren Kimball, Stimson and McCloy's opposition to the *Morgenthau Plan* was most effective because the War Department accepted most of the proposal, with the

exception of the pastoralization program. Kimball claims Morgenthau and Stimson's attitudes were similar with regard to all other aspects of the plan, apparently including the treatment of German war criminals. The president supported Morgenthau as a result of several factors: his own strong dislike of the Germans and his assumption that both the cabinet and the public would support the Treasury's policy. Kimball, *Swords or Ploughshares?*, 42.

49. Blum, *From the Morgenthau Diaries*, III, 335.

50. Kimball, *Swords or Ploughshares?*, 54.

51. Ibid. Also, see United States Department of State, *Foreign Relations of the United States: The Conferences at Malta and Yalta 1945* (Washington, D.C.: Government Printing Office, 1950), 968-973.

52. Acting Secretary of State Joseph C. Crew to Roosevelt, March 23, 1945, United States Department of State, *Foreign Relations of the United States, 1945*, 8 vols. (Washington, D.C.: Government Printing Office, 1968), III, 471-473. According to the memorandum, Germany would not be allowed to obtain credit, except in emergencies. In addition, the Allies also reserved for themselves the right to control all of Germany's financial transactions.

53. United States Department of State, *Germany 1947-1949: The Story in Documents* (Washington, D.C.: Government Printing Office, 1950), 28.

54. Ibid., 25.

55. Kimball, *Swords or Ploughshares?*, 60.

56. Hammond, "Directives for the Occupation of Germany: The Washington Controversy," in Stein, ed., *American Civil-Military Decisions*, 464.

57. Executive Order 9547, May 2, 1945, 10 *Federal Register*, 4961.

58. House Concurrent Resolution 39, May 7, 1945, *Congressional Record*, 79th Congress, 1st Session, 4281-4289.

59. *Foreign Relations of the United States, 1945*, III, 1162-1164.

60. Ibid., 1164.

61. "Report to the President by Robert H. Jackson, Chief Counsel for the United States," June 7, 1945, in Robert H. Jackson, *The Nürnberg Case* (New York: Knopf, 1947), 3-18. Also, see United States Department of State, *Bulletin*, June 10, 1945, 1071-1078. Jackson's misgivings about the slowness of progress on the diplomatic front were well founded. By the beginning of July the French and British had agreed with the U.S. position, but the Soviets had not. Jackson attributed this to a "deep difference in legal philosophy and attitude." *Foreign Relations of the United States, 1945*, III, 1167.

62. International Military Tribunal, *Trial of the Major War Criminals*, 42 vols. (Nuremberg: IMT, 1947), I, 11.

63. Ibid., 27-92.

64. Ibid., 16.

65. Control Council Law No. 10 put the London Agreement into effect and thus created "a uniform legal basis in Germany for the prosecution of war criminals and similar offenders." U.S. Military Government Ordinance No. 7 established the twelve additional American military courts on October 18, 1946. Nuremberg Military Tribunals, *Trials of War Criminals*, 15 vols. (Washington, D.C.: Government Printing Office, 1953), XV, 23-35.

66. Smith ascribes that name to the war crimes program. Smith, *The Road to Nuremberg*, 33.

67. Moltmann, "Zur Formulierung der amerikanischen Besatzungspolitik in Deutschland am Ende des Zweiten Weltkrieges," *Vierteljahrshefte für Zeitgeschichte* 15 (1967), 299-322.

2
Doubts about the U.S. War Crimes Program, 1946-1951

Although a majority of Americans apparently favored the punishment of war criminals in the immediate post-war era, the United States trial program was not without its domestic critics. As William J. Bosch has shown, several influential groups, ranging from conservative congressmen and newspapers opposed to the Roosevelt and Truman administrations to legal scholars, were highly critical of the policy.[1] To Bosch's list of outright opponents one must add a number of individuals intimately connected with the program, who entertained serious doubts about the way in which it was effected. Several justices of the U.S. Supreme Court, Secretary of the Army Kenneth C. Royall, the American Chief Counsel at Nuremberg Justice Jackson, the U.S. Military Governor in Germany Gen. Lucius D. Clay, as well as employees of the Army's War Crimes Branch, in time found fault with certain aspects of the trials.

The variety of reasons offered by the program's opponents and doubters were as diverse as the makeup of the above groups. Tom Bower has charged that some critics were motivated by their own anti-Semitic and pro-German biases, and not by concern for the integrity of the proceedings. These individuals, including several members of the U.S. Congress, used the highly publicized congressional inquiry into the Malmédy trial in 1949 to discredit the entire war crimes operations.[2] John Mendelsohn has also viewed congressional criticism (in addition to Malmédy, the Buchenwald trial was also the subject of an investigation) as important, but he has added other explanations directly related to the Cold War. These include the American media's admiration for the stamina of the citizens of Berlin during the Soviet blockade, coupled with the general belief that the possibility of a Nazi revival in the late 1940s seemed remote. Furthermore, the U.S. High Commission, established in 1949, actively sought a friendly relationship with the newly created Federal Republic, believing that the new German state was crucial to European and U.S. security interests in the face of Soviet aggression. The result of these developments, Mendelsohn believes, was "a more positive [American] attitude toward clemency for war criminals."[3] However, neither Bower's nor Mendelsohn's arguments provide a complete explanation. They have ignored other critics and doubters in the post-war era who had, or at least thought they had, legitimate grounds to question some elements of the war crimes program.

For civil courts in the United States, the trials of war criminals in Germany and the Far East brought up important constitutional questions, such as the defendant's right to challenge the jurisdiction of a tribunal or to an appeal, which the London Agreement denied. Court records also highlighted additional legal problems of the conspiracy and criminal organization indictments, which some historians see as a failure of the war crimes policy.[4] Aside from these considerations, members of the Truman administration questioned the sincerity of the Soviet prosecutors at the International Military Tribunal and the wisdom of trying defendants solely on the basis of violations of the rules and laws of war. Lastly, purely human factors also played a role in lessening the enthusiasm of U.S. officials to bring war criminals to justice. For example, by 1949 Gen. Clay admitted that he was tired of signing death warrants and confirming life sentences.

Although the Allies had begun to prosecute the first string of Nazi leaders at Nuremberg in late 1945, they still had to agree on future trials of war criminals, such as litigation against the German industrialists, Nazi bureaucrats and generals. One choice was to convene a second international court for further proceedings. The alternative was to prosecute these individuals unilaterally on a zonal basis. By May 1946 Justice Robert Jackson had become thoroughly disenchanted with the idea of staging additional international war crimes trials. Jackson had developed a strong dislike for the prosecutorial methods of his Soviet counterparts. The U.S. Chief Counsel suspected the Russians of using the Nuremberg Trial for political purposes rather than bringing the top Nazi perpetrators, like *Reichsmarschall* Hermann Goering, Foreign Minister Joachim von Ribbentrop and others, to justice. Jackson was particularly irritated by the fact that witnesses, whom the Americans and British had already interrogated, "have been questioned with lengthy futility by the Soviet prosecutors for reasons of home consumption." Consequently, the U.S. Supreme Court Justice recommended against American participation in a second international trial.[5] Gen. Clay fully supported Jackson's position. Clay preferred separate zonal trials to future international courts, fearing that ideological differences might render the war crimes program meaningless.[6]

The U.S. State Department viewed the matter somewhat differently. Secretary of State James F. Byrnes doubted that the United States could prevent another international trial. The Truman administration should not actively push for a second International Military Tribunal, Byrnes counseled, adding that should the other Allies insist on further multilateral courts "and are prepared to meet our requirements, we had better play along with them." In the latter case, the United States should at least ensure that a British or an American judge receive the presidency of the court.[7]

These doubts about the intentions and the style of Soviet prosecutors at the IMT had important consequences. After 1946 the United States unilaterally prosecuted other German war criminals before twelve American military tribunals at Nuremberg in the U.S. zone of occupation. These courts also adopted the rules of procedure as defined by the London Agreement of August 1945, which had been incorporated in Control Council Law No. 10. As a result, the United States created a third jurisdiction, in addition to the two existing ones, for war crimes cases. The Trial of the Major War Criminals had been the responsibility of all four major Allies. Furthermore, the Judge Advocate of U.S. Forces, European Theater (USFET)—redesignated European Command (EUCOM) on March 15, 1947—was charged with trying war criminals in cases involving the murder and mistreatment of American soldiers, mass atrocities in the area now comprising the U.S. zone of occupation and concentration camps which the Army had liberated. The Army's war crimes program, which held most of its trials at Dachau, prosecuted a total of 1,672 defendants, of whom 1,416 were convicted.[8]

The task of proceeding unilaterally against other major Nazi war criminals in subsequent tribunals fell to the U.S. Chief of Counsel for War Crimes at Nuremberg. When the International Military Tribunal (IMT) came to a close in October 1946, Brigadier General Telford Taylor replaced Jackson as the chief American prosecutor. Taylor became responsible for the prosecution of two groups of defendants: (1) the leaders of the European Axis powers and their principal agents and accessories (aside from those already sentenced by the IMT) and (2) members of organizations which the IMT had declared criminal.[9] During this phase of the war crimes program, twelve U.S. military courts at Nuremberg tried 185 defendants. The majority of these trials targeted members of specific groups, such as the *SS*, the German High Command, the mobile killing squads, the foreign and justice ministries, industrialists and others. These proceedings later became known officially as the Trials of War Criminals, but historians also refer to them as the Nuremberg program or the subsequent tribunals. Since the accused were convicted by purely American courts, they were eventually able to benefit from U.S. parole and clemency programs in the late 1940s and early 1950s. In addition, many defendants used the opportunity to challenge their convictions and sentences before courts in the United States. This contrasted starkly with the IMT, where any decisions affecting convicted defendants required the consensus of the three Western Allies and the Soviet Union.[10]

In the second half of the 1940s, the U.S. judiciary confronted two issues involving convicted war criminals: (1) whether American civil courts had the authority to accept petitions for writs of *habeas corpus* on behalf of enemy aliens sentenced by military tribunals operating under an international charter and (2) whether individuals, who had not been high-ranking Nazi government officials, should be indicted for participating in a conspiracy or common plan, an important issue in many U.S. trials of war criminals. With regard to the first point, none of the German or Japanese defendants succeeded in having American civil courts reverse the verdicts of the military tribunals. However, the lack of an appellate instance, as specified by Nuremberg procedure, clearly bothered many in the legal community, including justices on the U.S. Supreme Court. *U.S.* v. *Krauch et al.*, popularly called the I.G. Farben trial, highlighted the problems connected with the use of the conspiracy charge.[11]

The first case which reached the U.S. Supreme Court dealing with the issue of jurisdiction over enemy aliens convicted by U.S. military tribunals occurred in June 1942. That month, U.S. authorities captured eight German soldiers, who had come to the United States as saboteurs. A military court tried these individuals on charges that they had violated the laws of war. During the ensuing trial, seven defendants appealed to the Supreme Court for writs of *habeas corpus*, which the Court denied. In his opinion of October 1942, Chief Justice Harlan F. Stone argued that military courts were outside the meaning of the U.S. Constitution. Consequently, the constitutional protections for defendants before civil courts did not apply to the accused before military tribunals.[12]

Although Stone had rejected the arguments of the German saboteurs, others were encouraged by the Court's willingness to hear the case in the first place. Thus, in 1945 lawyers for Japanese Gen. Yamashita, whom an American military commission had convicted for war crimes, appealed to the Supreme Court on the grounds that the general had not received a fair trial as required by the Fifth Amendment. Stone and a majority on the Court turned Yamashita down. Two Justices, however, Frank Murphy and Wiley B. Rutledge, filed lengthy dissenting opinions. Murphy's dissent concluded that the Constitution's guarantee of due process applied to any person charged with the commission of a crime by the federal government or any of its agencies. Murphy made it clear that his interpretation also included war criminals, arguing that

no exception is made as to those who are accused of war crimes or as to those who possess the status of an enemy belligerent. Indeed, such an exception would be contrary to the whole philosophy of human rights which makes the Constitution the great living document that it is. The immutable rights of the individual, including those secured by the due process clause of the Fifth Amendment, belong not only to the members of those nations that excel on the battlefield or that subscribe to the democratic ideology. They belong to every person in the world, victor or vanquished, whatever may be his race, color or beliefs.[13]

Rutledge echoed Murphy's assessment that the United States was engaged in practicing victor's justice without regard for the requirements of the Constitution. For Rutledge, the emotional and physical wounds of the war were still too fresh to allow the victors to treat their former enemies wisely. Rutledge also viewed the trial and conviction of Yamashita as a departure from the American legal tradition. The justice viewed the concept of guilt by association as well as the application of what he considered to be *ex post facto* law in war crimes cases as completely incompatible with that tradition. As a result, Rutledge accused the military tribunal of lacking jurisdiction to try and to punish the general.[14]

Murphy and Rutledge's dissenting opinions undoubtedly encouraged convicted German war criminals to bring their cases before civil courts in the United States. As a consequence, many of those who had been found guilty by the Dachau and Nuremberg tribunals filed petitions for writs of *habeas corpus* in the late 1940s. During the October Term 1948 alone, fifty-eight Germans brought their cases before the Court. The U.S. Supreme Court continued refusing to assume jurisdiction, arguing that it lacked the power to review the judgments of military commissions. The majority of justices did not regard these tribunals as courts of the United States, but rather as courts of the Allied powers. Although the Court did not extend its jurisdiction to American war crimes trials, there were considerable differences among the justices. Four members of the Court were clearly troubled by the fact that the trial procedure to which the Allies had agreed forbade the review of verdicts and judgments of war crimes proceedings. Consequently, the Supreme Court engaged in a long series of close decisions. Murphy and Rutledge won the support of Justices Hugo L. Black and William O. Douglas in arguing that the Court should allow the filing of the petitions to determine what legal remedy the petitioners had. With Jackson, as the former U.S. chief prosecutor at Nuremberg, disqualifying himself, the Court denied many petitions for writs of *habeas corpus*, predominantly on four-to-four votes.[15]

The close decisions indicated that almost half the Court, or exactly half if one excludes Jackson, had doubts as to the constitutionality of the war crimes program and its rules of procedure, particularly the lack of a provision for an appellate instance. But even more damning than the obvious division on the Court concerning the jurisdictional question was the concurring opinion which Douglas filed in *Hirota* v. *MacArthur* in the summer of 1949. Six months earlier, the Supreme Court had denied the petitions of Hirota and other Japanese war criminals for writs of *habeas corpus*. That decision sent seven condemned offenders to the gallows. On December 20, 1948, the day of the vote, Douglas stated that he would submit his views on the case at a later time.[16]

In his concurring opinion of June 27, 1949, Douglas agreed with the majority that the Court lacked jurisdiction to consider Hirota's petition. Nonetheless, the justice used the opportunity to challenge the Allied war crimes program. International military tribunals were "an instrument of political power," Douglas argued, and did not act as free and independent judicial bodies, but rather as a tool of the executive to exert its will in the area of foreign policy.[17]

Douglas rejected the majority's notion that the legal actions of the Allied powers were completely off-limits to American civil courts. An American general who acted as the jailer of convicted war criminals derived his authority from the U.S. government and the Constitution, Douglas wrote, and consequently "it is our Constitution which he supports and defends. If there is evasion or violation of its obligations, it is no defense that he acts for another nation." Douglas concluded that the Court had indeed allowed American officials to commit unconstitutional acts by denying Hirota's petition on the grounds that the petitioners' American jailer acted on behalf of both the United States and other nations. This, Douglas argued, was an insufficient excuse for the Court's refusal to extend writs of *habeas corpus* to the petitioners.[18]

The United States Court of Appeals at Washington, D.C., soon extended this argument to other than Japanese war criminals. In *Eisenträger et al.* v. *Forrestal et al.*, the appeals court reversed a District Court's decision which had denied the petitions for writs of twenty-two German inmates of the American war crimes prison at Landsberg. Eisenträger was a particularly interesting case. Eisenträger and his co-defendants had been part of a German intelligence operation in the Far East and had continued to work against the Allies even after the end of the war in Europe. After capture by the Americans, they were tried for war crimes. Following their convictions by a military tribunal, the defendants ended up serving their sentences at Landsberg. In deciding this case, the court took issue with Chief Justice Stone's earlier interpretation of the German saboteurs case. The appeals court thought it perfectly proper for enemy aliens to use *habeas corpus* to challenge the jurisdiction of military tribunals. In fact, the appellate judges implied that the U.S. federal government had overstepped its authority by excluding a certain category of defendants from the right to employ the writ. Since Article I, Section 9 of the Constitution only permitted the suspension of this privilege in cases of rebellion or invasion, the Court of Appeals felt that government officials and the Congress had gone beyond their constitutional powers.[19] Despite these arguments, the Supreme Court denied the petitions in June 1950, with Justices Black, Douglas and Harold H. Burton dissenting.[20]

While the civil courts in the United States were quietly dealing with the question of the war crimes trials' constitutionality in the late 1940s, the U.S. war crimes program at Nuremberg was soon engulfed in public controversy. The scandal began when Iowa Supreme Court Justice Charles F. Wennerstrum, the presiding judge in the Hostage case (*U.S.* v. *List et al.*), surprised

U.S. authorities in Germany in February 1948 by strongly criticizing the war crimes program. In an interview with *Chicago Tribune* correspondent Hal Foust, Wennerstrum appeared to confirm German suspicions that the proceedings were nothing more than an expression of victor's justice. The judge accused the American prosecution of having veered from the original intent of the trial program, which he interpreted as the creation of a legal precedent to avoid future wars and the codification of the "rules for the conduct of governments and armies." Instead, Wennerstrum contended, the U.S. prosecutors had given the war crimes trials a highly nationalistic character. The Iowa Justice also viewed the absence of an appellate court for convicted defendants as a serious mistake, amounting to a denial of justice. Overall, the judge told Foust, his experience with U.S. war crimes policy in Germany had been so unpleasant that he "would have never come here," had he known what the tribunals were all about.[21]

Wennerstrum's statements were immediately denounced by U.S. Chief Counsel Taylor. Taylor questioned Wennerstrum's sincerity—citing his continuance as the presiding judge throughout the trial of the German generals despite his apparent misgivings—and accused the latter of providing propaganda material for the "worst elements in Germany." The prosecutor feared that Wennerstrum's public condemnation of the war crimes program would undermine American efforts to use the trials as a means to reeducate the Germans.[22] Just how serious the U.S. government and the Army took the incident to be became evident a few days later, when the news leaked out that the Army had intercepted Foust's transmission of the story from Germany to the United States in violation of American wire laws.[23]

In reality, the controversy should not have come as a surprise. Wennerstrum and the other two tribunal members in the Hostage Case, Edward F. Carter and George J. Burke, had earlier criticized aspects of the war crimes program. The three had deemed it regrettable that the court was composed only of judges from one victorious nation, the United States, and thus lacked a truly international character. For this, the American judges faulted the "lethargy of the world's statesmen," who had permitted international law to remain rather rudimentary in this area. This lack of sophistication with regard to international law had invited charges of unfairness. However, the judges did not see improvements in the current system as their responsibility, but as a challenge to political leaders. Wennerstrum, Carter and Burke claimed to have tried their best to preserve the trial's international character and to prevent it from deteriorating to a highly nationalistic level. Consequently, while the defendants in the Hostage Case had enjoyed a fair proceeding, the system as a whole required changes.[24]

Wennerstrum's remarks to the *Chicago Tribune* were welcomed by German opponents of the war crimes program. German lawyers for the defense during the trials against the industrialists and High Command generals seized on the Iowa justice's criticism and petitioned President Truman to ensure fair proceedings. American prosecutors, the defense claimed, had resorted to "intimidation and other illegal methods" to obtain evidence.[25] This proved to be the most disturbing result of the affair. For Wennerstrum's action, even if primarily aimed at an American audience, inevitably kindled further German anti-Nuremberg sentiment. For those Germans opposed to the trial program, the fact that the Americans were publicly debating these trials seemed to indicate decreasing U.S. commitment to the proceedings.

The Wennerstrum furor was not the last time that American judges at Nuremberg pinpointed perceived flaws in the war crimes program. In the summer of 1948, an American court handed down its judgment in *U.S. v. Krauch et al.*, the case against the directors of the chemical giant I.G. Farben, which had made extensive use of slave labor at its synthetic oil and rubber plant in Auschwitz. Although convicting thirteen of the twenty-three defendants, the court had exonerated the accused on two counts of the indictment: the planning and waging of aggressive war, and conspiracy to commit crimes against the peace. The dismissal of these charges resulted from the tribunal's conclusion that the I.G. Farben directors had been followers, but not the makers, of Nazi foreign policy.[26] That action led to strong disagreement among the judges. Tribunal member Paul M. Hebert, in his concurring opinion, charged that the court "misread the record in the direction of a too complete exoneration and an exculpation of even moral guilt to a degree which I consider unwarranted." For Hebert, the verdict of not guilty on the aggressive war and conspiracy counts was necessitated by the earlier judgment of the IMT and was not a testament to the moral innocence of the I.G. Farben defendants. The IMT had convicted Hitler successor Admiral Karl Dönitz on one of these counts for engaging in aggressive submarine warfare, but had found Armament Minister Albert Speer not guilty on the conspiracy and aggressive war charges.[27] Hebert considered it illogical to pronounce guilty verdicts for Krauch and his co-defendants on the same counts of which the IMT had cleared the head of the Armament Ministry himself.[28]

Hebert also objected to the American tribunal's ruling to convict only five of the defendants for having used slave labor at I.G. Farben's Auschwitz plant, while having acquitted fifteen members of the company's board on this charge. All directors, and not only the five most closely connected with Auschwitz, Hebert argued, were criminally responsible on this count. The judge thus disputed the defense notion, apparently accepted by the court, that the accused had only engaged in slave labor owing to fear of reprisals if they had refused to cooperate with the Nazis. According to Hebert, the I.G. Farben board had willingly worked with the *SS* in exploiting slave laborers. Thus, Hebert dissented from the tribunal's judgment on this count since, in his opinion, it was not supported by the evidence.[29]

Simultaneous with the American judiciary's involvement with the war crimes program, key conservative congressmen began to critize these proceedings. Unlike the judicial branch of government, the majority of the legislators critical of the operation were not concerned with constitutional issues. Conservative congressmen regarded American trials of German war criminals as a welcome partisan issue and a useful political tool to embarrass the Truman administration. The ink on the IMT verdicts had hardly dried, when Senator Robert A. Taft (R-Ohio) began to attack the Nuremberg Trial. Taft, however, was the laudable exception among the program's critics in the Congress. The Republican Senator appeared to be truly concerned about its constitutional implications.[30] The same cannot be said for other congressional opponents. In the opinions of these congressmen, the "Communist-inspired" trials were yet another expression of Truman's soft policy toward the Soviets. As a result, a number of senators and representatives did not hesitate to stoop to correspond with Landsberg prisoners and German critics of the program as part of an effort to discredit the administration.[31] These congressmen were remarkably successful in establishing a new Nuremberg philosophy. By the end of the 1940s, many in the United States had come to accept the conservative argument that the convicted Nazi perpetrators were not criminals, but were instead the victims of the Allied war crimes program. This attitude, which played greatly into the hands of the German anti-trial lobby, further lessened the commitment of U.S. authorities to carry out the program as originally intended.

Like Taft, the congressional hardliners did not wait long to criticize the war crimes program. For some, the trials of the "so-called war criminals" were the result of a desire for revenge on the part of aliens whom the U.S. government had employed to help investigate suspects. As a consequence, Congressmen Francis Case (R-South Dakota), Harold Knutson (R-Minnesota) and John Taber (R-New York) scolded the administration for continuing to prosecute individuals, even after the other Allies had allegedly stopped doing so.[32] Senator William Langer (R-North Dakota), one of the most outspoken critics, pointedly argued that the Soviets had devised the program. Comparing the Nuremberg proceedings to the Stalinist purge trials of the 1930s, Langer claimed that the Communists were using the war crimes program to destroy property rights, and thus capitalism and the Western world.[33]

In 1949 congressional conservatives readily exploited a new opportunity to raise public doubts about the trials. In that year, the American war crimes program suffered its most severe setback. The specific cause was the controversy surrounding the U.S. Army's trials of war criminals at Dachau. The largest proceeding of that program involved seventy-four members of the *SS* accused of having murdered a large number of American prisoners of war and civilians near the Belgian town of Malmédy. The incident had occurred during the Battle of the Bulge in December 1944. The massacre, which had once served to strengthen the American resolve to hold trials of war criminals,[34] now came back to haunt the United States by posing serious questions about the integrity of the war crimes program.[35]

The Malmédy trial had begun in May 1946 and had ended only two months later. The American tribunal had then found seventy-three of the defendants guilty and sentenced forty-three to death. During the trial, however, several of the accused had claimed to have been tortured and mistreated by American pre-trial interrogators wanting to extract statements. The defendants' court-appointed U.S. attorney, Willis M. Everett, Jr., had further charged in 1947 that 80 to 90 percent of the confessions had been obtained illegally by Army personnel, who had posed as bogus priests and had staged mock trials. In addition, Everett had blamed the court for permitting unfair and deceptive practices by the prosecution, which had made an effective defense impossible. Believing that his clients had not had a fair trial, Everett had petitioned the Army's Judge Advocate General Division (JAGD) to review the trial record.[36]

Not having much confidence that the Army could fairly investigate its own handling of military justice, on May 11, 1948, Everett had filed a petition for writs of *habeas corpus* on behalf of his German clients before the Supreme Court. The Court had turned down Everett's request within the week. However, the Court had again remained deeply divided on the issue and, in a rare hearing of the arguments behind closed doors, had denied the petition on yet another close four-to-four vote, arguing that it lacked jurisdiction.[37] The Army was thus well aware that, despite the Supreme Court decision, the defendants' allegations of illegal investigation and improper prosecution methods remained potentially controversial issues. Consequently, Secretary of the Army Royall had directed Theater Judge Advocate Brig. Gen. James L. Harbaugh to launch his own investigation into the matter.[38]

Harbaugh had already reviewed the Malmédy convictions and sentences once and had sent modification recommendations to Clay in March 1948. As a result, the U.S. Military Governor had commuted all but twelve of the forty-three life sentences and had released thirteen Malmédy war criminals from Landsberg.[39] Clay knew that his clemency decisions would not close the book on the Malmédy affair. Thus, in July 1948, the general had ordered his Administration of Justice Review Board to conduct yet another investigation into the trial. Clay's action did not satisfy the Secretary of the Army. During the same month, Royall sent Texas Supreme Court Justice Gordon Simpson, Pennsylvania judge Edward LeRoy Van Roden, and Lt. Col. Charles W. Lawrence of JAGD to Germany to review all sentences handed down during the Army's Dachau war crimes program.[40]

Royall obviously intended to cover all contingencies. For the summer of 1948, the Malmédy trial had clearly put the Army on the defensive. The press had already published reports detailing Everett's allegations of foul play. Now, the affair was developing into a serious controversy on both sides of the Atlantic Ocean. In Germany, a number of Catholic and Protestant bishops engaged in a lengthy campaign criticizing not only the Malmédy proceedings, but the entire Dachau program (see Chapter six).[41] In the United States,

Malmédy provided congressional and other opponents of the war crimes trials with the opportunity to harshly criticize the program.[42] Thus, it mattered little that Army Secretary Royall stayed the executions of those twelve whose sentences Clay had reaffirmed in March.

On September 14, 1948, Royall received the report of the Simpson Commission. This three-man investigative board had found "no general or systematic use of improper methods to secure prosecution evidence for use at the trials" of the Dachau program. The Commission did express its doubts about the staging of mock trials by the pre-trial investigators in order to extract statements and confessions. Simpson, Van Roden and Lawrence considered the remaining twelve Malmédy death sentences, which Clay had confirmed, justified. However, since the trial had been tinged with impropriety, the Simpson Commission recommended that the death sentences be commuted to life terms.[43]

The growing Malmédy controversy, as well as other charges that American military courts and prosecutors had not given German war criminals a fair trial, precipitated a crisis of confidence among those U.S. officials charged with carrying out the war crimes program.[44] Clay himself indicated that his responsibilities in that area were wearing on him. The general complained about his "lot to have had to sign many death warrants and to approve many life imprisonments."[45] Royall cited the conviction of Japanese General Tojo to state his own reservations about certain aspects of the program. The Army Secretary felt that war crimes trials based solely on the "waging aggressive war" indictment were wrong. Royall believed the proceedings to be fully justifiable for defendants accused of atrocities. Thus, Royall drew a conclusion similar to the one that the I.G. Farben tribunal also incorporated into its judgment in December 1948. American trials of war criminals, both in Germany and Japan, contained some worrisome features, which the secretary considered sufficiently serious to bring them to the attention of the president.[46]

To the annoyance of Malmédy defense counsel Everett, Clay was not yet tired enough of executions to consider commuting all death sentences.[47] But the military governor had to move quickly. Conservative congressmen were already preparing to launch an investigation into the Malmédy trial and the entire Dachau war crimes program. On February 11, 1948, Senator Langer informed Clay of his decision to introduce Senate Resolution 39[48] to examine the administration of U.S. military justice in occupied countries. Langer requested that Clay stop further executions until the Senate had acted on the resolution.[49]

Eager to get the remaining executions behind him, Clay received the report of his own Administration of Justice Review Board three days after Langer's cable. This report strengthened Clay's position. The board found that mock trials and violence had only been used sporadically to obtain confessions and blamed this more on the tough caliber of the defendants than the intentions

of the American investigators. It also concluded that the American interrogators had encouraged enlisted men to testify against their officers and
had placed stool pigeons in the prisoners' cells in order to make them talk.
Aside from these points, the board uncovered no evidence corroborating
other allegations of improper prosecution methods during the trial.[50]

In late March 1949, after two months of congressional squabbling as to
who should investigate the Malmédy trial, the job fell to a subcommittee of
the Senate Armed Services Committee chaired by Senator Raymond E. Baldwin (R-Connecticut), and including Senators Carey Estes Kefauver (D-Ten-
nessee) and Lester C. Hunt (D-Wyoming). Both Baldwin and Kefauver had
ties to members of the prosecution and interrogation teams at the Malmédy
trial through the law firms for which they had once worked. To gain additional credibility and quiet the more radical Army critics, the subcommittee
accordingly invited Senator Joseph McCarthy to become a visiting member.
McCarthy dominated the ensuing hearings for almost a month and sharply
attacked the Army. One historian, James F. Weingartner, has argued that
the presence of the Wisconsin Senator "made those hearings more meaning-
ful than they otherwise would have been."[51] Weingartner's assessment is
without merit. When the senator left the subcommittee in May 1949, his in-
quisitorial style and publicly proclaimed doubts about the honesty and integrity of the Army's War Crimes Branch personnel only caused cynicism and
fear among those engaged in the war crimes program.

A memorandum written by Theater Judge Advocate Col. Damon Gunn
to Clay's successor and EUCOM Commander in Chief Gen. Thomas T.
Handy in November 1950 best summarizes the impact of McCarthy's role in
the subcommittee's investigation. Gunn was listing the arguments for and
against prompt executions of the by then twenty-eight remaining condemned
war criminals. Among Gunn's most important considerations was the probable negative congressional response to additional executions. Consequently,
he reminded Handy that should the general delay the carrying out of the
death penalties until January 1951, when Congress would be in session, any
congressman "who makes any issue of anything which the administration
does" would become the center of attention. Gunn feared a particularly
negative reaction to additional executions of war criminals by the Army in
Germany. It would be better to do away with the last death row inmates at
Landsberg in November and December, Gunn counseled, since the elections
had only recently taken place and most congressmen would be on vacation,
thus limiting the potential for harsh criticism and interference from Congress.[52]

Gunn had good reason for his cynical assessment. The Baldwin subcommittee had begun its probe on April 18, 1948, and by then, the number of
Malmédy defendants still under death sentence had shrunk to six. Army Secretary Royall, the first witness to testify and eager to seek congressional cooperation, had invited the subcommittee's recommendations with regard to

these cases, promising that the administration would gladly take them into consideration. Senator McCarthy, however, was not impressed by the secretary's efforts to involve the Congress in war crimes decision-making, the Senator having already concluded that the Army was guilty of grave misconduct in the Malmédy investigation.[53]

Two days later, McCarthy had engaged in a heated confrontation with Col. Burton Ellis, the head of the Army prosecution team at the trial. The Wisconsin senator had used this occasion to charge for the first time that the subcommittee intended to whitewash the Army.[54] The low point of the hearings was reached three weeks later, when McCarthy insisted that William R. Perl, one of the American interrogators, take a lie detector test. That demand was unacceptable to the regular members of the subcommittee, who had so far permitted McCarthy to monopolize the inquiry.[55]

Despite McCarthy's outbursts at Army personnel, the hearings still managed to provide some startling revelations. Judge Van Roden, who, as a member of the Simpson Commission, had earlier given the Dachau war crimes program a clean bill of health, had apparently changed his mind. The February 1949 issue of *The Progressive* featured an article with the catchy title "American Atrocities in Germany." Although not the author, the story still carried Van Roden's by-line and the judge did accept payment from the magazine.[56] The article was actually a summarized version of remarks Van Roden had made during a speech earlier in the year and was only published under his name, the judge claimed, because he failed to realize what a by-line was.[57]

Nonetheless, "American Atrocities in Germany" seemed to confirm Everett and the defendants' allegations of physical and mental mistreatment. Van Roden claimed to have been concerned mainly that the use of beatings, mock trials and bogus priests by pre-trial investigators—charges which he now viewed as substantiated—would cause "permanent and irreparable damage" to "the prestige of America and American justice." To remedy the situation, Van Roden suggested that those U.S. interrogators guilty of such illegal acts should stand trial for having "abused the powers of victory and prostituted justice to vengeance."[58] The judge repeated this assessment of the Malmédy trial proceedings before the Baldwin subcommittee on May 4, 1949. And, most importantly, Van Roden also reinterpreted the events which had occurred in December 1944. While it had been generally believed that the SS had simply massacred its American POWs, Van Roden now told the committee that an attempted escape by the prisoners might have been the reason for the machine-gunning.[59]

Although Van Roden's damaging testimony should have given a second wind to McCarthy's campaign to discredit U.S. trials of German war criminals, the senator withdrew from the hearings on May 20. McCarthy did not leave the subcommittee without taking a parting shot at its chairman Baldwin and the other members. The Wisconsin senator openly accused the committee of whitewashing the Army's alleged resorting to "Gestapo and OGPU tactics." In McCarthy's opinion, Baldwin's refusal to come down harder on four Army investigators, whom the former had identified as the perpetrators, was particularly worrisome. The United States could hardly afford to "protest the use of these methods by totalitarian countries" as long as Congress tolerated the application of torture and mock trials during the Army's war crimes program.[60] McCarthy repeated these charges two months later on the Senate floor. This time, the Wisconsin senator insisted that Baldwin had been "criminally wrong" when assuming the subcommittee's chairmanship despite the fact of his earlier close professional connections with the head of a different U.S. interrogation team which had also extracted confessions from accused Nazis.[61]

Publishing its final report on October 13, 1949, the Baldwin subcommittee struck back at its accusers and critics of the war crimes trials both in the United States and in Germany. While conceding that some practices had been questionable and recommending a number of improvements,[62] the report in general exonerated the Army's program. More was at stake than the Army's conduct in this particular matter, the subcommittee warned, emphasizing that the "attacks on the war-crimes trials in general and the Malmédy case in particular" were meant to revive German nationalism and to cast doubt upon the U.S. occupation of Germany as a whole. In fact, the report cited evidence of the existence of groups in Germany seeking to have the United States withdraw its troops from Germany for two reasons: to pass a general amnesty for former Nazis convicted of war crimes and to establish close relations with the Soviet Union. The protests against the Malmédy trial were a part of this conspiracy, the report claimed, and were intended to exploit the controversy's potential to damage the image and reputation of the United States. Thus, those opposed to the American occupation—the subcommittee was careful not to name Senators McCarthy and Langer—had merely exploited the legitimate concerns of the defense for their own sinister political goals.[63]

Not all critics of the Dachau war crimes program and the Army's handling of the Malmédy trial fit that mold. In January 1951 Ben A. Smith, a former staff member of EUCOM's Judge Advocate Division, expressed his misgivings to Clay's successor Gen. Handy to prevent further executions of defendants condemned during the Army trials. Smith reminded the general that the majority of Dachau defendants were "small potatoes" and the "garden variety" of war criminals. The former War Crimes Branch employee, who had earlier recommended against commuting the death penalty in the case of one Landsberg prisoner then still on death row, now regretted this decision. Smith also considered the remaining Malmédy defendants under death sentence to be minor war criminals. Their executions, he wrote Handy, would be morally wrong and would not benefit the United States and its goals in any way.[64]

Neither the Baldwin subcommittee's conspiracy theory nor Smith's comments explain why U.S. Senators Langer and McCarthy had taken up such an apparent no-win issue as attacking the Army for prosecuting murderers of American POWs. McCarthy biographer Thomas C. Reeves argues that McCarthy became initially involved with Malmédy to make political gains, but that the latter's interest "quickly rose above his own political considerations and assumed characteristics of a personal crusade against the forces of evil."[65] According to historian Glenn H. Smith, Langer thought that the entire war crimes program, and not just Malmédy, was a big mistake. The North Dakota Senator felt that the United States should only have tried prominent Nazi party officials. This belief was coupled with Langer's contention that U.S. war crimes policy benefited communism and, at the same time, violated the American legal tradition.[66] William Bosch offers an additional explanation, which casts doubt upon Reeves's rather positive assessment of McCarthy's motivations. Bosch stresses that both Langer and McCarthy owed their political careers to constituencies which were predominantly of German descent and anti-Communist. Thus, Langer and McCarthy "desired to prove their first-class citizenship by opposition to" communism and the "Communist-inspired" war crimes trials.[67]

Langer and McCarthy's actions caused the most visible damage to the war crimes program. The Malmédy hearings recast the Nazi perpetrators, to the chagrin of EUCOM War Crimes Branch employees, as the victims of an alleged American injustice. This altered image had two important consequences. First, the senators' charges of wrongdoing and misconduct by Army investigators fueled the German anti-trial propaganda machine. This became increasingly clear when German foes of the U.S. war crimes policy were allowed to testify before the Baldwin subcommittee during the second phase of the hearings in the fall of 1949. Second, those charged with executing the program now knew that congressional support was shaky at best. Indeed, the Baldwin report itself might have been more critical of the Army had McCarthy refrained from his personal attacks against witnesses and committee members.

Still, there were other significant reasons for the declining U.S. commitment to its war crimes policy. As civil court records indicate, prominent members of the legal profession had come to conclude that the trials' procedural base had severe shortcomings. This is reflected in the debates over the defendants' rights to appeal the verdicts and the judgments, and to use writs of *habeas corpus*. For William O. Douglas, the trials had an even darker side. The Supreme Court Justice considered the program as merely an exercise in political power and a demonstration of victor's justice rather than an honest attempt to punish those guilty of horrendous crimes. The negative opinions of several justices and the U.S. Court of Appeals at Washington, in connection with the private reservations of Royall, Clay, Jackson, Wennerstrum and others, inevitably weakened the war crimes policy.

Only if all these points are taken together can one understand the reasons for the decline of the U.S. commitment to carry out the program as originally planned. A variety of factors, including constitutional and legal considerations, private regrets, differing interpretations of policy goals, and Cold War-inspired congressional and media rhetoric, contributed to the changed climate that weakened the operation. In fact, the increasing doubts of many participants regarding the legal and procedural aspects and the trials' integrity seemed more important to this change than the cold political calculation to embark on a softer policy toward Germany due to increasingly hostile U.S.-Soviet relations. Those executing and reviewing the war crimes program were particularly troubled by the lack of an appellate court to correct procedure and ensure sentence equalization. Consequently, U.S. authorities soon resorted to the use of executive clemency and sentence reviews as remedies.

NOTES

1. William J. Bosch, *Judgment on Nuremberg* (Chapel Hill: University of North Carolina Press, 1970).

2. Bower, *The Pledge Betrayed*, 249-258, 267-270.

3. Mendelsohn, "War Crimes Trials and Clemency in Germany and Japan," in Wolfe, ed., *Americans as Proconsuls*, 247-251.

4. Smith, *The Road to Nuremberg*, 249-250.

5. Jackson to Truman, May 13, 1946, President's Secretary's Files/Foreign Affairs File, Box 179, Germany-Nuremberg War Crimes Folder, Truman Library.

6. U.S. Deputy Military Governor Lucius D. Clay to Brig. Gen. George F. Schulgen, Civil Affairs Division, War Department, August 4, 1946, in Edward Jean Smith, ed., 2 vols., *The Papers of Lucius DuBignon Clay* (Bloomington: Indiana University Press, 1974), I, 247.

7. Brig. Gen. Telford Taylor, Assistant U.S. Chief Counsel for the Prosecution of Axis Criminality, to Jackson, June 27, 1946, PSF/Foreign Affairs File, Box 179, Germany-Nuremberg War Crimes Folder, Truman Library.

8. International Memorandum, August 17, 1949, War Crimes Branch, Judge Advocate Division (JAD), EUCOM, RG 338, The United States Army in World War II, The United States Army in Europe (USAREUR), Box 468, Policy 1952 File, Military Field Branch, Military Archives Division, Washington National Record Center, National Archives.

9. Ibid.

10. See Mendelsohn, "War Crimes Trials and Clemency in Germany and Japan," in Wolfe, ed., *Americans as Proconsuls*, 226-259.

11. *Trials of War Criminals*, VII-VIII.

12. Alfred H. Kelly, Winfred A. Harbison and Herman Belz, *The American Constitution: Its Origins and Development* (New York: Norton, 1983), 567.

13. In re Yamashita, February 4, 1946, 327 U.S. 1, 26.

14. Ibid., 43-45.

15. See Milch v. U.S., October 20, 1947, 332 U.S. 789; Brandt v. U.S., February 16, 1948, 333 U.S. 836; In re Eichel, April 5, 1948, 333 U.S. 864; and In re Muhlbauer, May 2, 1949, 336 U.S. 964.

16. "War Trials Doubts Stated by Douglas," *New York Times*, June 28, 1949, 8.

17. Concurring opinion of Justice Douglas, June 27, 1949, Hirota v. MacArthur, 338 U.S. 197, 215.

18. Ibid., 204.

19. Eisenträger et al. v. Forrestal et al., April 15, 1949, 174 *Federal Reporter*, 2nd Series, 961.

20. Johnson v. Eisenträger et al., June 5, 1950, 339 U.S. 763.

21. "Nazi Trial Judge Rips 'Injustice,' " *Chicago Tribune*, February 23, 1948, 1-2.

22. "Prosecutor Scores War-Crimes Judge," *New York Times*, February 23, 1948, 5.

23. "The Problem of Secrecy," *New York Times*, March 6, 1948, 6.

24. *Trials of War Criminals*, XI, 1318.

25. "Attorneys Appeal to Truman," *New York Times*, February 29, 1948, 10.

26. U.S. v. Krauch et al., *Trials of War Criminals*, VIII, 1125-28.

27. Bradley F. Smith states that, although Speer had been indicted on all four counts, "neither the prosecution nor most of the Court ever took the charges against him on Conspiracy or Crimes Against Peace very seriously." See Bradley F. Smith, *Reaching Judgment at Nuremberg* (New York: Basic Books, 1977), 218.

28. U.S. v. Krauch, *Trials of War Criminals*, VIII, 1306.

29. Ibid., 1307-1308.

30. Bosch, *Judgment on Nuremberg*, 76.

31. For example, Senator William Langer (R-North Dakota) lobbied on behalf of Martin Sandberger, who had been sentenced to death during the *Einsatzgruppen* case, on at least three different occasions. On May 25, June 1 and June 24, 1949, Langer sent the U.S. Military Government documents with the request that they be considered in Sandberger's case. Sandberger's sentence was eventually commuted to a life term. See RG 338, USAREUR, Box 464, Petition of Martin Sandberger File.

32. *Congressional Record*, December 16, 1947, 80th Congress, 2nd Session, 11468.

33. Ibid., December 18, 1950, 81st Congress, 2nd Session, 16708.

34. Smith, *The Road to Nuremberg*, 113-151.

35. See James F. Weingartner, *Crossroads of Death: The Story of the Malmédy Massacre and Trial* (Berkeley: University of California Press, 1979); Justus D. Doenecke, "Protest over Malmédy: A Case of Clemency," *Peace and Change* 4 (1977), 28-33; and Bower, *The Pledge Betrayed*, 248-271.

36. Petition for Review Requested by Willis M. Everett, defense counsel at the Malmédy trial, 1947, Milwaukee Public Library.

37. Everett v. Truman, May 18, 1948, 334 U.S. 824.

38. Col. Edward H. Young, War Crimes Branch, Department of the Army, to Theater Judge Advocate Brig. Gen. James L. Harbaugh, May 18, 1948, RG 338, USAREUR, Box 462, Supreme Court Opinion File.

39. Weingartner, *Crossroads of Death*, 184-185.

40. Clay to Harbaugh, July 19, 1948, in Smith, ed., *The Papers of General Lucius DuBignon Clay*, I, 742-743.

41. See the Army's files on Catholic Auxiliary Bishop Johann Neuhäusler and Protestant Bishop Theophil Wurm, RG 338, USAREUR, Box 464.

42. These critics included anti-Semitic, pro-German organizations, civil liberties watchdogs and strongly anti-Communist members of Congress like Senators Langer

and Joseph McCarthy (R-Wisconsin). With the exception of the civil libertarians, the majority of the Malmédy critics were more intent on discrediting the entire war crimes program, and thus the administration's foreign policy, than on safeguarding the defendants' rights to a fair trial. See Weingartner, *Crossroads of Death*, 197.

43. Simpson Commission Report, September 14, 1948, RG 338, USAREUR, Box 462, Simpson Report File.

44. Bigelow Boysen, Chief Legal Advisor, Office of the Staff Advocate, Munich Military Post, to Truman, October 19, 1948, Official File, Box 1008, Folder 325A, Truman Library. Boysen also charged that U.S. war crimes courts had used improper methods to convict one of his German clients.

45. Clay to Department of the Army, September 27, 1948, in Smith, ed., *The Papers of General Lucius DuBignon Clay*, I, 881.

46. Secretary of the Army Kenneth C. Royall to Secretary of Defense James Forrestal, November 23, 1948, Box 179, PSF/Foreign Affairs File, Germany-Nuremberg War Crimes Folder, Truman Library.

47. Everett to Truman, January 24, 1948, ibid.

48. S. Res. 39, January 27, 1949, *Congressional Record*, 81st Congress, 1st Session, 600.

49. Clay to Department of the Army, February 11, 1948, in Smith, ed., *The Papers of General Lucius DuBignon Clay*, II, 1012-1013.

50. The Administration of Justice Review Board report is cited in *Report of the Subcommittee of the Committee on Armed Services, United States Senate*, 81st Congress, 1st Session, Pursuant to S. Res. 42, October 13, 1949, 1197-1205.

51. Weingartner, *Crossroads of Death*, 201.

52. Theater Judge Advocate Col. Damon Gunn to EUCOM Commander in Chief Gen. Thomas T. Handy, November 10, 1950, RG 338, USAREUR, Box 537, Executions File.

53. Hearings before a Subcommittee of the Committee on Armed Services, United States Senate, 81st Congress, 1st Session, Pursuant to S. Res. 42, Investigation of Action of Army With Respect to Trial of Persons Responsible for the Massacre of American Soldiers, Battle of the Bulge, Near Malmédy, Belgium, December 1944 (henceforth: Malmédy Hearings), April 18, 1949, 3-26.

54. Ibid., April 20, 1949, 33-63.

55. Ibid., May 13, 1949, 630-633.

56. Doenecke, "Protest over Malmédy: A Case of Clemency," *Peace and Change* 4 (1977), 32.

57. Malmédy Hearings, May 4, 1949, 232.

58. "American Atrocities in Germany," *The Progressive*, February 1949, 21-22.

59. Malmédy Hearings, May 4, 1949, 256.

60. Ibid., May 20, 1949, 839-840.

61. The phrase "criminally wrong" was stricken from the *Congressional Record* after Senator Charles W. Tobey (R-New Hampshire) objected. "Malmédy Inquiry Held Whitewash," *New York Times*, July 27, 1949, 10.

62. The Baldwin subcommittee proposed that the United Nations adopt uniform rules of procedure and provide for greater civilian participation in future war crimes cases. Furthermore, all employees of the Departments of State and Defense involved in military government work and military employees of the war crimes program should be U.S. citizens for at least ten years. The senators also suggested that the Department

of Defense "institute a reserve program leading to the creation of a pool of trained investigators and lawyers for war crimes work who would be committed to serve beyond the cessation of hostilities." *Report of the Subcommittee of the Committee on Armed Services, United States Senate*, 81st Congress, 1st Session, Pursuant to S. Res. 42, October 13, 1949, 33-34.

63. Ibid.

64. Ben A. Smith, former War Crimes Branch official, to Handy, January 8, 1951, RG 338, USAREUR, Box 521, Cases Tried-Miscellaneous Administration File.

65. Thomas C. Reeves, *The Life and Times of Joe McCarthy: A Biography* (New York: Stein and Day, 1982), 166-167.

66. Glenn H. Smith, *Langer of North Dakota: A Study in Isolationism 1940-1959* (New York: Garland, 1979), 148-150.

67. Bosch, *Judgment on Nuremberg*, 85.

3

U.S. Post-Trial Programs for War Criminals, 1946-1951

In a series or articles during the 1970s, John Gimbel, the dean of occupation historians, warns against interpreting U.S. actions in post-war Germany solely as consequences of Cold War tensions. The policy of U.S. Military Government, he explains, was subject to a variety of influences such as the Congress and the two Western Allies, and was not merely the result of competing U.S.-Soviet interests in Germany. Gimbel uses several major events of the American occupation—including Clay's reparations stop of May 1946 and Secretary of State James Byrnes's Stuttgart speech of September 1946—to make his point.[1] The post-trial treatment of war criminals in the U.S. zone between 1946 and early 1951 supports Gimbel's argument. As the records of the Theater Judge Advocate Division and the High Commission show, U.S. policy in this area was also affected by various factors: the use of clemency in the French and British zones, the Congress, the security of U.S. forces in Germany, sentence equalization, defendants' rights and constitutional considerations. With regard to the Soviet Union, American war crimes authorities only insisted that the United States not consult the Soviets in matters of clemency, sentence review and parole.

In addition to these concerns, U.S. war crimes policy reflected changes in the priorities of the occupation as a whole. The overall U.S. policy for Germany had gradually discarded the punitive aspects of *JCS 1067*, resulting in the formulation of a new, more realistic occupation directive, *JCS 1779*, in 1947, primarily aimed at establishing German economic unification and self-government.[2] War crimes officials interpreted this adjustment as meaning that doing justice and ensuring fairness took precedence over merely inflicting punishment.

The concerns about the integrity and the constitutionality of the war crimes program in the United States, discussed in the previous chapter, most strongly affected the actions of U.S. authorities in Germany. No official was willing to extend the full protections of the U.S. Constitution such as the Fifth and Sixth Amendment guarantees of due process and a fair trial to German war criminals. This did not mean, however, that those executing the program were not concerned about questions of fairness with regard to both the trial and post-trial treatment of the perpetrators. For these officials, the main problem was that the war crimes procedures of the Dachau and Nuremberg programs did not allow for appellate reviews of the judgments and verdicts. As a result, U.S. occupation authorities increasingly resorted to administrative processes and to granting executive clemency to ensure equal sentences for comparable offenses and procedural consistency. Between 1946 and 1951 the Army's European Command and, after June 1949, the U.S. High Commission established a number of clemency and modification boards with authority to go beyond the automatic review of all sentences.[3]

American occupation officials also felt that their efforts to ensure fairness in trying and sentencing war criminals served an additional purpose. If the trials of war criminals were meant to aid in the democratization and re-education of the German people, why not use the former's post-trial treatment for the same purpose? This, U.S. authorities were certain, would help to demonstrate to their liberated subjects the superior moral standards of a democratic society.[4] Owing to the complexity of the sentence review and modification programs instituted by the United States, however, the German reaction will be dealt with in a later chapter.

The review and clemency operations lasted from 1946 until 1958, when the United States released its last war criminal. During these twelve years, the motivations of U.S. authorities changed. Initially, during the first five years, legal considerations predominanted. The offices of EUCOM's War Crimes Branch and the Theater Judge Advocate Division were sincerely concerned to ensure that justice had indeed been done. Roughly after January 1951 the purely political desire to dispose of the war crimes program in order to set the stage for German sovereignty and rearmament replaced the legal concerns. Accordingly, this chapter will focus on the first phase of the clemency and review operation.

The United States began the permanent phase of its occupation of Germany in July 1945. Until then, the Theater Judge Advocate Division had been responsible for handling war crimes cases involving the murder and mistreatment of Allied military personnel as well as mass atrocities in concentration camps located in what was now the American zone of occupation. That role was reaffirmed in September 1945 with the implementation of *JCS 1023/10*, a Joint Chiefs of Staff directive on the treatment of war criminals. The directive's primary goals were to regulate the extradition of suspected war criminals and to try and punish German perpetrators who were not major war criminals within the meaning of the London Agreement.[5] *JCS 1023/10* also permitted Army prosecutors to seek indictments on the basis of the conspiracy charge, a departure from normal U.S. military justice procedure.[6] This explanation of prosecutorial powers became a major factor in a second congressional investigation of the war crimes program focusing on the Army's Buchenwald trial.

The Army used the 1928 Manual for Courts-Martial as the procedural basis for its war crimes program. In the absence of an appellate court, all sentences were subject to automatic reexamination.[7] After the conclusion of a trial, the record went to the Deputy Theater Judge Advocate for War Crimes as the first step in the review process. His office then issued a document containing an examination of the trial and a recommendation for the theater judge advocate, including requests for clemency or petitions for review filed by the defense. The theater judge advocate, taking into consideration the report of his deputy, had authority to reaffirm or reduce prison sentences. Those cases where defendants faced the death penalty were brought before the commander in chief of the Army's EUCOM. Thus, the execution of death sentences was subject to at least three reviews and could only be carried out with the consent of the highest military authorities.[8]

During the Dachau war crimes program, the Army accumulated a truly vast caseload. A total of 3,887 cases were opened as a result of Army investigations. Although only 1,672 eventually went to trial and even fewer defendants (1,416) were ultimately convicted, the War Crimes Branch of the Theater Judge Advocate Division possessed twelve tons of records in August 1949, after an additional eighteen tons had already been shipped to Army Intelligence.[9] By December 31, 1947, the proposed closeout date for the Dachau program's trial phase, 489 trials had been held. The overwhelming paperwork and the large number of cases seems to have contributed to the decision of U.S. authorities in Germany to devise a procedure outside the normal sentence review process. In the summer of 1946 two military officers and two civilian attorneys within the War Crimes Branch began to formulate plans for a clemency program. At the time, the Army was primarily interested in ensuring equal sentences for comparable offenses. Owing to the multitude of cases and tribunals, the punishments for similar crimes often varied. Thus, the equalization of sentences was to be the foremost goal of a future clemency program. The War Crimes Branch had also concluded that five additional factors should be taken into account when considering sentence reductions: (1) the defendant's pre-war record, (2) his age and physical condition, (3) his behavior in prison, (4) his family situation and (5) his willingness to learn a worthwhile trade or occupation while in prison. The latter suggestions bordered on recommendations normally considered during parole board hearings and bore little relationship to the more urgent desire to equalize sentences.[10]

In early 1947 the military governor, General Joseph R. McNarney, did establish a Board of Clemency, but not in the way originally intended by the War Crimes Branch. U.S. Military Government (OMGUS) General Order

No. 3 made the Board the "final reviewing authority for granting clemency, parole, or commutation of sentence" for individuals convicted and imprisoned in the American zone. However, the newly created body did not have jurisdiction over death sentences and defendants whom military tribunals had found guilty of war crimes and crimes against humanity.[11]

For obvious reasons, the OMGUS Board of Clemency did nothing to relieve the pressure on the War Crimes Branch and particularly the military governor himself. In October 1946 the latter had also become the final reviewing authority for the twelve subsequent military tribunals at Nuremberg. Several months earlier, President Truman had ordered that once Jackson retired, his office, which had so far operated independently, was to become a function of OMGUS. Thus, it was the Military Governor's task to select Brig. Gen. Telford Taylor as Jackson's successor for the subsequent Nuremberg tribunals.[12] In addition, the rules of procedure to be used during the trials involving the second string of prominent former Nazis called for the forwarding of the records of each case to the military governor. The head of OMGUS had the power "to mitigate, reduce or otherwise alter the sentence imposed by the tribunal."[13] The regulations permitted the defendant and his counsel to submit a petition for sentence reduction after the judgment.[14] The first reviewing instances for the Nuremberg program were joint sessions of the military tribunals and they were mainly intended to ensure procedural consistency.[15] The military governor retained the final authority to review cases in which the court had imposed the death penalty. In all other cases, the deputy military governor was authorized either to confirm or to reduce sentences.[16]

In early 1947 the theater judge advocate also found himself under increasing pressure, but not because of an expanding workload so much as an overly ambitious closeout date for the trial phase of the Army's war crimes program. After an inquiry by EUCOM Chief of Staff Maj. Gen. Clarence R. Huebner, Theater Judge Advocate Col. C.B. Mickelwait estimated that his part of the program could end as early as December 31, 1947, and the entire operation by June 30, 1948, allowing time for sentence reviews and record processing. Mickelwait attributed the Army's rush to the "diminishing interest of the public in general in this field." Thus, although he acknowledged not having received new orders from his superiors with regard to war crimes trials, Mickelwait suggested that "the avowed purposes of Military Government may best be served by a gradual shift in emphasis from punishment for past misdeeds to guidance along appropriate paths of future conduct."[17]

Mickelwait's successor, Brigadier General James Harbaugh, did not share his predecessor's optimism regarding the speedy phasing out of the program. Harbaugh reminded Huebner that the records for the Mauthausen and Flossenburg concentration camp trials alone contained some 13,000 pages. The new theater judge advocate considered it impossible that he, as one of the reviewing authorities, could examine these trial records as well as the files of

1,230 other defendants by himself within the proposed timetable. The volume of paper waiting to be examined was only one reason for Harbaugh's protest. The EUCOM judge advocate also had reservations about aspects of the procedure itself. His particular concern centered on the deputy theater judge advocate's responsibility as the first reviewing authority in view of the fact that he was also the chief prosecutor in Army war crimes trials. Harbaugh thought it unfair that his deputy "should be the sole judge of the legality and the justness of his own work." In fact, the current arrangement forced the theater judge advocate to reexamine each case personally before making recommendations to the commander in chief. To eliminate any hint of impropriety, Harbaugh proposed the creation of a Board of Review, consisting of three experienced lawyers, "whose sole duty will be to process, review, and advise the Judge Advocate as to the action to be taken in war crimes cases."[18]

On August 21, 1947, Huebner approved Harbaugh's recommendation to establish the first Board of Review, and eventually five such bodies operated in the office of the theater judge advocate. The board's task was to ensure that defendants in war crimes cases had had a fair trial. Furthermore, the Board of Review was directed to pay particular attention to the reports of the deputy theater judge advocate for war crimes, especially his recommendations for sentencing and the completeness of the review of the evidence.[19] The Board of Review's role, however, was not limited to examining the trial record. In fact, in January 1949 Board No. 2 also investigated the charges of prisoner mistreatment and objectionable prosecution methods which German Protestant Bishop Hans Meiser had leveled against both the Nuremberg and the Dachau programs. This obviously went far beyond the initially planned function of the boards.[20]

The early sentence review process had its greatest impact in the area of capital punishment for war criminals. As a consequence of the initial examination by the deputy theater judge advocate, the Boards of Review, the theater judge advocate and the military governor, the number of court-assessed death sentences fell from 426 to 298. Due to this drop, the number of life terms rose slightly from 199 to 221. The average length of other term sentences (26 to 50 years, 11 to 15 years, 6 to 10 years, 5 years or less) was reduced during the review process. Altogether, the theater judge advocate and the military governor rejected only sixty-nine recommendations for sentence reduction.[21]

In May 1948 General Lucius D. Clay, McNarney's successor as military governor, faced with an increase in the number of reviews due to the Nuremberg tribunals now under way, committed a rather macabre accounting error with important consequences. Owing to the backlog in the Army's review process, Clay had earlier stayed the executions of those war criminals who had been sentenced to death so that they could petition the United States Supreme Court for writs of *habeau corpus*. The military governor had wrongly concluded that the U.S. officials in Germany would have to execute over 500 prisoners once the Court had turned down their requests. Clay, who was apprehensive about the prospect of having to stage a mass execution, informed the Army Department that he was leaning toward commuting a large numbere of death sentences to life terms. However, the general did not want to make a decision of this magnitude without consulting Washington. Thus, while admitting that the "question rests entirely in my hands," Clay requested to hear Secretary Royall's views on the matter.[22]

To solve Clay's problem, the Army Department recommended that a board of three to five prominent jurists be created with authority to make recommendations to the military governor.[23] Only several days later, Clay realized that there were actually only 150 instead of 550 prisoners on death row and recognized that a clemency board might not be as urgently needed as he had initially expected. He then apologized to the Department of the Army for the error and affirmed his ability to deal with this smaller number without the help of a clemency board. Nonetheless, even in light of a smaller than anticipated caseload, Clay continued to support the concept of a committee of legal experts empowered to examine sentences and to make recommendations for eventual acts of clemency in addition to the review process already in place.[24]

The military governor had good reason to ask for more expert help. In the fall of 1948 the Army's war crimes program, already plagued by the steadily growing Malmédy scandal, became the subject of yet another congressional investigation. While the 1949 Malmédy probe eventually focused on questionable interrogation and prosecution methods, the 1948 hearings before the Senate Investigations Subcommittee of the Committee on Expenditures in the Executive Departments, chaired by Homer Ferguson (R-Michigan), dealt with how the Army reviewed war crimes sentences. The subcommittee's decision to examine sentence reviews had been precipitated by disclosures during the trial of thirty-one individuals before a U.S. military court for their involvement with the Buchenwald concentration camp. Among the defendants was the former camp commander's wife, Ilse Koch, who had gained particular notoriety due to accusations that she had ordered lamp shades made from human skin. Despite the seriousness of the charges against Koch, Clay had reduced her original court-assessed punishment of life imprisonment to four years. The Army's decision not to publicize the sentence reduction only worsened matters and led to considerable criticism of the war crimes program, especially once the story had leaked to the press.[25]

Koch and her co-defendants were officially charged for "violations of the laws and usages of war" and the common design to participate in the running of the camp, particularly the mistreatment and murder of its inmates. The prosecution focused only on crimes committed against non-German victims.[26] Two lawyers in JAD's War Crimes Branch, Harold E. Kuhn and Richard A. Schneider, were the first to review the Koch trial. On November

15, 1947, in their recommendations to the deputy theater judge advocate, Kuhn and Schneider upheld Koch's conviction for taking part in the common design. However, the two found the military court's sentence for the defendant too harsh and argued that the extent of Koch's participation in the running of Buchenwald did not warrant life imprisonment. Nonetheless, they recommended approval of the judgment and the original sentence, and, at the same time, urged the reduction of the life term to four years imprisonment, commencing on October 18, 1945.[27]

Both the theater judge advocate and Clay approved the recommendations, but the decision apparently touched on some nerves in Washington. Army Secretary Royall, bypassing the usual review process, requested an evaluation of the case and Koch's reduced sentence from Judge Advocate General Thomas H. Green. Green reported to Royall that evidence existed for and against Koch's acquisition and use of human skin. However, the judge advocate general pointed out that, in his opinion, the evidence clearing Koch of this particular charge was more convincing. Green considered the defendant's conviction and a substantial prison term justified due to credible proof that Koch participated in the administration of Buchenwald, struck inmates and repeatedly reported them for punishment. Despite his own feelings that Koch should have served a long sentence, Green discovered no irregularities in the review process and "no abuse of discretion" in the rather surprising reduction of the court's initial punishment.[28]

The Ferguson subcommittee, however, viewed the matter differently. In their report, the committee members saw no justification for the rather generous sentence reduction. Among other points, the senators particularly faulted the relationship between the charges of the indictment against Koch and the review practices. Unlike Theater Judge Advocate Harbaugh, who thought that the process gave the prosecution an unfair advantage, the subcommittee argued that in this case the reexamination of the trial record had grossly favored the defendants. In contrast to the indictment's accusations of participation in the common design, the reviewing lawyers had concentrated on individual criminal acts, and thus the exact opposite. Therefore, the subcommittee felt, the prosecutor would undoubtedly have put greater emphasis on specific crimes committed by Koch, had he known that this would be crucial during the review stage.[29]

In addition to calling for better cooperation between war crimes prosecutors and reviewing authorities, the subcommittee demanded improvements in another area of the sentence reexamination process, wherein the theater judge advocate and Clay based their rulings solely on the report which the War Crimes Branch attorneys had prepared on the trial record. Although the summarization of the transcripts was an accepted practice—no one could expect the military governor to read several thousand pages of the trial record—the Ferguson subcommittee suspected that the recapitulations of the facts in Koch's case had contributed to the serious error.[30]

Fortunately, for Clay, not all was lost. The military governor rejected the recommendation to retry Koch before a U.S. military court since this would have violated the principle of double jeopardy. However, he could still urge German authorities to prosecute Koch for crimes against German Buchenwald prisoners since the American prosecutors had only focused on offenses against non-German nationals. Consequently, Clay urged the minister president of Bavaria to send a representative to work out charges against Koch with JAD's War Crimes Branch personnel, centering on crimes against German citizens.[31]

Crucial changes in the policy of the United States and the other Western Allies toward Germany in 1948 and 1949 also affected how German war criminals convicted by American courts were to be handled. Unable to reach an agreement with the Soviets on the German question, Britain, France, the United States and the Benelux countries decided in June 1948 to establish a German government for the Western zones of occupation. Although several of these countries, particularly France, continued to have serious doubts about German political unification, two Soviet actions in the spring of 1948 appeared to underscore the need for an economically and politically unified Germany. On March 10, Czechoslovakia's independence ended with the murder of its foreign minister, followed by the Soviet Union's leaving the Control Council for Germany only ten days later. These incidents raised serious questions about the security of the West, thus greatly facilitating the move toward unification of the three Western zones.[32]

In 1949 the Department of State took over the administration of the American zone from the Department of the Army with the establishment of the U.S. High Commission for Germany (HICOG). In June of that year former Assistant Secretary of War John J. McCloy became the first American High Commissioner and the U.S. representative to the Allied High Commission for Germany (AHC).[33] Three months later, France, Great Britain and the United States merged their zones of occupation into a new German state, the Federal Republic of Germany, and with the creation of the Federal Republic, the Allied Occupation Statute went into effect. The statute limited the powers of the West German government, headed by Chancellor Konrad Adenauer, and retained important rights for the Allied High Commission in vital areas such as foreign policy, trade and law-making. The document also underscored the limits of Allied trust in the new Germany, particularly with regard to war criminals. As a result, the Allies reserved for themselves the exclusive authority over questions of clemency, amnesty and pardons for those convicted by Allied war crimes courts.[34] Nevertheless, the events of 1949 were to have significant consequences regarding this particular problem. For Adenauer, who was committed to full German integration in the West, the existence of German inmates in the three Allied war crimes prisons Landsberg (U.S.), Wittlich (France) and Werl (Britain) became a major obstacle to the achievement of his foreign political goals. As a result, the war criminals problem evolved in the following years into a thorny issue, which both the Allied and German governments viewed as blocking the Federal Republic's path toward integration, rearmament and, ultimately, sovereignty.

The establishment of HICOG also brought about important changes in the area of jurisdiction over war criminals. In July 1950, Executive Order No. 10144 officially made the U.S. High Commissioner responsible for executing the sentences of and granting clemency to the defendants before the twelve subsequent Nuremberg tribunals, although McCloy believed he had jurisdiction over these cases as soon as HICOG began to function. In contrast, the EUCOM commander in chief retained jurisdiction over prisoners who had been convicted and sentenced by Army war crimes courts.[35] Clay, in addition to his role as military governor, had also held this position. Clay's successor as EUCOM commander was now General Thomas T. Handy. The split into HICOG and EUCOM prisoners was to have important consequences and provoked a good deal of in-fighting between U.S. military and civilian authorities in Germany. The Germans regarded McCloy as more lenient, which often caused EUCOM to disagree with the high commissioner and resist HICOG initiatives.

At this point, in the summer of 1949, EUCOM Judge Advocate's office began preparations for the formation of a new clemency board. The Simpson Commission, which had investigated the Malmédy trial, had recommended that a permanent body be created to consider petitions for clemency and pardons. The EUCOM War Crimes Branch committee, which studied the proposal, had mixed feelings about the long-term installation of such a board and rejected the idea of a general amnesty for war criminals outright. Instead, the War Crimes Branch considered it desirable that "sentences should be reduced to minimum levels consistent with maintaining respect for the occupying powers who represent the victorious United Nations." Furthermore, the penalties for war criminals should remain harsh enough to serve as punishment for the perpetrators and as deterrents for "future would-be violators." The committee suggested instituting a system providing for good conduct time, even if this would only lead to better prisoner behavior. The Army still had to overcome other serious problems. A permanent clemency board could run into trouble with the other Allies. To avoid this, the United States should consult with France and Great Britain, "if not the USSR," since many of those countries' citizens had been the victims of the German defendants before Army courts. In addition, the paperwork involved was forbidding. The committee estimated that the board would have to review the trial records of some 400 individuals. Finally, the War Crimes Branch feared a negative German reaction. Calling attention to the persistent German criticism of Allied war crimes trials in the past, the committee recommended that a U.S. government agency not connected with the program should conduct a post-trial clemency operation.[36]

The War Crimes Branch committee submitted its final draft to new Theater Judge Advocate Col. Damon M. Gunn in July 1949. It urged the Army to set up a clemency board consisting of five members, either officers with legal training and/or civilian attorneys. This board's most important task was to equalize sentences by reviewing each individual case. Defendants and their attorneys were granted the right to submit petitions in the form of legal briefs and other documentary evidence before the date on which the prisoner's case came up for consideration. The proposed clemency commission could also act as a medical parole board for those prisoners whose physical condition warranted their release. Despite all these provisions, the War Crimes Branch committee did not feel that the creation of a clemency board would suffice. Consequently, it urged Gunn to institute a system of good conduct time to coincide with the board's establishment. The Army's priorities with regard to the implementation of the review program also pointed to obvious biases. The proposal's timetable scheduled parent concentration camp cases (such as Buchenwald and Dachau) first, followed by trials involving the numerous smaller subcamps. Those who had mistreated or murdered American military personnel, the so-called "flier cases," were to be considered last.[37]

Not everybody within the Theater Judge Advocate Division concurred with these recommendations. One of the proposal's reviewers objected to the suggestion that the clemency board consider medical parole. Lt. Col. John H. Awtry, Assistant Chief of the War Crimes Branch, viewed this particular proposition as exceeding the commission's function of merely reviewing trial records. In Awtry's opinion, to discuss questions of medical parole would amount to a new trial, lead to further criticism of the war crimes program in Germany and the United States and flood the board with requests for medical hearings. Awtry was also worried that the Army was about to proceed unilaterally with regard to sentence reviews. Since the United States had always regarded the war crimes program as a joint Allied undertaking, Awtry suggested that EUCOM should hold talks with the French and the British before the clemency board began its work. Awtry's concern for Allied cooperation was limited to the Western powers, emphasizing "that no efforts be made to secure and that no consideration be given to the views of the Soviet Union with respect to this matter."[38]

The head of the War Crimes Branch himself, Col. Wade M. Fleischer, predicted that the EUCOM clemency board would adversely affect occupation policy. Observing that most of the Dachau war crimes program's prisoners had been *SS* concentration camp guards, members of *SS* elite fighting units, trustee inmates (*Kapos*), habitual criminals and low- to mid-level party and police officials, Fleischer voiced concern that the proposed policy might backfire on U.S. goals in Germany. Fleischer warned that the gradual release of entire segments of the Landsberg prison population, who had proven their potential for violence and fanaticism in the past, might have serious consequences. These individuals were likely to assume their former roles in their communities and "they will undoubtedly commence to work against the occupation authorities in Western Germany." To minimize this problem, the War Crimes Branch chief recommended that U.S. intelligence agencies continue to monitor the prisoners closely.[39]

Despite these serious reservations, both the U.S. High Commission and EUCOM's Judge Advocate Division continued their search for viable clemency programs in the fall of 1949. During a conference between HICOG and EUCOM officials, Gunn announced that the Army's clemency program, now called the War Crimes Modification Board, would soon become reality. Since the board would only be responsible for the sentences of prisoners convicted by Army courts, the theater judge advocate wished to coordinate good conduct time, medical parole and compassionate leave policy with the U.S. High Commission.[40] Most of the discussion centered on the question of good conduct time. The British had recently increased the good conduct time allowance for war criminals imprisoned at Werl to ten days a month. This action encouraged the HICOG representatives to propose the adoption of the U.S. federal prison system's sliding scale ranging from five to ten days. The HICOG proposal exceeded Gunn's willingness to allow for five days per month. However, agreement was reached permitting occupation authorities to forfeit accumulated good conduct time and to remand prisoners who committed criminal acts after their release based on good conduct time.[41]

EUCOM created the War Crimes Modification Board on November 28, 1949, with General Order No. 106. The clemency committee first met two months later to decide on a docket to establish a priority of cases up for review and to lay out procedure for the board's work. It voted to implement the timetable proposed earlier and to consider the parent concentration camp trials first and the flier cases last. The Theater Judge Advocate Division was to prepare detailed reviews of each case for consideration by the board.[42] Several factors were to be weighed, ranging from membership and rank in Nazi organizations to the nature of the defendant's crimes to mitigating circumstances. In addition, the committee also had to consider the original sentence, any prior modifications thereof, and the severity of the sentence compared to the punishment of others accused of the same or similar offenses. A third category was the defendant's conduct while in prison and other character references.[43] One problem remained unsolved, however. The EUCOM order specified that the judge advocate was to serve as a member of the committee and, simultaneously, as the final authority to act on the War Crimes Modification Board's recommendation in all cases, except those involving the death penalty. Gunn considered this arrangement improper and urged Handy to revise it.[44]

With the EUCOM board in place, the U.S. High Commission continued to make plans for its own clemency commission. Armed with his legal counsel's opinion that HICOG had jurisdiction over the Nuremberg tribunals, McCloy saw a great need for some kind of clemency action. General Clay had reduced the sentences of three prisoners from the Nuremberg program before McCloy took over. The high commissioner deemed this hardly enough in view of his intent, when assuming his new position, to create a friendly relationship with the Adenauer government and to pacify West German public opinion on the war crimes issue.[45] Consequently, in a meeting with his French and British counterparts on December 16, 1949, McCloy announced that he and Handy had instituted a good time conduct program which would result in a number of releases before Christmas. As a result of this new parole policy, a total of sixty German war criminals were released in 1949.[46] Good conduct time credit was fixed at five days as of December 20, 1949,[47] but was expanded to ten days per month on August 25, 1950.[48] The December action was only the beginning. McCloy also told the Allied High Commission about his intentions to appoint a committee to draw up plans for a permanent system of clemency and parole for war criminals in his custody.[49]

McCloy immediately informed German officials about his plans. During a visit with the highest-ranking bishop of the German Catholic Church, Cologne's Josef Cardinal Frings, McCloy promised to review the sentences of all prisoners who had been sentenced by American courts, including war criminals. The U.S. High Commissioner could not tell the cardinal anything binding due to the complexity of the issue, particularly his fear of a negative public reaction in the United States. Nonetheless, McCloy confided to Frings HICOG's and the State Department's plans to have three prominent American jurists come to Germany in early 1950 to work out a practical solution, but he rejected suggestions to involve German officials in clemency decisions.[50]

McCloy had good reason to adhere to his original idea to have only American jurists in charge of examining the Nuremberg cases. Since his arrival in June 1949, lawyers for the Landsberg prisoners had flooded HICOG with clemency requests. There was nothing wrong with submitting petitions on behalf of one's client, but McCloy soon discovered that an all too friendly attitude was bound to become a liability rather than an asset in establishing good HICOG-German relations. In January 1950, McCloy expressed his disappointment about the fact that many of the clemency petitions attacked the procedural soundness of the American war crimes program. A second point of irritation for the high commissioner was continued German demands for a general amnesty for convicted war criminals. McCloy believed that world opinion would oppose such a move and reject the premise "that the German people should now be allowed to forget" the war crimes.[51]

Despite these negative experiences, McCloy did not cease to work to establish a clemency board and thus toward helping the Germans forget Nazi atrocities. In a January 27, 1950, meeting with Undersecretary of the Army Tracy Vorhees in Washington, McCloy in effect countermanded Vorhees's agreement with General Handy, underscoring his distrust for EUCOM's War Crimes Modification Board. Having concluded that the EUCOM board would not work quickly enough, McCloy proposed that Vorhees appoint a three-member committee to review the cases of prisoners under both HICOG and EUCOM jurisdiction. Such a board should consist of a former judge, a lawyer and a layman, and would act as an advisory body to Handy and McCloy.[52]

McCloy's latest proposal failed to make friends at EUCOM. For the Army, the issue was crystal clear. The Nuremberg program was the result of essentially *ex post facto* laws. In contrast, the Dachau trials had focused on violations of established rules and laws of war, a matter with which the Army was familiar. EUCOM advised Handy to adhere to the current setup and to rely only on the War Crimes Modification Board. Any other arrangement, such as coordinating the sentence review process with HICOG, could curtail Handy's powers or, even worse, might lead to an embarrassing leak, in case one of the members of McCloy's proposed board took his case " 'to the people.' "[53] Handy accepted this advice. The EUCOM commander in chief informed Vorhees that he would not tolerate any interference or limitations of his powers to affirm or reduce sentences. If the Department of the Army had no confidence in current process, it should assume the responsibility for sentence confirmation or reduction itself.[54]

Handy found an unlikely ally in Secretary of State Dean Acheson, who also opposed the creation of a common clemency board. Acheson told McCloy that he disagreed with the latter on several important points. For one, the State Department shared EUCOM's opinion that the Nuremberg and Dachau war crimes programs were very different. More important, Acheson did not want to see McCloy and the HICOG review process become involved in the reconsideration of the Malmédy trial and other cases under Army jurisdiction. This would ask for trouble, given the controversies surrounding the Army's proceedings. Acheson also disliked McCloy's suggestion for a "board of calibre" to process the clemency requests. Such an action, Acheson feared, could create the impression that the legal basis and procedure, and not just the sentences, of the Nuremberg tribunals were under review.[55]

A rebuffed McCloy went to see Handy on February 8, 1950, to discuss Acheson's views on the matter. The two decided to create a separate HICOG board. However, Handy and McCloy did agree to coordinate the timing of their individual clemency decisions which would result from the work of the two committees. This was most likely meant to impress upon the Germans that American authorities stood united on the war crimes program. To undercut Acheson's reservations that the boards might be mistakenly perceived as also reviewing procedure, judgments and verdicts, the high commissioner and the EUCOM commander promised to embark on a publicity campaign. Having reached a mutual agreement, McCloy cabled Acheson and urged him to help create the HICOG board as early as possible. Any further delays, the High Commissioner warned, would make the task of reviewing the Nuremberg sentences increasingly difficult.[56]

McCloy established his Advisory Board on Clemency for War Criminals in March 1950. It consisted of David W. Peck, presiding justice of the New York state appeals court, Frederick A. Moran, chairman of the New York Board of Parole and Brigadier General Conrad E. Snow, assistant legal advisor in the State Department. The board spent several months studying the cases and the Nuremberg tribunals' judgments. On July 11, Moran, Peck and Snow began to consider petitions for clemency by the defendants in all twelve trials. All in all, McCloy's advisory committee claimed to have read the files of the 104 defendants still in prison and interviewed fifty defense counsel representing ninety of the prisoners.[57] HICOG specifically did not allow the board to review the jurisdiction and composition of the Nuremberg court as well as questions of fact and law. In one point, however, its instructions varied significantly from those of the Army's War Crimes Modification Board. The Advisory Committee on Clemency had permission to consider the physical condition and family situation of the petitioner. This came dangerously close to a parole board function.[58]

On August 28, 1950, the HICOG Advisory Board submitted its report to McCloy. After a lengthy introduction covering the nature of Nazi crimes as well as the precedent-setting and educational character of the American trial program, the committee members expressed their disappointment that many defendants still believed what they had done was right. They were equally disturbed by the tendency of most prisoners to blame their offenses on orders from a higher authority. The board dismissed the defense argument that the Allies had relied on *ex post facto* law and it defended the courts' practice to hold individuals responsible for the criminal acts committed by organizations they had joined. Peck, Moran and Snow also professed to having taken every mitigating circumstance into account and pointed out that "if we have erred, we have erred on the side of leniency." However, even this leniency had its limitations, the three claimed. The board rejected the idea of executive clemency for those guilty of mass murder, arguing "it would undo what Nuremberg has accomplished."[59]

Regrettably, the board's report did not square with its actions. In a memorandum to McCloy, HICOG General Counsel Robert R. Bowie complained that the Advisory Board's recommendations were too lenient. Bowie considered forty-six clemency proposals unwarranted. In an additional twenty-two cases, he found the board's reasons for its recommendations suspect. Bowie was surprised to discover that the committee had referred to the trial record of only two of the twelve tribunals and to having instead relied on affidavits and petitions submitted by the defense. Bowie found even more surprising the Advisory Board's conclusion that certain convictions, such as those in the *Einsatzgruppen* trial, were improper having considered them based on hearsay and other shaky evidence. A seemingly sarcastic Bowie claimed to appreciate the fact that the clemency committee had excluded these findings, which would have cast renewed doubt on the validity of the judgments and the verdicts, from its final, public report.[60]

On January 31, 1951, Handy and McCloy announced the review decisions they had reached in following the recommendations of their respective clemency boards. The result was a mass sentence commutation for German war criminals. The EUCOM commander in chief reduced the number of death sentences under his jurisdiction from thirteen to two. Handy took great care to point out the elaborate review process, including the Judge Advocate General and the Simpson Commission, which his prisoners on death row had enjoyed. Among the reprieved were all six remaining defendants sentenced to death at the conclusion of the Malmédy trial. The two prisoners whose punishment Handy did not commute to life terms were a roll call leader of a Dachau subcamp and the adjutant to the Buchenwald concentration camp commander. Both had been convicted for the murder and abuse of several hundred victims. Handy saw "no basis for clemency" in either case. As reasons for the commutations of the other death sentences, Handy pointed to the individuals' relatively subordinate position in concentration camps or the discovery of additional mitigating evidence. The Malmédy defendants actually received the most favorable evaluation. The general found their "offenses . . . associated with a confused; fluid; and desperate combat action, a last attempt to turn the tide of Allied successes and to reestablish a more favorable tactical position for the German Army. The crimes are definitely distinguishable from the more deliberate killings in concentration camps."[61]

McCloy's highly advertised clemency decisions were more far reaching. The German industrialists, who had faced the Nuremberg tribunals in the Flick, I.G. Farben and Krupp trials, benefited most. By the time of McCloy's announcement, all defendants in the Flick and I.G. Farben cases had already been released from Landsberg or were now scheduled for release. With regard to the Krupp trial, the U.S. High Commissioner generously reduced the sentences of all prisoners from term sentences to time served. Alfred Krupp even found himself in possession of his properties again, which the American court had earlier confiscated. McCloy was not quite as forthcoming in the nine other cases. After much soul-searching, he let stand five of the remaining fifteen death sentences under HICOG jurisdiction. The five were Oswald Pohl, head of the *SS* Economic and Administrative Main Office, and four leaders of the *Einsatzgruppen*. According to former American occupation authorities, the decision to go ahead with the executions of these prisoners bore heavily on the high commissioner. George N. Shuster, the former *land* commissioner for Bavaria, reports that McCloy was pacing the floor "day after day, night after night."[62] Former HICOG advisor Charles W. Thayer writes that McCloy locked himself in his study and became rather irritable in the weeks preceding the announcements.[63] Although these accounts differ, it is nevertheless evident that the U.S. High Commissioner did not make these decisions easily. McCloy considered it impossible to commute the sentence of Pohl, whose office had overseen and run the entire concentration camp system, and the others, whose mobile killing squads had murdered two million victims in the wake of the German army's advance into the Soviet Union. All in all, however, McCloy reduced the punishment of seventy-eight of the eighty-seven Nuremberg defendants held in Landsberg. Despite these high figures, McCloy emphasized that his decision to extend clemency to 87 percent of the HICOG prisoners was not meant simply as a nice gesture for the Germans, but rather an educational tool. McCloy particularly underscored his efforts "to apply standards of executive clemency as they are understood in a democratic society."[64]

Handy's and McCloy's January 1951 sentence reductions are a convenient dividing line in the history of the post-trial treatment of German war criminals. Between 1946 and 1951 American authorities in Germany had been primarily concerned with preserving the judicial integrity of the war crimes program. As the hearings before the Baldwin and Ferguson subcommittees showed, the trial operation contained a number of serious flaws. The congressional investigations had also uncovered serious inconsistencies in the initial sentence review processes, which, in accordance with regulations, were automatic. In addition, the Baldwin subcommittee admitted that irregularities had occurred. These shortcomings violated the sense of justice on the part of the professional attorneys who staffed EUCOM's War Crimes Branch and HICOG's Office of Legal Counsel. In the absence of a regular appellate court to rectify matters, U.S. occupation authorities instituted far-reaching administrative sentence reviews and executive clemency to secure the rights of the defendants. These post-trial programs were also intended to reduce the risk of additional controversies. Unfortunately, the elaborate process, which, in cases of capital punishment, included five or more reviewing instances, could also lead to wrong impressions, namely that American authorities themselves had lost faith in the war crimes program and were revising judgments and verdicts.

Most importantly, these operations put in place a mechanism which made the political abuse of sentence reviews and clemency possible in the coming years. It is not surprising that the Allies and the Germans decided to rely on this method of sentence reduction after January 1951. There is evidence that McCloy attempted to use clemency to establish good relations with the Adenauer government between 1949 and 1951. For the most part, however, McCloy like Generals Clay and Handy, granted pardons to ensure equity in sentencing and to correct procedural inconsistencies during this period. The negotiations regarding West Germany's rearmament and sovereignty, which began in 1951, changed all this. Clemency and sentence modification thereafter became convenient means insofar as they permitted dismantling of the war crimes program without public scrutiny.

NOTES

1. See John Gimbel's essays "Cold War Historians and the Occupation of Germany," in Schmitt, ed., *U.S. Occupation of Europe after World War II*, 86-102; "The American Reparations Stop in Germany. An Essay on the Political Uses of History," *Historian* 37 (1974/75), 276-296; and "Byrnes' Stuttgarter Rede und die amerikanische Nachkriegspolitik in Deutschland," *Vierteljahrshefte für Zeitgeschichte* 20 (1972), 39-62.

2. U.S. Department of State, *Germany: The Story in Documents*, 34-41.

3. John Mendelsohn describes some of these programs in Mendelsohn, "War Crimes Trials and Clemency in Germany and Japan," in Wolfe, ed., *Americans as Proconsuls*, 226-247.

4. Ordinary Military Government courts had been used to this effect since the beginning of the occupation. See Eli E. Nobleman, "American Military Courts in Germany," *The Annals of the American Academy of Political and Social Sciences* 267 (January 1950), 91.

5. Lt. Col. William F. Fratcher, Chief, War Crimes Branch, OMGUS, to the director of the Legal Division, OMGUS, May 31, 1946, RG 338, USAREUR, Box 462, Cases Tried-General Administration 1946 File.

6. Ziemke, *The U.S. Army in the Occupation of Germany*, 169-173.

7. Gen. M. S. Eddy, Commander in Chief, USAREUR, to Handy, October 4, 1952, RG 338, USAREUR, Box 465, History File.

8. Lt. Col. Peter Peters, Assistant Adjutant General, to Commanding General, U.S. Third Army Area, October 14, 1946, ibid., Box 468, Policy 1952 File. Also, see Clay to Army Department, September 27, 1948, in Smith, ed., *The Papers of General Lucius DuBignon Clay*, 881.

9. Internal memorandum "War Crimes Activities, Theater Judge Advocate," August 17, 1949, RG 338, USAREUR, Box 468, Policy 1952 File.

10. Gunn to Commander in Chief, EUCOM, May 10, 1946, ibid., Box 465, History File.

11. OMGUS General Order No. 3, January 17, 1947, ibid., Box 517, Cases Tried-Miscellaneous Clemency File.

12. Executive Order No. 9679, January 16, 1946, *Federal Register*, 703.

13. U.S. Military Government Ordinance No. 7, October 18, 1946, in *Trials of War Criminals*, XV, 28.

14. Regulation No. 1 under Military Government Ordinance No. 7 as amended by Military Government Ordinance No. 11, April 11, 1947, ibid., 1151.

15. Military Government Ordinance No. 11, February 17, 1947, ibid., 35.

16. Ibid., 1153-1154.

17. Theater Judge Advocate Col. C.B. Mickelwait to EUCOM Chief of Staff Maj. Gen. Clarence R. Huebner, February 21, 1947, RG 338, USAREUR, Box 534, Organization File.

18. Harbaugh to Huebner, August 5, 1947, ibid.

19. Internal War Crimes Branch memorandum "Establishment of Board of Review for War Crimes Cases," August 29, 1947, ibid.

20. Report of War Crimes Board of Review No. 2, January 5, 1949, ibid., Box 467, Bishop Meiser File.

21. Eddy to Handy, October 4, 1952, ibid., Cases Tried—General Administration File.

22. Clay to Draper, May 24, 1948, in Smith, ed., *The Papers of General Lucius DuBignon Clay*, I, 658-659.

23. Draper to Clay, May 25, 1948, ibid.

24. Clay to Draper, May 31, 1948, ibid., 661.

25. Mendelsohn, "War Crimes Trials and Clemency in Germany and Japan," in Wolfe, ed., *Americans as Proconsuls*, 247-248.

26. *Conduct of Ilse Koch War Crimes Trial*, Investigations Subcommittee of the Committee on Expenditures in the Executive Departments Pursuant to S. Res. 189, 80th Congress, 2nd Session, 1254-1255.

27. Ibid., 1235-1236.

28. Ibid., 1254.

29. *Conduct of Ilse Koch War Crimes Trial*, Interim Report of the Investigations Subcommittee of the Committee on Expenditures in the Executive Departments Pursuant to S. Res. 189, December 17, 1948, *Senate Reports*, Report No. 1775, Part 3, 80th Congress, 2nd Session, 23.

30. Ibid.

31. Clay to Army Department, February 7, 1949, in Smith, ed., *The Papers of General Lucius DuBignon Clay*, II, 1007-1008.

32. Ziemke, "The Formulation and Initial Implementation of U.S. Occupation Policy in Germany," in Schmitt, ed., *U.S. Occupation in Europe after World War II*, 40.

33. Executive Order No. 10062, June 6, 1949, *Federal Register*, 2965.

34. Internal Route Slip by Robert F. Corrigan, foreign service officer, February 11, 1949, RG 338, USAREUR, Box 542, Clemency 1949 File.

35. Executive Order No. 10144, July 22, 1950, *Federal Register*, 4705.

36. War Crimes Branch, EUCOM, to the Judge Advocate General, June 1, 1949, RG 338, USAREUR, Box 493, Miscellaneous File.

37. Memorandum for the record by Col. Wade M. Fleischer, Chief, War Crimes Branch, EUCOM, July 18, 1949, ibid.

38. Memorandum for the record by Lt. Col. John H. Awtry, Assistant Chief, War Crimes Branch, EUCOM, July 28, 1949, ibid.

39. Memorandum for the record by Col. Fleischer, October 5, 1949, ibid., Box 542, Clemency 1949 File.

40. On October 11, 1949, HICOG's Office of General Counsel had assured U.S. High Commissioner for Germany John J. McCloy that he had jurisdiction over the prisoners sentenced before the Nuremberg tribunals. Mortimer Kollander, acting chief, Administration of Justice Division, HICOG, to HICOG general counsel, October 11, 1949, RG 466, U.S. High Commission for Germany, Papers of John J. McCloy, Classified General Records 1949-1952, D (49) 278, Civil Archives Branch, Washington National Record Center, National Archives. Executive Order No. 10144 would eventually confirm this opinion several months later.

41. Maj. Joseph L. Haefele, War Crimes Branch, EUCOM, to Gunn, November 17, 1949, RG 338, USAREUR, Box 542, Clemency 1949 File.

42. Minutes of War Crimes Modification Board meeting on January 23, 1950, ibid., Box 517, Cases Tried-Miscellaneous Clemency File.

43. Haefele to Col. Stanley W. Jones, Deputy Judge Advocate for War Crimes, EUCOM, July 14, 1950, ibid., Box 542, Clemency 1949-50 File.

44. Internal Route Slip by Gunn, January 24, 1950, ibid.

45. Mendelsohn, "War Crimes Trials and Clemency in Germany and Japan," in Wolfe, ed., *Americans as Proconsuls*, 251-252.

46. McCloy to Secretary of State Dean Acheson, December 21, 1949, RG 446, U.S. High Commission for Germany, Security-Segregated General Records 1949-1952, Box 28, 321.6, War Criminals File.

47. Lt. Col. W.F. Smith, Assistant Adjutant General, EUCOM, to Handy, December 15, 1949, RG 338, USAREUR, Box 542, Clemency File. Handy and McCloy jointly instituted the good conduct time program to promote institutional discipline among the Landsberg inmates. McCloy to Acheson, December 28, 1949, RG 466, U.S. High Commission for Germany, Security-Segregated General Records 1949-1952, 321.6, War Criminals File.

48. Col. P.B. Mayson, Assistant Adjutant General, EUCOM, to Handy, August 15, 1950. McCloy later justified the move with the argument that "ten days is the average normal credit in penal institutions in the United States and is also the credit allowed for war criminals in British prisons and under the jurisdiction of the United States Army in Japan." McCloy to Manfred George, ed., *Der Aufbau*, August 28, 1950, RG 466, Papers of John J. McCloy, Classified General Records 1949-1952, Box 18, D (5) 2065. General Douglas MacArthur established good conduct time credit for Japanese war criminals in March 1950. Circular No. 5, March 7, 1950 General Headquarters, Supreme Commander for the Allied Powers, RG 338, USAREUR, Box 461, General Administration File. McCloy and Handy also agreed that prisoners deserved credit for pre-trial confinement. Normally, the war crimes courts had given such credit during sentencing. However, in December 1950, EUCOM's Judge Advocate Division came across twenty-two cases where the tribunals had not taken the defendants' stay in prison prior to the trial into consideration. To the Army, this discovery confirmed the impression that sentences for the same or comparable offenses had been uneven, depending on how early or how late the proceedings had occurred in the Dachau program. Consequently, the JAD urged the War Crimes Modification Board to hand these cases to the commander in chief with the request that Handy give these prisoners credit for pre-trial confinement to ensure equity. Lt. Col. T.A. Borom, JAD, EUCOM, to Col. Mark McClure, Chairman, War Crimes Modification Board, December 10, 1950, ibid., Box 541, Landsberg 201 File.

49. Minutes of Tenth Meeting of the Council of the Allied High Commissioners, December 16, 1949, RG 466, Papers of John J. McCloy, Classified General Records 1949-1952, Box 5, D (49) 447B.

50. Internal Memorandum by Alfons Wahl, Federal Justice Ministry, January 30, 1950, *Bundeszwischenarchiv* St. Augustin/Hangelar, Akten des *Bundesjustizministerium*, B141-9576, 1. McCloy's actual proposal was still rather moderate. As early as January 1950 attorneys consulted by the Department of Defense suggested the creation of a board consisting of American lawyers, representatives from neutral countries and "at least one outstanding German jurist." McCloy, however, was not yet willing to go this far and to consider the recommendations of a German regarding war criminals. See, memorandum for the record by Lt. Col. H.A. Gerhardt, HICOG, January 28, 1950, RG 466, Papers of John J. McCloy, Classified General Records 1949-1952, Box 7, D (50) 203.

51. McCloy to the Rev. A.J. Muench, Regent, Apostolic Nunciature in Germany, January 11, 1950, ibid., Box 6, D (50) 57.

52. Undersecretary of the Army Tracy Vorhees to Handy, January 30, 1950, RG 338, USAREUR, Box 534, Organization 1950 File.

53. Memorandum for Handy, January 31, 1950, ibid.

54. Handy to Vorhees, January 31, 1950, ibid.

55. Acheson to McCloy, February 8, 1950, RG 466, U.S. High Commission for Germany, Security-Segregated General Records 1949-1952, Box 28, 321.6, War Criminals File.

56. McCloy to Acheson, February 17, 1950, ibid.

57. Advisory Committee on Clemency members David W. Peck, Conrad E. Snow and Frederick A. Moran to McCloy, August 29, 1950, RG 466, Papers of John J. McCloy, Classified General Records 1949-1952, Box 18, D (50) 2063.

58. Staff Announcement No. 117, HICOG, July 18, 1950, RG 338, USAREUR, Box 462, Major Haefele File.

59. Report of the Advisory Committee on Clemency for War Criminals to the United States High Commission for Germany, August 28, 1950, RG 466, Papers of John J. McCloy, Classified General Records 1949-1952, Box 18, D (50) 2063a.

60. HICOG General Counsel Robert R. Bowie to McCloy, October 31, 1950, RG 466, U.S. High Commission for Germany, Security-Segregated General Records 1949-1952, Box 28, 321.6, War Criminals File.

61. EUCOM Release No. 51-91, Public Information Division, EUCOM, January 31, 1951, ibid., RG 338, USAREUR, Box 461, Execution of War Criminals File.

62. George N. Shuster, *The Ground I Walked On* (Notre Dame: University of Notre Dame Press, 1961), 228.

63. Charles W. Thayer, *The Unquiet Germans* (New York: Harper, 1957), 233-234.

64. Public Relations Division, HICOG, January 31, 1951, RG 338, USAREUR, Box 461, Execution of War Criminals File.

4

The Rearmament of Germany and the U.S. War Crimes Program, 1951-1955

The clemency program of the American war crimes operation can be divided into two parts. During the first phase from 1946 to January 1951, as the previous chapters have shown, U.S. occupation authorities relied upon administrative procedures as substitutes for an appellate court. Because defendants were denied the right to appeal their convictions, those in charge of the trial operation sought to apply at least some American legal standards. Most of the employees of the Theater Judge Advocate Division and McCloy's Office of Legal Counsel were professional alwyers. For the most part, their records indicate their concerns as professionals to ensure the integrity of a controversial undertaking, which had already been rocked by two congressional investigations. American officials thought that the early clemency programs should also serve another useful purpose. Since U.S. authorities in Germany viewed the war crimes program as an important function in their effort to reform and reeducate the German people, the post-trial treatment of war criminals, in addition to the trials themselves, became a vital part of this educational device. The United States intended to use the proceedings against war criminals to demonstrate to the Germans the horrendous crimes Nazism had inflicted on its victims. Many U.S. officials believed that Germany's perceived preference for militarism and authoritarianism over democracy and pluralism had greatly facilitated the commission of these crimes. In contrast, sentence review and clemency were meant to promote the superior values of democratic society, which entitled even the perpetrators of mass murder to fair treatment.

The second phase of the modification and clemency operation, which lasted roughly from 1951 to 1955, took on entirely different characteristics. Its purpose was no longer to educate the German people and to ensure justice but to end the war crimes program as quickly as possible without causing a storm of protest in the Allied countries. Cold War political considerations dominated this period.[1] The reason was the perceived need for a German contribution to the defense of the West. Obviously, the Western Allies would have to pay for this by restoring the sovereignty of Germany. As a consequence, the imprisoned war criminals became an uncomfortable burden to both the Allies and the Adenauer government, then in the process of making the Federal Republic an equal partner militarily and politically.

The decision to promote German participation in the defense of Western Europe led to the dismantling of the war crimes program. However, the files of the West German foreign office and justice ministry as well as the records of the U.S. High Commission show that the imprisoned war criminals were a considerable obstacle to the normalization of Allied-German relations. There was no single, simple solution to this problem. Allied trust in the stability of the young Federal Republic's democracy was limited, despite the plans for German rearmament and integration. U.S. officials, both in Washington and in Germany, continued to fear a revival of Nazism.[2] The controversial war criminals issue was hardly suited to reassure the Western Allies that they had indeed acted wisely in uniting their zones into a new state. The German right demanded that remilitarizing the Federal Republic be connected with a general amnesty. Yet, the fulfillment of this demand would have provoked considerable domestic opposition in France, Britain and the United States. The Adenauer government advocated a more moderate position. Since the war crimes program was one of the last vestiges of exclusive Allied authority, the chancellor pushed for German involvement in the clemency process. Neither U.S. nor German officials, however, had specific plans regarding the future operation of the war crimes program at the beginning of the decade. Because of this, the program's fate came to be determined on an *ad hoc* basis. In this chapter, I will deal with the relationship between German rearmament and the post-trial treatment of convicted war criminals.

The creation of an East German paramilitary force in 1949 and the outbreak of the Korean War in June 1950 forced the Western Allies to rethink their positions on the question of German rearmament. President Truman's National Security Council (NSC) studied the issue for three months. On September 11, 1950, the president approved *NSC 82*, which called for the early creation of an integrated European defense force, with West German participation, against a possible Soviet attack.[3] The administration realized that a German contribution to European security would pose significant problems. Many European countries, particularly France, were bound to become nervous over the militarization of their troublesome neighbor.[4] Furthermore, Adenauer responded to the call for the rearming of Germany, which he himself very much desired, by demanding changes in the occupation regime. As a result, Secretary of State Acheson urged President Truman to allow the Federal Republic to run its own affairs. Such a step required that the American mission be modified from that of an occupying power to providing military assistance to an equal partner. Eventually, this shift culminated in the abolition of the Allied High Commission and the exchange of ambassadors between the Western powers and West Germany.[5]

The United States and France spent much of the fall of 1950 arguing over the nature of German participation in the defense of the West, and ultimately the French defined the best attainable solution. On October 26 the French National Assembly approved Minister President René Pleven's plan to establish a fully integrated European army under the guidance of a European defense ministry. Negotiations between Allied and German military experts regarding the creation of the European Defense Community (EDC)—the name for the Pleven Plan after July 1951—began in January 1951. At the same time, the Western Allies and the Federal Republic also initiated a second round of talks designed to put their relations on a contractual basis, as Acheson had suggested and Adenauer had demanded several months earlier. These efforts resulted in the separate signings of the EDC treaty and the Allied-German contractual agreements in May 1952. The EDC, however, never became reality since the French parliament refused to ratify the agreements in August 1954. Less than a year later, however, the Federal Republic did become sovereign and joined the North Atlantic Treaty Organization (NATO) with its own national army.[6]

The question of what to do with the convicted German war criminals came up almost simultaneously with the inception of negotiations regarding West Germany's rearmament. On January 30, 1951, the German representatives to the talks, Generals Adolf Heusinger and Hans Speidel, made a last-minute attempt to persuade the U.S. High Commission to announce a general amnesty for its Landsberg prisoners. In addition, the two threatened that a German contribution to Western defense would be impossible if the Americans insisted on executing the remaining Landsberg death row inmates. The generals considered the imprisonment of high-ranking military men for war crimes as defaming the entire German officer corps, whose "honor" they wanted to see restored. Heusinger and Speidel's protests were too late. McCloy had already made up his mind and announced his decisions on the following day.[7] However, the Landsberg war criminals were a public relations nuisance not only for Heusinger and Speidel. The Truman administration was also very much aware of the potential damage which the prisoners could cause. Thus, the State Department advised McCloy that it had successfully delayed congressional action on the termination of the state of war with Germany until after the scheduled executions of Oswald Pohl and the six others on June 7. The State Department thought it unwise to take such an important foreign policy step affecting the Federal Republic as long as the Landsberg gallows were still in business.[8]

In the late summer of 1951, having disposed of the last condemned war criminals, the three major Western foreign ministers gave the Allied High Commissioners a draft directive concerning the Allied-German contractual arrangements. The foreign ministers wanted to maintain the offices of the high commissioners in order to deal only with the future of individuals convicted for offenses against Allied personnel, administration or property. The right to grant clemency or parole in all other cases should be handed over to German authorities.[9] In contrast, the draft directive submitted by the Adenauer government was more radical and proposed to transfer clemency and parole powers for all Landsberg, Werl and Wittlich prisoners to the Germans. This had the appearance of a German attempt to usurp the Allies' exclusive authority with regard to war criminals. However, the U.S. High Commission gave the Adenauer government the benefit of the doubt and speculated that its proposal had "probably inadvertently" failed to exclude war criminals.[20] That seemed unlikely considering the importance which the German chancellor attached to a solution of the war criminals problem.

The desire for speedy German rearmament moved the Allied governments to share Adenauer's sense of urgency on this point. During their September 1951 meeting to discuss the German defense contribution, the foreign ministers and high commissioners attempted to find ways to eliminate the by now very irritating war criminals question. Acheson proposed to turn the prisoners over to German custody and to create a special clemency board with Allied and German members. Such an arrangement was acceptable to French Foreign Minister Robert Schuman but ran into problems with the British. Britain's delegation feared a negative public reaction at home, should the Allies decide to give German authorities custody over the imprisoned war criminals. The British instead suggested that full Allied authority continue in this area and that the remaining cases be reviewed every three years. But the Allies also feared a negative response by Adenauer unless they devised a formula acceptable to the German chancellor. British High Commissioner Ivone Kirkpatrick, noting the problem was now purely political and not legal, predicted that Adenauer would attack the Allied High Commission in the event that the Western Powers insisted on maintaining the present situation.[11] The foreign ministers, unable to come to an agreement during this particular meeting, placed the burden of making "urgent" recommendations on the high commissioners.[12]

The foreign ministers' call for a speedy resolution of this very complicated issue, but more importantly the impression that the Germans were trading rearmament for war criminals, caused resentment within the U.S. High Commission and the Army's European Command. Officials in HICOG's Office of Legal Counsel reacted sharply to German suggestions that former generals who were now Landsberg inmates receive special treatment. The U.S. High Commission rejected German claims that remilitarization would suffer unless the imprisoned generals were granted special concessions. Such an action would only amount to laying the foundation for a whitewash of the German officer corps and general staff.[13] A similar mood predominanted at

EUCOM. Handy's War Crimes Modification Board had only recently completed its review of all cases under EUCOM jurisdiction. As a consequence, the EUCOM commander decided to limit further reviews to those individual cases which, in the general's estimation, merited special consideration. Preserving his clemency board for such sentence reviews, Handy sought to avert German attempts at blackmail by requiring his own personal order before the board could act.[14]

While American authorities in Germany appeared to adopt a harsher stance, German officials in the fall of 1951 drafted their own more lenient plans to end the war criminals problem. In October, the Adenauer government received a proposal from a private interest group, the *Heidelberger Juristenkreis* (Heidelberg Circle of Jurists), which had a keen interest in the issue as well as excellent government connections. The *Juristenkreis* recommended that a mixed Allied-German board should be established in the near future to decide matters of clememcy.[15] In November the mixed commission proposal was endorsed by the German parliament's Committee for the Occupation Statute and Foreign Affairs. The chancellor subsequently accepted this concept as official German policy during the contractual agreements negotiations with the Western Allies, aimed at normalizing Allied-German relations.[16]

The beginning of the new year witnessed a frantic search on the part of both the Allies and the Germans for an acceptable way to deal with the war criminals in Allied custody. The issue now appeared to threaten the efforts toward German rearmament and the establishment of a contractual relationship. As a result, the Allied High Commission set up a special study committee to find a solution which all sides would consider satisfactory. The idea of a mixed clemency board was accepted by the United States. On January 12, 1952, HICOG Political Advisor Samuel Reber proposed to the British and French the creation of an Advisory Clemency Tribunal with equal German and Allied representation. The American proposal reserved the right of the convicting power to grant clemency. In addition, it gradually increased the board's function from that of an advisory body to one which would eventually make binding decisions.[17]

At McCloy's request, the Council of the High Commissioners considered the question two weeks later. While not finally deciding to support the mixed clemency board proposal, the high commissioners did agree on other important points. McCloy, Kirkpatrick and François-Poncet concluded that the Germans could only assume custody of the prisoners by recognizing the validity of the war crimes program's judgments and verdicts, an unlikely prospect.[18] This exceeded McCloy's initial suggestion to hand the war criminals over to the Federal Republic if the Adenauer government merely promised not to attack the legality of the courts and the trials. Unfortunately for the high commissioner, General Handy still advocated a sterner approach. The EUCOM commander promptly recommended that the prisoners remain in Allied custody. To McCloy's annoyance, the general further insisted that the Germans defray the costs of maintaining Landsberg and its inmates, while the U.S. ran the prison administration. Finally, Handy opposed any change in the current policy until after plans for the withdrawal of American troops from Germany had been completed.[19] Handy's position derived from the Baldwin subcommittee report on the Malmédy controversy and thus was in accordance with the recommendations of the Congress.

In spite of Handy's reservations, McCloy went ahead and continued negotiations with the British and the French on future clemency policy for war criminals. On January 30, 1952, the special study committee of the high commissioners came to terms on the makeup of the proposed mixed board. Consisting of six members, three Germans and one from each major Western Ally, the pardon commission would act independently of the appointing governments. Furthermore, no one who had previously taken part in the occupation or in a different function was eligible to serve on the board. The Allies informed Adenauer a week later about their plan to establish the mixed board as part of the contractual agreements.[20] Furthermore, the three high commissioners recommended to their governments that Adenauer be invited to the upcoming foreign ministers' meeting in London scheduled for February. Adenauer, in addition to his duties as chancellor, had also become the head of the Federal Republic's foreign office, the *Auswärtiges Amt*, in March 1951. To treat him as an equal, the high commissioners argued, would help to speed up the resolution of the remaining disputed points in the EDC and contractuals negotiations.[21] Such an approach seemed particularly appropriate with regard to the war criminals question where German agitation was still attempting to make rearmament dependent on a resolution of this problem.[22]

The opportunity to make the gradual emancipation of the Federal Republic and its chancellor acceptable to public opinion in France, Britain and the United States came with the death of British King George VI on February 6, 1952. Adenauer's decision to attend the monarch's funeral in London led him to expect an invitation from his counterparts to participate in the talks following the funeral, even though he had not been officially informed about the plans of the foreign ministers to ask him to participate in the meeting. For this purpose, the German foreign office had prepared a sixty-page memorandum on the war criminals problem for Adenauer. The *Auswärtiges Amt* acknowledged that by October 1951, 50 percent of the war criminals imprisoned in Germany had been released. However, the Germans were disappointed with the developments in the American zone and charged that not much had happened since the mass commutations a year ago, and were particularly concerned with Handy's stubborn attitude. The *Auswärtiges Amt* called the general's release policy and the activities of his War Crimes Modification Board "unsatisfactory." As a result, the foreign office suggested that Adenauer present the Allied foreign ministers with several German demands for the release of the remaining 659 prisoners. The chancellor should press for the creation of not just one but several mixed clemency commissions. In addition, the Allies should parole all those who had served one-third of their sentences. The foreign office, however, was not overly enthusiastic about having the war criminals transferred to German custody since this would be tantamount to an official German recognition of the judgments and the verdicts. This, the agency felt, should be avoided at all cost.[23]

Adenauer finally met with his Western Allied counterparts on February 18, 1952, to discuss the war criminals situation. The four agreed on the creation of one mixed commission, whose recommendations, if unanimous, would be binding on the convicting power. The board would become part of the contractual agreements and the Federal Republic would assume custody once the former began its work. Adenauer succeeded in convincing the Allies that he needed to be able to show improvements regarding the problem to impress the Germans upon his return to Bonn. Consequently, the foreign ministers acceded to Adenauer's request for a communiqué focusing on the establishment of the mixed board rather than Germany's obligations under the EDC treaty and the contractuals. The chancellor also had a recipe for his critics in the German veterans organizations and conservative parties who wanted greater Allied concessions, such as a general amnesty for war criminals. Adenauer announced his intention to publish the prisoners' pre-war criminal records to show the German public their truly criminal character. This, the chancellor hoped, would prevent calls for a solution beyond the envisaged Allied-German clemency commission.[24]

Adenauer did not have to wait for criticism from the right to encounter complications at home. His own justice ministry, headed by Thomas Dehler, faulted many of the London meeting's provisions. The agency was disappointed that only one board was to be established and estimated that the reviewing process would drag on for years. The provision calling for German custody, however, provoked the strongest reaction. The West German constitution, the Basic Law, in addition to outlawing capital punishment and the extradition of German citizens, also forbade the use of special courts and *ex post facto* laws. In the opinion of the justice ministry, the Allied war crimes program had relied on both. These constitutional concerns, the ministry acknowledged, could be circumvented if the chancellor petitioned the parliament to recognize the verdicts and the judgments of the war crimes courts. However, the justice ministry doubted that such an effort would succeed.[25]

A concerned Dehler quickly informed the chancellor of his agency's misgivings. The justice minister was convinced that a custody transfer would violate the Basic Law. More importantly, Dehler feared that the Allies might view such a move as a *de facto* German recognition of the war crimes program.[26] Emphasizing that the HICOG and EUCOM clemency boards had not led to the desired results, Dehler urged Adenauer to push for additional Allied concessions. The chancellor should press for the release of prisoners who had served one-third of their sentences and an Allied promise not to open new investigations of individuals suspected of war crimes. The chancellor should couple the latter demand with a request to stop all court proceedings now in progress if the maximum punishment was twenty years imprisonment or less.[27]

Adenauer took the concerns regarding the constitutionality of German custody of the Landsberg, Wittlich and Werl inmates straight to the Allied High Commission. McCloy was still convinced that the Germans could be put in charge of executing the Allied sentences. However, HICOG was unwilling to let this question delay the work on the EDC treaty and the contractuals, which were nearing completion. As a consequence, the high commissioners agreed with the chancellor to maintain their custody until it was legally possible for the Federal Republic to take over. This necessitated a renewed statement in the contractuals recognizing the Allies' supreme authority over war criminals. Although this uncomfortable reminder of Allied powers limited the Federal Republic's areas of competence, Adenauer gladly supported it. The chancellor preferred to leave the impression that he had made a minor concession to the Allies rather than stand accused of violating the Basic Law by assuming control over the prisoners.[28]

There were additional problems with the foreign ministers' London agreement, particularly Adenauer's plan to publish the pre-war criminal records of the war criminals. During a conference between HICOG and EUCOM officials in February, the former proposed to expand this information by listing offenses for which the individual had been sentenced by American tribunals.[29] Handy, however, did not think much of the entire idea. The general feared that supplying the Germans (except the prisoners' attorneys) with such data would lead to further attacks on the Army's war crimes program. EUCOM's problem was that in many cases the Army had successfully prosecuted many defendants on conspiracy charges owing to a lack of evidence of their specific individual guilt. Handy used the Malmédy trial to make his point. The court had convicted the leader of the SS combat group, Col. Joachim Peiper, without any proof that he had actually shot an American POW. Thus, Handy recommended that the Adenauer government proceed and publish pre-war convictions if it wanted to go through the trouble to search for them in the files. EUCOM, however, would refrain from handing out sensitive information on its convictions.[30]

The Western Allies and the Federal Republic finally signed the contractual agreements and the EDC treaty on May 26 and 27, 1952, respectively. The contractuals practically guaranteed German sovereignty by abolishing the Occupation Statute and integrating West Germany as an equal partner in the West. However, the agreement would not go into effect unless the EDC treaty was also ratified by all four parties. This proved to be a most fateful provision, which not only delayed the achievement of German independence until 1955 but also dragged out the war criminals problem to the annoyance of everyone involved. The treaties addressed the question of the Allied prisoners in Article 6 of the Convention on the Settlement of Matters Arising out of the War and the Occupation. This article called for the establishment of a mixed six-member clemency board with equal German and Allied representation, and reserved the Allies' exclusive right to grant pardons. Whenever unanimous, however, the board's recommendation would be binding on the convicting power.[31] This last point became part of Article 6 despite new objections by the Adenauer government, which preferred a simple majority as binding.[32]

Although May 1952 should have been a time for rejoicing over the resolution of the thorny issues of German rehabilitation and rearmament to the apparent satisfaction of all parties, the question of ratification soon cast doubt on the future of the agreements. As early as May 12 the State Department gave Truman the disturbing news that the EDC and the contractuals might not survive in the French parliament. The Paris government, according to its foreign office, did not command the majority needed to ratify the treaties. Consequently, the government did not intend to submit the documents to the National Assembly for a first reading until October. The final vote was not planned until after the November 1952 presidential elections in the United States. Even more upsetting was the reason which the French provided for the EDC's current troubles. The defense community, which had evolved out of the French Pleven Plan, was no longer seen as that country's initiative. Instead, many lawmakers in the National Assembly now believed that the Truman administration had forced the French into the arrangement.[33] The problem was that any delay with regard to the parliamentary approval of the EDC also prevented the contractual agreements from becoming effective.

Across the Rhine, Adenauer presented the treaties to his parliament in the summer of 1952. To fill in the time between the signing and the anticipated ratification by all four signatories, the Germans drew up additional plans to tackle the war criminals problem. The goal was to reduce the number of prisoners so that the Article 6 mixed board, once it began its work, could consider the remaining cases more speedily. As a result, the German government considered urging McCloy and Handy to revive their respective clemency commissions. Justice Minister Dehler recommended that McCloy and Handy should be warned that the German public, press and legislature would oppose a German defense contribution unless pardons were more generously granted. Dehler claimed that the recent period of inactivity on the part of HICOG and EUCOM boards might ultimately lead to a parliamentary defeat of the EDC treaty and the contractuals.[34]

The justice ministry's own records indicate the weakness of Dehler's argument. Between December 1951 and June 1952 the Landsberg population had shrunk from 458 to 345, a twenty-five percent reduction. Yet, the justice ministry complained about the American failure to release individuals who had served one-third of their sentences. Current U.S. policy provided for release after prisoners served two-thirds of a sentence. As usual, Handy was the prime target of the criticism. The Federal Justice Ministry was disappointed that the general was not nearly as forthcoming as McCloy. Furthermore, the agency continued to view the EUCOM War Crimes Modification Board as somewhat of a hoax. While McCloy had shipped independent jurists to Germany to work on his advisory commission, Handy, in the justice ministry's opinion, had relied only on individuals connected with the war crimes program. The obvious implication was that cases before the EUCOM board did not receive a fair hearing.[35]

The Adenauer government also focused during the annual summer lull in West German politics on the question of jurisdiction under the war crimes program. The Federal Republic suddenly considered it possible to transfer some of the prisoners into its custody, but only after the mixed board in Article 6 of the contractuals had completed its work. This was undoubtedly intended as an incentive for the Allies to ratify the treaties quickly. In return, the Germans would quickly follow ratification with assuming jurisdiction over, and thus the cost for, the inmates and the prisons. The government found a simple explanation to make this unexpected change in attitude plausible for the German public. Without mentioning names or specifics, it reasoned that only the "true" criminals would remain in prison once the board had reviewed all cases. These individuals would also have been prosecuted and sentenced on the basis of German law. Thus, it was logical and constitutional for the Adenauer government to execute their sentences.[36]

The German government's willingness to take responsibility for the prisoners at some point in the future did not mean that it was prepared to compromise in other areas of the war criminals question. Adenauer himself increased the pressure on the Allies, particularly the United States, by promising German journalists that the problem would soon be solved. The *Auswärtiges Amt* sensed, or at least claimed to sense, public dissatisfaction with the alleged delays in releasing additional war criminals.[37] Adenauer promptly requested again that McCloy and Handy be more lenient in their release practices. The U.S. High Commissioner, nearing the end of his tenure, rejected the notion that he and the general had adopted a policy of refusing all clemency requests until the contractual agreements, and thus the mixed board, went into effect. McCloy admitted that neither he nor Handy considered it appropriate to conduct a second general review at this time. However, both HICOG and EUCOM were still willing to examine individual cases if the circumstances warranted such action.[38]

McCloy's comments confirmed the impression that U.S. authorities in Germany were making additional large-scale releases dependent upon ratification of the EDC treaty and the contractuals by the Allied and German parliaments. However, the State Department in Washington was already formulating plans to address at least one of Adenauer's concerns. The Germans continued to have strong reservations about the unanimity clause in Article 6. This provision did not deal with those cases in which a simple majority of the mixed board's members would recommend release. Theoretically, such individuals could remain in prison or could be released depending on the preference of the convicting power. With regard to the Landsberg prisoners, the State Department proposed that Truman form an additional board in the United States consisting of officials from the Departments of Justice, Defense and State with authority to consider the clemency requests of war criminals who did not obtain unanimous recommendations.[39]

In the fall of 1952 Adenauer intensified his lobbying of the Allies to end the war criminals problem, just in time to coincide with the second reading of the treaties in the *Bundestag*. The chancellor continued to argue that the German public expected to see the issue solved. The new U.S. High Commissioner, Walter J. Donnelly, also noted an ever-increasing campaign by the German press and prominent politicians demanding the release of war criminals in return for German rearmament.[40] After asking Acheson and French High Commissioner François-Poncet for concessions,[41] Adenauer found at least one important ally. NATO commander General Matthew Ridgway, obviously not quite in tune with the policies of his own government, declared that the annoying issue should be disposed of even before the treaties became effective. Worse, Ridgway played right into the hands of those German elements, particularly the veterans groups, which were attempting to exchange war criminals for remilitarization. The general shared the sentiment that the German soldier should not be asked to bear arms while his former "comrades" remained in the prisons of nations belonging to the EDC.[42] Although the German government cautioned that Ridgway had not called for the release of every imprisoned war criminal, the statement was certainly water on its own propaganda mills.

These official and unofficial pressures on the Allies soon brought results. On October 12, 1952, Donnelly gave EUCOM a new memorandum on the treatment of war criminals, thus setting the stage for yet another feud between the High Commission and the Army. The document suggested that EUCOM undertake more reviews of individual cases, show greater generosity, institute a medical parole program and consider increasing good conduct time.[43] These proposals, evidently aimed at pleasing the Germans, drew an uncompromising response from Army authorities and forced Donnelly to retreat. The U.S. High Commissioner was quick to agree that the present good conduct time system and Handy's review policy was satisfactory. Donnelly pointed out that he did not question the Army's policies. In fact, the high commissioner confessed to having acted on State Department orders to check up on EUCOM. Despite the obvious mistrust between the State Department and HICOG on the one hand and EUCOM on the other, Donnelly urged cooperation between U.S. officials in Germany. His reason was simple: Donnelly expected increasing German demands for the premature convening of the Article 6 mixed board even though France was unlikely to ratify the EDC and contractual agreements in the near future.[44]

By January 1953 the State Department also became increasingly concerned with West Germany's, in addition to France's, delay in ratifying the treaties. The held-up ratification process in the Federal Republic's legislature had two causes. Adenauer's Social Democratic opponents tested the constitutionality of the EDC and the contractual agreements before the Federal Constitutional Court. The other reason was the increasing irritation among many lawmakers regarding the war criminals problem, whose solution was now perceived as a "psychological prerequisite" for German rearmament. There was little the United States could do about the former. On the issue of imprisoned war criminals, however, Acheson was prepared to adopt measures going beyond the still unratified Article 6 to bring about at least the "liquidation [of the] US aspect of this serious irritant to Allied-German relations." In view of Dwight D. Eisenhower's victory in the 1952 presidential election, time was running out for the Truman administration. The same was apparently true with regard to fresh ideas on the future treatment of war criminals within the State Department. Therefore, Acheson informed the U.S. High Commission that the administration would gladly accept "any suggestions" from HICOG.[45]

Acheson's call for new approaches won an enthusiastic response in both West Germany and the United States. In the Federal Republic the *Heidelberger Juristenkreis* urged Adenauer to push for the creation of an interim mixed board to prepare for the Article 6 clemency commission before the latter was finally convened. Such an interim board was necessary, the *Juristenkreis* argued, due to the large volume of material and the multitude of remaining problems, such as procedure. The German side should begin its work immediately so that "precious time" was not lost.[46] The most important aspect of this proposal was its call for an interim measure, which more and more seemed necessary.

Within HICOG and the State Department, the most noticeable development was a new tougher attitude toward the British and the French. Secretary of State John Foster Dulles' patience with Paris, in particular, was clearly limited. Consequently, the United States put increasing pressure on France and Great Britain to convene the Article 6 board before the final ratification of the treaties by all parties. The new U.S. High Commissioner, James B. Conant, who replaced Donnelly after his brief four-month tenure, attempted to convince his counterparts Kirkpatrick and François-Poncet that the political atmosphere in the Federal Republic demanded such a step. Thus, the three powers should agree to establish the board once Germany had ratified the EDC and the contractuals. This was only part of the new American approach. The United States was also willing to introduce a system of parole for war criminals over the objections of the French and British. Conant was even prepared to include a German on the parole board since, in his opinion, this would force the Germans to shoulder some responsibility. In addition, the Federal Republic would inevitably discover that most of the imprisoned war criminals were in effect common criminals by any standard.[47] Nonetheless, the United States was preparing to release them.

German ratification of the treaties in the spring of 1953 removed one significant obstacle and only deepened the American resolve to use a tough-line approach vis-à-vis the British and the French. Visiting Eisenhower in April, Adenauer urged him to convene the Article 6 board early even though French ratification was in limbo. In June Eisenhower decided to try one last time to persuade the two Allies to establish the mixed German-Allied commission as provided for in the contractuals. The administration assured the Germans that should this attempt fail, it would unilaterally introduce a general parole system for the Landsberg prisoners.[48] For U.S. authorities, the use of parole offered numerous advantages anyway. Such an arrangement was already in place for Japanese war criminals and thus the Americans could rely on the experience gathered in the Far East. In Germany, it would help to reduce the political pressure on the Allies and Adenauer by leading to the release of a number of prisoners.[49] Most importantly, from the American standpoint, parole proceedings would not question the validity and judgments of the war crimes trials. In addition, HICOG and the State Department had concluded that clemency reviews had been conducted all too often. Should the United States continue to rely only on this method of sentence modification, the whole idea of clemency would soon become a "mockery." A parole system would help to avert such a development.[50]

As usual, the Army opposed the State Department and HICOG plans. Dating from 1953, General Charles L. Bolte, the commander in chief of the United States Army, Europe (USAREUR), was in charge of the war criminals under Army jurisdiction, having replaced EUCOM's Gen. Handy in that role. Bolte did not oppose the introduction of a parole system but differed in two important aspects with the High Commission's positions. Bolte rejected the idea of German membership on the proposed parole board and was at most willing to tolerate Germans in an advisory function. Jealously guarding its turf and seeking to prevent the State Department and HICOG from meddling with the Army's Landsberg prisoners, USAREUR pressed for the establishment of two separate boards, one for the High Commission and one for the Army.[51]

The decisive breakthrough regarding the lingering war criminals question came on July 7, 1953, but not because of an American idea. The French, whose delay in ratifying the agreements was causing great concern within the Eisenhower administration and the German government, surprised everyone by proposing a solution. François-Poncet suggested to Kirkpatrick and Conant to forget the Article 6 mixed board for the time being. Instead, the French desired three interim clemency commissions, one for each Western zone of occupation. With this approach, the Paris government could save face at home by preventing any provisions of the two treaties from going into effect prematurely, before French ratification. A second advantage was that the irritating war criminals issue would not stay around indefinitely. Third, the French, in anticipation of pressure for holding up progress on the EDC, wanted the prisoners removed as an agenda item from the upcoming Washington foreign ministers conference.[52] Fourth, France had already experimented with an interim mixed board for the war criminals in its custody, an arrangement which had apparently satisfied both the German and French governments.[53]

Conant liked the French proposal and recommended that the United States endorse the idea. To avoid difficulties with the Army, the high commissioner urged Dulles to discuss the matter directly with the Defense Department and make a decision at the highest level, thus bypassing the stubborn commanders of EUCOM and USAREUR.[54] Conant's worries about Army reaction were well founded. When informed of this latest development, Gen. Bolte suddenly announced his concerns about making the full trial records available to the foreign members of the interim mixed boards. The Army feared that this would result in further controversy and unwanted criticism of the war crimes program. Bolte told the High Commission that he did not want to proceed on his own authority. USAREUR preferred that the Defense Department decide the issue of record availability.[55]

Bolte did not hesitate to make his reservations known to Secretary of Defense Charles Wilson. In addition to the concerns about the trial records, the Army wanted to limit the function of German board members to an advisory status and thus give the convicting power the exclusive authority to grant clemency and parole.[56] The U.S. High Commission immediately protested. Convinced that American authorities in Germany would become the targets of criticism if USAREUR's recommendations were adopted, HICOG expected the suggested curtailment of the availability of the trial records to create very serious problems with the Germans.[57]

The administration took both HICOG's and USAREUR's considerations into account. On July 11, 1953, at the Washington foreign ministers meeting, the United States officially agreed with the French proposal to establish three interim mixed boards on a zonal basis. The Allies aimed at having the three clemency commissions resemble the Article 6 German-Allied board as closely as possible. Now that the Allies were in agreement, it was time to help out the German chancellor who was about to face the voters in the upcoming September 1953 federal elections. To ensure that the war criminals problem would not cause Adenauer's downfall, the Allies decided to make an announcement on the zonal boards at the earliest possible moment.[58] The Allied High Commission notified the chancellor about the foreign ministers' decision a few days later. Several provisions still ran counter to Adenauer's wishes. The zonal boards were to be advisory only and, in accordance with the Army's viewpoint, even their unanimous recommendations were not binding. Furthermore, Allied representatives would outnumber German members, a significant departure from Article 6. Despite these shortcomings, as far as the Germans were concerned, the Allied action was better than the nerve-racking wait for French ratification of the EDC treaty and the contractuals.[59]

For obvious reasons, the German government was also very eager to have the zonal clemency boards convene before the September election.[60] However, the Germans still had to resolve one important problem themselves. The Allies feared that convicted war criminals who were released on parole, and thus on their word of honor, would escape to foreign countries.[61] To prevent this, the United States wanted assurances that German authorities would participate in the arrest and detention of parole violators. This demand posed potential constitutional problems for the Adenauer government since it required the extradition of such individuals to Allied custody. The Basic Law, however, prohibited the deportation of German citizens, and until then the government had always given preference to the Basic Law over the Allied Occupation Statute. This obstacle could be circumvented if German officials instead relied on the provisions of the Occupation Statute, giving Allied parole officers the right to issue orders to German agencies.[62] The Adenauer government was relieved that it had found a solution which permitted it to ignore the Basic Law in this particular instance. The Federal Republic's newly discovered love for the Occupation Statute, which most likely came as a surprise to U.S. officials in Germany, meant that the mixed boards could begin their work as soon as a procedure had been drafted.[63] Adenauer's willingness to commit a potentially unconstitutional act also demonstrated the eagerness of the Germans to get rid of the problem once and for all.

On August 31, 1953, six days before the German election, Conant and General Bolte announced the establishment of the Interim Mixed Parole and Clemency Board (IMPAC) for war criminals in American custody (the British and the French followed with similar actions in their zones of occupation). IMPAC was to consist of five members, three from the United States and two from the Federal Republic. The board operated as had earlier U.S. clemency commissions. It focused on sentence equalization, the defendant's criminal record, behavior while in prison, prospects for rehabilitation as well as age and physical condition. In contrast to previous programs, which had been conducted only under the aspect of clemency, IMPAC could also make parole recommendations. As Adenauer already knew, unanimity would not be binding. This was a significant difference between IMPAC and the mixed commission of the contractuals' Article 6. The IMPAC order also showed the haste with which the Allies and the Germans wanted to dispose of the war criminals problem, aggravated further by their desire to ensure the chancellor's reelection. Consequently, Conant and Bolte left the procedural details to IMPAC once it convened.[64] In fact, U.S. officials did not even have time to find a suitable chairman for the board, thereby causing additional delays to the dismay of the German government.[65] Nevertheless, the chancellor won at the polls. Just how much the IMPAC announcement contributed to Adenauer's victory is difficult to determine.

Not until October 21, 1953, did U.S. authorities appoint the five-member board.[66] Adenauer, eager to have IMPAC begin its work, was quick to promise the full cooperation of the German federal government and individual *länder* concerning the planned parole program.[67] Nonetheless, the pace of events following the initial announcement of IMPAC in August continued to dismay the Germans. As a result, the *Auswärtiges Amt* used every opportunity to press the Allies for speedy action. By the end of the year, while all three zonal mixed boards were in session they had yet to inform the Federal Republic about the results of their sentence reviews. Thus, all Adenauer could hope for was the generous granting of Christmas amnesties in December 1953.[68]

In reality, there were no grounds for German dissatisfaction. Within the first year of IMPAC's existence alone, the United States released more than 60 percent of the Landsberg war criminals, reducing the prison population from 228 to 112.[69] The political events of 1954 showed that the Germans should have been particularly grateful for the interim zonal boards. In August the French National Assembly did what by now everyone had all along expected. The parliament turned down the EDC and the contractual agreements and thus killed, for the time being, the Article 6 Allied-German mixed board. Clearly, a new formula for the rearmament of the Federal Republic and the restoration of its sovereignty had to be found. British Prime Minister Winston Churchill had already urged Eisenhower to integrate Germany's future military force in NATO if the EDC failed.[70] These plans became reality in a new series of Allied-German treaties, the Paris conventions, which were signed in October. With regard to the war criminals problem, the Paris treaties adopted Article 6 of the old contractual agreements. This meant that, once the conventions went into effect, the interim zonal boards would cease to function and would be replaced by the originally intended mixed German-Allied board operating on a supra-zonal basis. The Federal Republic finally became sovereign on May 5, 1955, and participated in a meeting of the NATO council for the first time four days later. As a consequence, the mixed board of the Paris conventions replaced IMPAC and the French and British interim commissions on July 1.

When the IMPAC operation came to a close only forty-five "hard core" war criminals remained at Landsberg. Thus, the interim board released approximately 85 percent of the prisoners since the beginning of its work. All in all, IMPAC considered a total of 487 cases. Many of these were applications by war criminals seeking changes in their conditional release status. A large number of individuals applied for parole and clemency several times. The final report of American board member Edwin A. Plitt, a career diplomat, submitted to the State Department, disclosed that IMPAC had led to results which were more sweeping than Handy's and McCloy's January 1951 mass commutations. However, Plitt was interested in more than merely supplying the administration with statistical information. In making recommendations for a possible future U.S. war crimes program, Plitt blamed many of the difficulties on the American authorities themselves. Excessive sentence reductions such as commuting a death sentence to a six-year term were bound to create the impression that injustices had taken place. Plitt also faulted the United States for treating regular prisoners of war harshly. For example, the Americans had stripped both war criminals and POWs of their ranks and their uniforms. Therefore, Plitt alleged, large segments of the German population had come to believe that the two groups were in effect identical, and consequently, never accepted the concept of war crimes. Lastly, Plitt criticized the use of the same witnesses in several different concentration camp trials. Some of these individuals, Plitt contended, "willfully or unconsciously gave false testimony." As a result, IMPAC had taken this "discredited testimony" into consideration while reviewing cases. Plitt obviously believed that the war crimes program could have succeeded had U.S. authorities paid closer attention to these details early on.[71]

Although IMPAC did not release all war criminals from American custody, it sufficiently reduced the problem so that German rearmament and sovereignty were no longer in jeopardy. The United States had sold out its war crimes program—so had the British and the French. Thus, the trial operation, which was to punish the perpetrators and, at the same time, teach the Germans the virtues of democracy by demonstrating the evils of Nazism, simply fell by the wayside. For the historian, there remain a few rather interesting and, at times amusing, points underscoring the purely political considerations which caused the war crimes program's demise. The German government was evidently not interested in justice but only in a political solution to the problem. Adenauer's bureaucrats were even willing to prefer the otherwise dreaded Occupation Statute to Germany's own Basic Law to ensure the quick release of the prisoners on parole. This approach was not only unique and ingenious. It was also a potential violation of the Federal Republic's constitution. Nonetheless, the chancellor achieved his most important goal by convincing the Allies to allow German participation in clemency and parole decisions.

In addition, the Landsberg prisoners offered a perfect means for the Germans and the Allies to blackmail each other. West German participation in the EDC would be impossible, Adenauer and his government had emphasized, without the resolution of the war criminals problem. In return, U.S. authorities used the issue to speed up German ratification of the EDC treaty and the contractuals. The records indicate that American officials slowed down clemency proceedings in 1952 and early 1953. In part, the United States reacted angrily to the repeated German attempts to make rearmament dependent upon the release of the Landsberg inmates. However, by granting pardons less generously, the U.S. High Commission and the Army hoped to force German ratification since the contractuals contained the much desired answer to the war criminals question in Article 6.

NOTES

1. Rückerl, *NS-Verbrechen vor Gericht*, 130.

2. Hans Wilhelm Gatzke, *Germany and the United States: A Special Relationship?* (Cambridge: Harvard University Press, 1980), 279; and Thomas A. Schwartz, "The 'Skeleton Key'—American Foreign Policy, European Unity, and German Rearmament, 1949-54," *Central European History* 19 (1986), 369-385.

3. Report to the National Security Council by the executive secretary, James S. Lay, on United States Position Regarding Strengthening the Defense of Europe and the Nature of Germany's Defense Thereto, September 11, 1950, Memorandum Approvals 359 File, Document 63, Truman Library.

4. Ibid.

5. Acheson and Under Secretary of State Robert Lovett to Truman, July 30, 1951, PSF-Subject File, Box 178, Germany Folder 2, Truman Library.

6. For more information on German rearmament and the EDC negotiations, see Gerhard Wettig, *Entmilitarisierung und Wiederbewaffnung in Deutschland 1943-1955. Internationale Auseinandersetzung um die Rolle der Deutschen in Europa* (Munich: Oldenbourg, 1967) and F. Roy Willis, *France, Germany and the New Europe, 1945-1967* (Palo Alto: Stanford University Press, 1968), 130-184. French contemporary views on the issue are presented in Daniel Lerner and Raymond Aron, eds., *France Defeats EDC* (New York: Praeger, 1957). American interests and goals are discussed in Robert McGeehan, *The German Rearmament Question: American Diplomacy and European Defense after World War II* (Urbana: University of Illinois Press, 1971) and Schwartz, "The 'Skeleton Key'—American Foreign Policy, European Unity, and German Rearmament, 1949-54," *Central European History* 19 (1986), 369-385. For a presentation of the German side, see Arnulf Baring, *Außenpolitik in Adenauers Kanzlerdemokratie* (Munich: Oldenbourg, 1965), 76-162.

7. Baring, *Außenpolitik in Adenauers Kanzlerdemokratie*, 99; and Thayer, *The Unquiet Germans*, 234.

8. State Department to McCloy, May 11, 1951, RG 466, Papers of John J. McCloy, Eyes Only File, E.O. (51) 48.

9. Draft Directive from the Foreign Minister to the Allied High Commission on Contractual Agreements, August 21, 1951, RG 466, Papers of John J. McCloy, Classified General Records 1949-1952, Box 30, D (50) 1271.

10. Comments on German Draft Directive, September 2, 1951, ibid., Box 31, D (50) 1320.

11. Meeting of the U.S., U.K., French Foreign Ministers, Minutes of the Fifth Meeting, September 13, 1951, ibid., D (51) 1375.

12. Instruction from the Three Foreign Ministers to the Allied High Commission, September 13, 1951, ibid., D (51) 1373.

13. Richard C. Hagan, Records Officer, HICOG, to E.W. Debevoise, General Counsel, HICOG, September 24, 1951, RG 466, U.S. High Commission for Germany, Security-Segregated General Records 1949-1952, Box 28, 321.6, War Criminals File.

14. Internal Route Slip by Col. O'Neill, EUCOM Deputy Chief of Staff for Administration, October 10, 1951, RG 338, USAREUR, Box 518, War Criminals Modification Board File.

15. *Heidelberger Juristenkreis* to the Subcommittee "Prisoners of War" of the *Bundestag* Committee for the Occupation Statute and Foreign Affairs, October 23, 1951, *Politisches Archiv des Auswärtigen Amtes* (henceforth: *Auswärtiges Amt*), File 515-00 h II, unnumbered/51, Bonn, West Germany.

16. Carlo Schmid, chairman, Committee for the Occupation Statute and Foreign Affairs, to Adenauer, November 15, 1951, ibid., Document 14296/51.

17. Samuel Reber, director, Political Affairs, HICOG, to McCloy, January 12, 1952, RG 466, Papers of John J. McCloy, Classified General Records 1949-1952, Box 35, D (52) 106.

18. McCloy to State, January 24, 1952, ibid., Box 36, D (52) 223.

19. McCloy to State, January 27, 1952, ibid., D (52) 227.

20. McCloy to State, February 4, 1952, RG 466, U.S. High Commission for Germany, Security-Segregated General Records 1949-1952, Box 28, 321.6, War Criminals File.

21. McCloy to State, February 7, 1952, RG 466, Papers of John J. McCloy, Classified General Records 1949-1952, Box 36, D (52) 356.

22. Gen. MacArthur to Handy, January 30, 1952, ibid., D (52) 267; and Federal Justice Minister Thomas Dehler to Adenauer, February 9, 1952, *Auswärtiges Amt*, File 515-11 II, Document 6103/52.

23. *Material für die London-Reise des Herrn Bundeskanzlers* by Wilhelm Hoppe, German foreign officer, February 13, 1952, *Auswärtiges Amt*, File 515-00 h II, Document 2019/52.

24. State Department Briefs, February 19, 1952, Truman Papers, Naval Aide Files, Box 23, Truman Library.

25. *Stellungnahme zu dem deutsch-alliierten Entwurf "betreffend Kriegsverbrecher," London*, 18.2.1952, *Bundeszwischenarchiv*, File B141-9576, 131-135; 141-144.

26. Justice Minister Thomas Dehler to Adenauer, March 12, 1952, *Auswärtiges Amt*, File 515-11 II, Document 6103/52.

27. *Vorschlag zur Behandlung des Kriegsverbrecherproblems* by Dehler, March 12, 1952, ibid.

28. McCloy to Acheson, May 3, 1952, RG 466, Papers of John J. McCloy, Classified General Records 1949-1952, Box 41, D (52) 1078.

29. Memorandum for the record by Edgar M. Gerlach, HICOG, February 29, 1952, RG 338, USAREUR, Box 462, General Administration-Policy File.

30. Transcript of a telephone conversation between Handy and Deputy U.S. High Commissioner for Germany Maj. Gen. George P. Hays, March 25, 1952, ibid., Box 461, General Administration File.

31. Convention on the Settlement of Matters Arising out of the War and the Occupation, *Bundesgesetzblatt, 1955, Teil II*, 411-413.

32. McCloy to State, May 14, 1952, RG 466, Papers of John J. McCloy, Classified General Records 1949-1952, Box 41, D (52) 1184.

33. State Department Briefs, May 12, 1952, Truman Papers, Naval Aide Files, Box 24, Truman Library.

34. Dehler to Adenauer, June 26, 1952; and draft letter by Dehler prepared for Adenauer to be sent to McCloy, June 24, 1952, *Auswärtiges Amt*, File 515-11 II, Documents 8797/52, 9798/52.

35. *Stand der Begnadigungen durch die drei alliierten Besatzungsmächte* by Margarete Bitter, German justice ministry official, June 23, 1952, ibid., Document 8796/52.

36. *Diplomatische Korrespondenz*, June 14, *Jahrgang II*, No. 38.

37. Hoppe to Deputy Foreign Minister Walter Hallstein, June 25, 1952, *Auswärtiges Amt*, File 515-11 II, Document 8465/52.

38. McCloy to Adenauer, July 3, 1952, ibid., Document 9081/52.

39. State Department to HICOG, August 26, 1952, RG 338, USAREUR, Box 466, Cables File.

40. U.S. High Commissioner for Germany Walter J. Donnelly to State Department, September 10, 1952, ibid.

41. German consulate, New York, to Adenauer advisor Herbert Blankenhorn, September 9, 1952, *Auswärtiges Amt*, File 210-01/80 II g, Document 51/52; and Adenauer to French High Commissioner for Germany André François-Poncet, September 13, 1952, *Auswärtiges Amt*, File 515-11 II, Document 12007/52.

42. *Internationale Diplomatische Information*, September 11, 1952, 1.

43. Eddy to Donnelly, October 27, 1952, RG 466, U.S. High Commission for Germany, Security-Segregated General Records 1949-1952, 321.6, War Criminals File.

44. Donnelly to Eddy, November 6, 1952, ibid.

45. Acheson to Acting High Commissioner Samuel Reber, January 7, 1953, RG 466, U.S. High Commission for Germany, Security-Segregated General Records 1953-1955, Box 164, 321.6, War Criminals—Mixed Board File.

46. *Heidelberger Juristenkreis* to Adenauer, March 1953, *Auswärtiges Amt*, File 515-11 II, Document 3299/53.

47. U.S. High Commissioner for Germany James B. Conant to Secretary of State John Foster Dulles, April 1, 1953; and Dulles to Conant, April 3, 1953, RG 466, U.S. High Commission for Germany, Security-Segregated General Records 1953-1955, Box 164, 321.6, War Criminals—Mixed Board File.

48. Dulles to Conant, Handy, NATO Commander Matthew Ridgway and Gen. Charles L. Bolte, Commander in Chief, USAREUR, June 25, 1953, ibid.

49. Memorandum regarding Proposed U.S. Parole System for German War Criminals, Bureau of German Affairs, State Department, June 5, 1953, RG 338, USAREUR, Box 461, General Administration File.

50. Memorandum regarding Proposal Parole Board for German War Criminals, June 4, 1953, ibid.

51. Conant to Dulles, July 6, 1953, RG 466, U.S. High Commission for Germany, Security-Segregated General Records 1953-1955, Box 164, 321.6, War Criminals—Mixed Board File.

52. Conant to Dulles, July 7, 1953, ibid.

53. United States Department of State, *Foreign Relations of the United States, 1952-1954*, 16 vols. (Washington, D.C.: Government Printing Office, 1983), V, Part 2, 1629-1630.

54. Ibid.

55. HICOG to Dulles, July 8, 1953, ibid.

56. USAREUR to Secretary of Defense Charles Wilson, July 9, 1953, ibid.

57. HICOG to Dulles, July 9, 1953, ibid.

58. Dulles to Conant, July 14, 1953; and July 17, 1953, ibid.

59. British High Commissioner for Germany Ivone Kirkpatrick to Adenauer, July 20, 1953, *Auswärtiges Amt*, File 515-11/01 II, Document 20188/53.

60. Heinz v. Trützschler, German foreign officer, to Hallstein, August 17, 1953, ibid., Document 20466/53.

61. Memorandum for the record by Dr. Brückner, German foreign officer, July 31, 1953, ibid., Document 20291/53.

62. Protocol of a meeting between officials of the justice ministry, the *Auswärtiges Amt* and the interior ministry, August 26, 1953, *Bundeszwischenarchiv*, File B141-9578, 98-100.

63. Hallstein to Conant, August 28, 1953, ibid., 77-79.

64. Order concerning Interim Mixed Parole and Clemency Board by Conant, August 31, 1953, RG 338, USAREUR, Box 461, General Administration File.

65. Conant to Dulles, September 1953, U.S. High Commission for Germany, Security-Segregated General Records 1953-1955, Box 164, 321.6, War Criminals—Mixed Board File.

66. USAREUR Release No. 53-830, October 21, 1953, RG 338, USAREUR, Box 461, General Administration File.

67. Adenauer to Conant, November 7, 1953, ibid.

68. *Zwischenbericht über die Tätigkeit der gemischten Beratungsausschüsse und über den Stand des sogenannten Kriegsverbrecherproblems im allgemeinen*, December 17, 1953, *Auswärtiges Amt*, File 515-00 h II, Document 22250/53.

69. *Statistiken der Zentralen Rechtsschutzstelle*, October 1, 1955, *Auswärtiges Amt*, File 204/515-00 k II, Document 3734/53.

70. 205th Meeting of the National Security Council, July 1, 1954, Ann Whitman File, NSC Series, Eisenhower Library, Abilene, Kansas.

71. IMPAC Board member Edwin A. Plitt to State Department, September 15, 1955, RG 466, U.S. High Commission for Germany, Security-Segregated General Records 1953-1955, Box 164, 321.6, War Criminals—Mixed Board File.

5

Private German Lobbies and Convicted War Criminals

So far, this study has focused to a great extent on the American side of the war crimes program and its diplomatic implications. To determine why the operation failed to impress the Germans with its mountains of evidence of atrocities and organized mass murder committed by the convicted war criminals, the German end of the reeducation process must also be examined. A HICOG survey, titled "Current West German Views on the War Criminals Issue," of September 1952 found that only one in ten Germans supported the war crimes trials.[1] The opinion poll provided the clearest indication yet to the Americans that the use of the trials for educational purposes was a failure. This posed important questions for U.S. authorities in Germany at the time. It also poses a significant challenge to historians. Why did the Germans not support the efforts to punish those proven guilty of the murder of millions of Jews and other victims? Why did the Germans refuse to believe that their society with its history of militarism and authoritarianism was indeed in need of reform? The culprit, I submit, was German nationalism.

In 1950 the U.S. High Commission concluded that German nationalism had not died in 1945. Rather, it had taken on a different, more moderate form.[2] Most historians agree with this assessment, although some have pointed out that right wing fringe groups continued to threaten the stability of the Federal Republic for some time.[3] Nonetheless, German nationalism between 1946 and 1955, the period of this study, differed from its aggressive predecessor during the Third Reich, although it bore some features which were reminiscent of the widespread post-World War I reaction to the Treaty of Versailles. Morgenthau had wanted to prevent this at all cost. The Germans did not think that their actions in the East were considerably different from what other powers had done in the countries they had occupied.[4] This was coupled with a tendency to blame Germany's post-war problems, such as the loss of the Eastern territories and the economic hardships of the immediate post-war years, on an Allied conspiracy instead of viewing them as the consequences of military defeat.[5] In short, the Germans saw themselves as a victimized nation.

Such an interpretation of the recent past was bound to affect the war crimes program. As early as 1946 there were indications that even the average German was at least indifferent, if not opposed, to American education attempts in that area.[6] Here, the historian encounters the usual dilemma of trying to gauge public opinion. Surveys, including those conducted by U.S. occupation authorities, have inherent weaknesses.[7]

Fortunately, many groups with a strong interest in the war criminals problem have left posterity with sufficient records. The documents show that post-war German nationalism did not translate into an acceptance of responsibility for the crimes of the Third Reich by those who were in a position to influence public opinion considerably. The war crimes program was opposed by the Adenauer government, almost all political parties, the Catholic and Protestant churches, seemingly respectable experts on international law as well as such right wing organizations with mass appeal as veterans and refugee groups. Each individual subgroup, with few exceptions, widely publicized its objections to the proceedings. It is safe to say that this bombardment of negative publicity about the trials and the imprisonment of war criminals affected the average German at one point or another, which would explain why only ten percent ultimately backed the program.

In this chapter, I will deal with the non-governmental and non-parliamentary foes of the war crimes program. In the last two chapters, I shall discuss the attitude of the German government and the *Bundestag*. Although this distinction is somewhat artificial, because of the close relationship between church and state in Germany for example, it is nonetheless necessary owing to the great volume of material. I will begin with church reactions to war crimes trials since Germany's bishops, both Catholic and Protestant, were among the first to voice their criticism.

The German Catholic Church spent the first year and a half of the post-war period attempting to define its position on the Holocaust and the extent of the German people's guilt. By the end of 1946 the church hierarchy had decided to dismiss the notion of collective guilt. This allowed the bishops to cover up their own failure to act decisively on behalf of millions of the Nazi regime's innocent victims, although they had possessed accurate information about the annihilation of the Jews and the murder of others in the occupied territories. Instead, Germany's Catholic leadership chose to assume the offensive by criticizing the Allied, and particularly the American, war crimes trial program, which was an uncomfortable reminder of the past. On the Catholic side, two bishops were most active. One was Cologne's Cardinal Josef Frings, who, as the chairman of the Fulda Bishops Conference, served as the highest-ranking Catholic clergyman in Germany. The other was Munich

Auxiliary Bishop Johannes Neuhäusler, who had a keen interest in the war criminals issue since he oversaw the spiritual affairs at Landsberg, the American prison for war criminals.

Frings, in his New Year's Eve sermon on December 31, 1946, rather arrogantly took the Allies to task for what he saw as Allied attempts to hold the German people as a whole responsible for the crimes of the Nazi era. In addition, the Cologne cardinal was not at all enthusiastic about the Nuremberg Trial, which had come to an end only a few months earlier. Frings expressed his deep concern that the International Military Tribunal had relied on *ex post facto* law to convict the major Nazi war criminals. However, his reminder of the legal principle *nulla poena sine lege* was only a front. In reality, Frings strongly opposed the entire concept of bringing the perpetrators to justice. The cardinal announced that, when it came to determining guilt, God was the last and the only true instance. That line of reasoning led Frings to conclude that the Allies had followed a "pagan and naive" optimism for taking it upon themselves to make judgments on guilt or innocence.[8]

Neuhäusler's involvement was the result of the controversy surrounding the U.S. Army's Dachau war crimes program, particularly the Malmédy trial. The fact that American Senators like Langer and McCarthy, as well as major newspapers such as the *Chicago Tribune*, condemned the trial operation undoubtedly encouraged Neuhäusler to speak out on behalf of the war criminals. The Baldwin subcommittee, while investigating the allegations of improprieties which had occurred during the Malmédy trial, suspected that the interest of many German clergymen in the scandal consisted of more than mere Christian concern for the defendants' spiritual well-being. Instead, it found that the German clergy's attacks had already expanded to include the entire war crimes program and the administration of Landsberg.[9] Neuhäusler's activities more than justified this assessment. From 1948 to 1951, the auxiliary bishop intensively lobbied American authorities on behalf of convicted German war criminals. He continued to demand further examinations of the Malmédy trial, which had already been the subject of a half dozen investigations, and the Dachau program as a whole. Neuhäusler's other efforts focused on preventing the United States from executing condemned war criminals.

In March 1948, Neuhäusler wrote to five members of Congress to express his misgivings about the Army's handling of the Malmédy trial. Emphasizing his own imprisonment in a Nazi concentration camp, Neuhäusler reiterated the defendants' charges of torture, mistreatment and calculated injustice, which the American investigators had allegedly committed. Thus, he urged the legislators to press for further investigations into the matter and to suspend the execution of the forty-three death sentences.[10]

Neuhäusler tried a different approach with the Office of U.S. Military Government (OMGUS) in Germany. To widen his attack against the war crimes program, the auxiliary bishop also accused American prosecutors of having relied on "professional witnesses." To prove this point, he submitted a list of fourteen witnesses who had testified at the Flossenburg trial. Neuhäusler emphasized certain alleged character traits of these witnesses so as to strike a chord with OMGUS personnel. Consequently, he described them as homosexuals, child abusers, pimps, Communists and career criminals.[11]

By the summer of 1948, Neuhäusler was no longer content with a mere reexamination of Army war crimes trials. Now, the bishop also called for the establishment of a clemency board for the 150 condemned prisoners under General Clay's jurisdiction. Neuhäusler viewed the function of such a board as an appellate court; had this procedure been adopted, it would have violated war crimes procedure. The bishop wanted the clemency commission to focus on procedural irregularities, perjury by German witnesses and American authorities, and the trial documents. Apparently, he desired a review of the verdicts, not merely a modification of the sentences. On this last point, on August 26, 1948, the Fulda Bishops Conference officially backed Neuhäusler by demanding the establishment of a regular appellate court for convicted war criminals and protesting the Nuremberg and Dachau programs. Consequently, the fight against American war crimes trials was now the official policy of the German Catholic Church.[12]

The pressure by Neuhäusler and some of his Protestant counterparts paid off. On October 25, 1948, Clay barred the executions of those Landsberg prisoners who had been sentenced to death during the Malmédy trial. Clay's order resulted from what the *New York Times* called a "barrage" of protests from Catholic and Protestant clergymen.[13] Soon it became apparent that the German Catholic bishops acted with the support of the papacy. In December, the Rev. Edmund J. Walsh, S.J., the Apostolic Delegate in Washington, handed Army Secretary Royall a papal memorandum emphasizing "the desire of the Holy See to present to the Allied authorities a plea of mercy in behalf of the German nationals condemned to death."[14] The Pope's message convinced Clay that it was time to remind the Catholic Church of the crimes for which the Landsberg prisoners had been convicted. Thus, the U.S. military governor asked the Department of War to inform Walsh that Army courts had applied the death penalty only in cases of cold-blooded murder. Clay tried to soften his statement by implying that the Church was the victim of misinformation supplied by German clergymen like Neuhäusler. For the general, most of the charges against the Army's Dachau program were clearly unfounded and a consequence of carefully planned propaganda on the part of Germany's Catholic leadership.[15]

Despite Clay's assurances that the Army's trial program had been fair to the defendants, many of whom were guilty of horrendous crimes, Cardinal Frings continued to criticize the war crimes trials in his sermons. On December 31, 1948, Frings reminded German Catholics of the "plight" of several hundred Germans who had been sentenced for war crimes in the zones of occupation and individual European countries. The cardinal particularly condemned the Allied decision not to allow reviews of the verdicts and to release prisoners only on the basis of clemency.[16] Such a practice was not only slower, but also stifled the debates concerning the validity of the judgments and verdicts, in which Frings had a strong interest.

Frings shared Neuhäusler's concern about the possibility that the Americans might soon resume executions of those war criminals condemned during the Dachau program. The cardinal decided to deal with the matter in a less public and less aggressive manner than the Munich bishop. Frings also preferred to work with High Commissioner McCloy whose attitude was at first friendlier than that of EUCOM commanders like Clay and Handy. In November 1949, Frings reminded the U.S. high commissioner of the prisoners' long stay in solitary confinement, which led him to believe that they had already repented. Furthermore, he urged McCloy to prevent the execution of those who had acted on orders from a higher authority and without criminal intent. The German public would consider the liquidation of such individuals as particularly harsh, Frings argued, especially since "common criminals" were already benefiting from the Federal Republic's prohibition of capital punishment.[17]

McCloy, well aware that additional executions could damage the Allied image in Germany, went to see the cardinal in December. The high commissioner pointed out that his jurisdiction was limited to the more prominent defendants sentenced by the subsequent Nuremberg tribunals. The cases cited by Frings and Neuhäusler were all part of the Army war crimes program and thus under the jurisdiction of the EUCOM commander, Gen. Handy.[18] But McCloy did have some good news. He informed the cardinal of his plans to bring prominent American jurists to Germany in 1950 for an advisory clemency commission to review all sentences and to work out a practical solution to the war criminals problem. The last part, McCloy cautioned, was particularly difficult. McCloy personally appeared willing to concede to some of the German demands, but emphasized that HICOG had to consider public opinion in the United States. The American public, he told Frings, would have to be taken into account regarding decisions for large-scale sentence commutations and clemency actions by U.S. authorities in Germany.[19]

Frings made sure to inform the Adenauer government about McCloy's statements. In January 1950, Alfons Wahl, a high-ranking member of the Federal Justice Ministry, met with Frings and the chancellor of the Archbishopric of Cologne, Dr. Heribert Knott, to discuss the imprisoned war criminals. The three agreed to coordinate the efforts of the cardinal with those of the German government. Frings thereafter continued to intervene in extremely urgent cases with foreign governments and the three Western high commissioners on behalf of Germans facing execution. In turn, Adenauer sought improvements for the other imprisoned war criminals on a long-term basis with the Allied High Commission and the Allied governments.[20]

The Vatican wholeheartedly supported Frings's efforts to prevent the U.S. High Commission and the Army's European Command from carrying out the remaining executions. Pope Pius XII decided to try to influence Gen. Handy, who appeared much less inclined to show leniency toward German war criminals than McCloy. The Pope pleaded for mercy on behalf of the condemned prisoners under Handy's jurisdiction. In contrast to Neuhäusler's more aggressive approach, the Vatican did not attack the integrity of the Dachau war crimes program. Instead, while pointing out its assumption that the war crimes trials had actually served justice, the Church claimed that it had a long-standing tradition of attempting to modify justice with mercy and to act for "even the worst of criminals."[21]

The Vatican's more moderate tone did not prevent Neuhäusler from proceeding along his established lines. In fact, it appears that the papacy's action further encouraged the Munich bishop. As a result, Neuhäusler presented American authorities with a series of new criticisms. He wished to see the input of the prisoners and their attorneys in the Army's sentence review process. More important, Neuhäusler accused the Americans of applying different standards to defendants of the Nuremberg trial program, now under HICOG jurisdiction, and those sentenced by the Army's Dachau courts. Prisoners in Army custody, Neuhäusler alleged, were at a disadvantage. The prosecution had failed to inform the accused of the charges against them until the main trial. That, in the bishop's opinion, was too late to prepare an efficient defense. In addition, the Army's trial transcripts were allegedly not as detailed as the Nuremberg ones. Thus, Neuhäusler complained, the Dachau defendants found it more difficult to submit effective clemency petitions.[22]

McCloy and Handy's January 1951 mass sentence commutations, which left only seven of twenty-eight Landsberg inmates on death row, brought out another dimension of Neuhäusler's interest in the issue. So far, the auxiliary bishop had fought for prisoners who had once held low- to mid-level Nazi party, police and military positions and whose trials before U.S. Army courts had been engulfed in controversy. Thus, one might view the bishop's engagement for the defendants under EUCOM jurisdiction as the result of his sincere belief that injustices had indeed taken place and needed to be addressed. This changed with McCloy and Handy's clemency actions. Neuhäusler began to lobby American officials on behalf of the last condemned, among them Pohl and four leaders of the mobile killing squads. The crimes of these prisoners had led to the murder of millions of victims. After emphasizing his own opposition to Nazism and his disgust with the crimes which these individuals had committed, the bishop nonetheless asked that their lives be spared.[23]

Not all German bishops opposed the war crimes program. Nonetheless, those who agreed with the Allies that war criminals deserved punishment did not publicize their views. Ironically, Neuhäusler's immediate superior, Munich's Cardinal Michael Faulhaber, appeared to support the Allied treatment of war criminals. In early January 1952, U.S. *land* commissioner for Bavaria, Oron J. Hale, paid a courtesy visit to the cardinal. In Faulhaber's opinion, a convicted war criminal was a sinner who had to pay for his sins. Faulhaber, dismissing compassion as a trait best left to "weeping women," insisted that the law had to be fulfillled. Hale was certainly glad to hear such reassuring words, especially since they came from the superior of one of the war crimes program's most persistent Church critics. The *land* commissioner interpreted Faulhaber's comments as support for the correctness of the trials and the justice of the sentences.[24] Why, then, did Faulhaber not attempt to curb Neuhäusler's activities? There are several possible answers. The auxiliary bishop did have Frings's protection and enjoyed the support of the Fulda Bishops Conference. Second, the aging Faulhaber most likely did not want to cause friction within the Catholic clergy by publicly agreeing with the war crimes program. After all, Frings also had the Vatican's backing. A third possibility is, as former *land* commissioner for Bavaria George N. Shuster implies, that the cardinal was no longer in full command of his mental faculties.[25] However, HICOG's records do not confirm this assessment of the state of Faulhaber's mind in early 1952.

Frings and Neuhäusler's intense public lobbying on behalf of convicted war criminals in the American zone of occupation decreased considerably after 1951. Frings in particular was now more concerned with the fate of perpetrators in France proper, some of whom still had not gone on trial for war crimes owing to the slowness of French criminal procedure. In addition, the Allied-German negotiations with respect to the European Defense Community and the contractuals appeared to bring about resolution of the issue. Nonetheless, the Cologne cardinal remained dissatisfied with the pace of events. When McCloy's successor Donnelly visited Frings in August 1952, the latter used the opportunity to press the U.S. high commissioner to relax his war criminals policy. Donnelly was irritated with that request. The high commissioner already had the impression that the Federal Republic was trying to trade the ratification of the Allied-German agreements for the release of all war criminals. Consequently, Frings's question came at the wrong time. Donnelly shot back that the ratification of the EDC treaty and the contractuals would solve the problem. The Germans, he told Frings, should work toward ensuring passage of the agreements in their parliament instead of pressing the Allies for further concessions with regard to war criminals.[26]

When it came to opposing Allied trials of war criminals, the two major religious hierarchies in Germany shared identical views. The issue, like few others, united Catholic and Protestant clergymen. For the Protestant Church, two bishops, Hans Meiser of Munich and Theophil Wurm of Stuttgart, led the protest against the American war crimes program. Meiser and Wurm, moreover, commanded the full support of the highest-ranking Protestant clergyman, Berlin's Otto Dibelius, who served as the president of the German Evangelical Church Council.

Initially, the Protestant Church appeared to respond much more favorably to Allied attempts to reform German society. During its Stuttgart conference in the fall of 1945, ten members of the German Protestant Church Council issued a declaration of guilt. The document conveyed the impression that the church supported the goals of the American occupation.[27] In reality, however, the statement was a preventive measure. The clergymen thought that U.S. officials might back down from their reeducation program now that the Protestant hierarchy had admitted guilt for not opposing the Nazi government more vigorously. Other parts of the Stuttgart declaration were intended to appeal to the average German. The Protestant Church left out references to the collective guilt of the German people for Nazi crimes by arguing that "guilt is something very personal."[28]

Like their Catholic counterparts, Meiser and Wurm at first focused much of their attack on the perceived inadequacies of the Army's Dachau trial program such as discrimination against the defense, the influencing of witnesses, the arbitrary choice of defendants and the reliance on *ex post facto* law. The bishops viewed the latter not only as a violation of international law but also the American Constitution, which, they charged, had incorporated the principle *nulla poena sine lege*. To rectify these alleged illegalities, the Evangelical Church urged the United States to allow the Dachau defendants to appeal their convictions. Thus, a Wurm telegram of June 1948 called for the creation of an appellate court for the Dachau program, accompanied by the demand that the military governor halt all executions of condemned war criminals "until the definite clearance through an appointed court of appeals."[29] Clay had no intention of abandoning the existing, elaborate EUCOM review procedure (consisting of the deputy judge advocate for war crimes, EUCOM Board of Review, theater judge advocate, military governor) and replacing it with an ordinary appeals court. In Clay's opinion, the present sentence review process was sufficient to guarantee fairness to all defendants under his jurisdiction.[30] Clay knew precisely that the interest within certain circles in Germany, among them the churches, in a court of appeals was to question the verdicts and the judgments, and thus the legality of war crimes trials as a whole.

Wurm's cable coincided with the sending of a letter to Clay, signed by Wurm himself and four other bishops, detailing the Evangelical Church's additional misgivings about the Nuremberg trials of more prominent war criminals such as the former officials of the German High Command and the ministries. All in all, the bishops criticized eleven aspects of the Nuremberg program. The Protestant clergymen noted that these proceedings, which had been intended to be international in character like the Trial of the Major War Criminals, were now a purely American affair since the other victor nations had withdrawn. They then charged that the trials were comparable to Hitler's treatment of the German officers involved in the July 20, 1944, attempt on the *Führer's* life. This absurd comparison was advanced on the grounds that both Hitler and the Americans had stripped their respective defendants of their military ranks and had civilians judge over them. Despite the insulting words, the Protestant bishops closed on a softer note emphasizing that "the love of our Lord Jesus Christ urges us to make every effort that the desperate, sceptical [sic] and nihilistic humanity regains confidence in public order."[31]

Clearly upset by the accusations, Clay rebutted the bishops' statement point by point. The military governor was deeply disappointed that even Germany's bishops, as the highest moral authorities, had learned little or nothing from the tragic evidence presented at the trials. The Allies had held war crimes proceedings to demonstrate "the evil which comes from an abuse of power" and to deter future aggressors. Clay argued he could not understand how the review of the evidence could lead the Evangelical Church to sympathize with the perpetrators of mass murder. Although some regrettable irregularities had taken place, Clay rightly put the bishops in their place for displaying no feelings for the victims of these war criminals and instead attacking the United States for its efforts to do justice.[32]

As one might expect, Clay's remarks did not have the desired effect. In 1949 the Evangelical Church officially pushed for the establishment of a court of appeals for the defendants before the twelve subsequent Nuremberg tribunals. It regarded the latter as military courts in name only since they had been staffed with civilian American judges, and urged the reexamination of the Nuremberg sentences before an appellate body.[33] Furthermore, Wurm did not back away from his charges and, in correspondence with the Assistant U.S. Chief Counsel at Nuremberg, Robert M.W. Kempner, and other American officials, continued to criticize the war crimes program. The bishop acted as a clearinghouse for the complaints of German war criminals' defense attorneys. Wurm's constant criticism as well as his demand for an appellate court for the Dachau operation provoked angry reaction within EUCOM's Judge Advocate Division. Theater Judge Advocate Harbaugh at first ignored the recurring allegations altogether, but then he decided to inform at least the EUCOM chief of staff about Wurm's activities.[34] After investigating the bishop's accusations, EUCOM's War Crimes Branch finally dismissed them as "a planned and concerted attack upon American occupation policies." The War Crimes Branch depicted Wurm as the driving force behind the Evangelical Church's negative position toward the U.S. war crimes operation and the occupation as a whole. The bishop substantiated this assessment himself when complaining that trying German war criminals actually absolved the Soviet Union of its own crimes. EUCOM viewed this particular point as "an interesting theory [which] involves political decisions at the highest level, and criticism of American policy in this respect is an attack on basic occupational policies."[35]

Wurm may have been the driving force behind the Protestant opposition to the U.S. war crimes program, but he was by no means the only bishop who, employing his position as a religious leader, forwarded the complaints of the defendants and their counsel to American authorities. During 1948, Bishop Meiser submitted eleven sets of documents from various sources, all highly critical of U.S. war crimes trials. The bishop believed their arguments and made his own charges of procedural improprieties and prisoner mistreatment in an interview with Judge Advocate General Thomas Green. This prompted an investigation by EUCOM's Board of Review No. 2. The board, consisting of three War Crimes Branch officers, gave Meiser the benefit of the doubt and assumed that he was the victim of misinformation. Errors had occurred during the trials, the officers admitted, but these had been rectified during the long series of reviews following each case. But the board also displayed the usual American insecurity whenever defending the operation against outside critics. It believed Meiser's charges of "unlawful, inhumane and sadistic" behavior on the part of American personnel of some internment camps where the Army had held suspected war criminals immediately after the surrender. Irrespective of whether these individuals would ever be charged, their prosecution would have no effect on the trials of German war criminals. Nonetheless, the board recommended filing charges of war crimes against Americans who had mistreated prisoners because they had brought "serious discredit to the Army and the United States."[36]

The record does not indicate whether Meiser ever received word of the board's investigation, particularly its accusation that American military personnel had severely mistreated war criminals at certain internment camps. The Board of Review report would undoubtedly have been of great value to the German anti-war crimes program propaganda. But the bishops did not really need such confidential information to criticize the operation. Fortunately for them, there were the Malmédy hearings in the United States in the spring and fall of 1949, which lent themselves to this purpose. The German Protestant bishops became downright theatrical during this phase of the Malmédy controversy. The *Christian Century* quoted Wurm as saying "never will the people of Schwäbisch Hall (the place of internment for the Malmédy defendants), who in the nights heard the cries of pain of the tortured beyond the prison walls, be made to believe that these investigators were servants of justice and not servants of revenge." The Evangelical Church's attitude toward the Nuremberg program was equally clear. Bishop Dibelius pointed out that "as Christians we refuse to recognize the Nuremberg verdicts as justice, but we have to accept them, as a defeated people, as acts of reprisal imposed by the victor."[37] These remarks clearly showed that U.S. efforts to use the trials to reeducate the Germans were in serious trouble. American officials, convinced that National Socialism had resulted from Germany's authoritarian and militaristic past, hoped that the war crimes program would underscore the need to democratize German society. In contrast, the Germans interpreted war crimes trials as attempts to prove their collective guilt. Wurm and Dibelius's attitudes confirmed that the Germans viewed themselves as victims of arbitrary and cruel occupation policies, and not as a people ready and willing to assume responsibility for the Holocaust and other Nazi atrocities.

The comments also explain why Germany's Protestant bishops, like their Catholic counterparts, showed little support for General Handy and Commissioner McCloy's January 1951 mass sentence reductions. After all, seven inmates remained on death row, thus giving Wurm new cause to lament about the war crimes program.[38] In addition, the sentence commutations were clemency decisions on the part of American authorities and not the result of the appellate court review for which the bishops had lobbied. The paper trail of communications between prominent Protestant bishops and the heads of EUCOM and HICOG largely ended in 1951, when a new political authority, in the form of the Adenauer government, assumed responsibility for the issue. But more importantly, both the Catholic and Protestant churches decided to work through a little-known private interest group and reduce their inflammatory public and private rhetoric. As members of the *Heidelberger Juristenkreis* the churches remained intimately connected with the war criminals problem, although outwardly this arrangement enabled them to hide the extent of their involvement. Sensing that publicly attacking the U.S. war crimes program would not lead to the desired results, the bishops opted for a new strategy.

The *Juristenkreis* had been founded in the summer of 1949 under the leadership of Christian Democratic lawmaker Eduard Wahl. Due to his expertise as a professor of international law at the University of Heidelberg, Wahl had served as a consultant for the defense in *U.S. v. Krauch*, the I.G. Farben case. The other members of the *Juristenkreis* were representatives from the Catholic and Evangelical churches in Germany, war crimes trial defense counsel, legislators and high-ranking jurists from the federal and *land* courts.[39] The group maintained close ties with Adenauer and his government, and it carried enough political weight to arrange for conferences with American occupation authorities. This allowed the *Juristenkreis* to work as a clearinghouse for information and to draw up policy proposals for the German government regarding possible solutions of the war criminals problem. As a result, this secretive organization credited itself with two major developments in the early 1950s: the Article 6 Allied-German mixed clemency commission in 1952 and the concept of interim mixed boards in 1953 after the French delay in ratifying the EDC and the contractuals prevented the implementation of the former.

By its own admission, the goal of the *Juristenkreis* was to revise the war crimes trial verdicts. The group denied having any interest in excusing the crimes of the Nazi era or those war criminals who had been convicted as a result of ''unobjectionable proceedings.'' Instead, the *Kreis* demanded justice for defendants it considered innocent and the reduction of sentences it deemed too high.[40] Evidently though, the *Juristenkreis* found very few trials unobjectionable. Wahl himself saw Control Council Law No. 10, the legal basis for Allied war crimes trials, as violating existing international law. In addition, Wahl did exactly what his organization had promised not to do—search for excuses for Nazi crimes. German troops had had to act in a particularly brutal manner in the East, Wahl believed, to retaliate for the brutality of Soviet partisans during World War II. Furthermore, the mental confusion (*Geistesverwirrung*) caused by the Hitler regime and the war was a mitigating circumstance in any case. Wahl predicted dire consequences for the Western Allies and their plans for a German defense contribution because of the war crimes trials. The prisoners had the sympathy of their former comrades since "nothing binds as much as a mutual war experience." This could spell trouble for German rearmament, unless the Allies and the Adenauer government quickly agreed on a solution.[41]

The *Juristenkreis* sold itself to the Americans as an organization which feared and wanted to help prevent a revival of extreme German nationalism because of the convicted war criminals at Landsberg. The *Kreis* claimed it operated behind closed doors so as to quietly suppress an issue which might inflame German nationalism. On February 10, 1951, Wahl gave a party for the members of the *Juristenkreis* and employees of EUCOM's War Crimes Branch. The German participants used the occasion to criticize the procedure of the Army's War Crimes Modification Board as too slow and unfair to the defendants whose cases were being considered. The *Kreis* proposed a number of improvements to "take away from the growing nationalistic movement a cheap argument for their increasing activity and to reduce the possibility for political success they had during the last weeks."[42] The good showing of the neo-Nazi *Sozialistische Reichspartei* (Socialist Reichs Party: SRP), which gained in excess of 350,000 votes during *Land* elections in Lower Saxony in May 1951, appeared to underscore the correctness of the last argument. Nevertheless, the success of the SRP, which the *Juristenkreis* blamed on the unresolved war criminals problem, did not prompt EUCOM to revise its clemency board's procedure. This caused the *Kreis* to threaten to publicize its demands, an indication that the organization's self-portrayal as a harmless assembly of experts who were only interested in "justice" was indeed insincere.[43]

During its September 17, 1951, meeting the *Kreis* discussed the possibility of exerting public pressure on the Allies by stirring up German nationalism and further anti-Allied sentiment. Some, like Wahl, strongly objected to the proposals to publicize the organization's efforts on behalf of German war criminals and the alleged slow Allied response thereto. Until then, McCloy had been the only high commissioner who had met with the group. The British and the French had refused. Nonetheless, Wahl was concerned that any publicity about the *Juristenkreis* and its current feud with Allied war crimes authorities would damage the negotiations between the Allies and the Adenauer government with respect to German rearmament and the establishment of contractual relations. Wahl viewed a revision of the Occupation Statute reducing Allied war crimes authority as the only way to improve the situation. Such a change could only be made at the highest diplomatic level. Thus, the *Kreis* should not undertake anything which might appear as attempts to blackmail the Allies into concessions since the latter were bound to react accordingly.[44]

Wahl's call for caution and moderation did not prevent individual members of the Heidelberg group from assuming the offensive. Rudolf Weeber, a high-ranking official in the Evangelical Church, and Freiherr von Hodenberg, a Lower Saxony appeals court justice, launched an angry attack against the Army. The two held Theater Judge Advocate Damon Gunn personally responsible for the failure to improve the operations of the War Crimes Modification Board as the *Kreis* had demanded earlier. Weeber and Hodenberg accused Gunn of willfully misinterpreting the intentions of the *Juristenkreis* to ensure speedy and fair sentence reviews for war criminals as symptoms of collective guilt. Consequently, it was Gunn's fault, they charged, that "the horror of past German atrocities is fading on account of a strong sense of wrong and unfairness in the procedure of some US courts."[45] Gunn's reassurances that the War Crimes Modification Board had only recently finished the review of all cases under Army jurisdiction, resulting in the release of more than 100 prisoners from Landsberg, helped cool tempers a bit.[46] Nonetheless, EUCOM's relations with the *Juristenkreis* were clearly strained.

In the fall of 1951 the attention of the *Kreis* also began to focus on other priorities, mainly the group's proposal to establish a mixed clemency commission. After selling the idea successfully to the *Bundestag's* Committee for the Occupation Statute and Foreign Affairs, the *Juristenkreis* discussed it with Adenauer in January 1952. The chancellor should use the German-Allied negotiations regarding the EDC and the contractuals to remove this "thorny issue for all concerned." Furthermore, the group assured Adenauer that its objectives were noble. The Allied trials of war criminals, the *Kreis* explained to the chancellor, had resulted in injustices, which had caused many Germans to lose their respect for the law. This erosion of the public belief in the law could make the past war crimes proceedings and the continued imprisonment of war criminals issues for right wing radical propaganda, and a threat to the stability of the Federal Republic.[47] Well aware of this danger, Adenauer made the idea of a mixed commission the official German position in the treaty negotiations.

In addition to Adenauer's adoption of its mixed board concept, the *Juristenkreis* scored a second important success over the issue of the treatment of war criminals in France. The *Kreis* coordinated the activities of the German Catholic and Evangelical churches with their French counterparts in an effort to influence that country's public opinion. The vast majority of Frenchmen favored harsh punishment for convicted perpetrators of war crimes. However, by July 1952 the *Juristenkreis* noticed a softening at least in the attitudes of French government officials toward German war criminals and their collaborators.[48] But while the situation in France was encouraging, the *Kreis* continued to have problems with U.S. Army authorities in the American zone.

On October 2, 1952, Col. Edgar H. Snodgrass replaced the hated Gunn as EUCOM theater judge advocate. The change in personnel encouraged the *Heidelberger Juristenkreis* to try its luck with the new head of the Judge Advocate Division by asking for an appointment with the commander in chief. Snodgrass promptly arranged a preliminary meeting between himself, Wahl and four other *Kreis* members. The group presented the Americans with a number of proposals ranging from an increase in good conduct time to special considerations for former soldiers who had been convicted of war crimes such as the Malmédy defendants.[49] Despite the long list of suggestions, Snodgrass recommended that the new EUCOM commander in chief, Lt. Gen. Manton S. Eddy, meet with the *Kreis* "in the interest of international relations and in the light of the current importance of the war criminals problem."[50]

The meeting took place a short time later. From the outset, Eddy indicated that he shared the uncompromising stance of his predecessors, Clay and Handy. The general told the *Juristenkreis* that he was unwilling to review each case under his jurisdiction for clemency again. General Handy had already done this. In addition, Handy had also taken care of the other points the group wished to see addressed. Eddy also flatly ruled out a mass clemency action on his part. The only encouraging news which the *Juristenkreis* heard was Eddy's plan to release four prisoners on medical parole and to grant Christmas amnesties to five percent of the Landsberg population (the U.S. High Commission and the Army released 123 prisoners shortly before Christmas 1952).[51] For obvious reasons, the *Juristenkreis* was dissatisfied with the meager results of the meeting.[52] However, Wahl and his organization also knew that Eddy's position was not likely to change. As a consequence, the *Juristenkreis* concluded that only the convening of the Article 6 mixed board would eventually solve the war criminals problem. Since delays in ratifying the EDC treaty and the contractuals had so far prevented this from happening, the *Kreis* began to focus on a new project, the formulation of proposals for an interim solution.[53] These efforts ultimately resulted in the French proposal for, and the establishment of, three interim zonal boards in the late summer of 1953.

A second group composed of lawyers and lawmakers strongly interested in eliminating the war criminals issue was the *Vorbereitender Ausschuß für die Herbeiführung einer Generalamnestie* (Preparatory Committee To Bring about a General Amnesty), usually referred to as the Essen Amnesty Committee. Unlike the *Heidelberger Juristenkreis*, which could boast of having a respectable membership, good connections and relatively moderate goals, the Essen Amnesty Committee included some rather shady individuals from what McCloy liked to call the "right wing lunatic fringe." Its leader was Essen lawyer and Free Democratic politician Ernst Achenbach. During the war, Achenbach had officially served as a political advisor to the German ambassador in Paris. In reality, Achenbach had also arranged the deportation of thousands of French Jews to extermination camps in the East.[54] Evidently, his wartime activities did not lead to an indictment before a war crimes court. Instead, Achenbach became counsel for the defense during several trials, including two subsequent Nuremberg tribunals, the I.G. Farben case and the Ministries case.[55] Aside from the background of its founder, additional factors explain why the Essen Amnesty Committee never achieved the same degree of trust with the Adenauer government and American occupation authorities as the *Heidelberger Juristenkreis*. As a foreign policy expert for the Free Democratic Party, Achenbach strongly opposed Adenauer's program of European integration and Franco-German reconciliation.[56] Furthermore, in 1953 even his own party doubted Achenbach's intentions. He stood accused of having encouraged former Nazis to join the party in order to undermine it and to take over its leadership.[57] Most imporantly, however, Achenbach and his group were attempting to whip up German nationalistic sentiment on the issue of war criminals. Obviously, neither Adenauer nor the Americans appreciated this tactic. It also contrasted starkly with the methods of the *Heidelberger Juristenkreis*, which preferred to operate behind the scenes.

The Essen Amnesty Committee's brain was Freiburg law professor Friedrich Grimm, a persistent proponent of a general amnesty for war criminals. Grimm claimed to have helped the government of the Weimar Republic negotiate a treaty with the Allies in 1924, releasing all those Germans who had been tried and imprisoned for war crimes after the First World War. Second, Grimm revealed that he was a member of an earlier Essen Amnesty Committee in 1929 and 1930 that had also included leading churchmen and politicians, three former Weimar chancellors and, most significantly, Konrad Adenauer himself. According to the law professor, this group successfully lobbied for a 1930 law granting a general amnesty to individuals who had been convicted of crimes committed during the uprisings of the early 1920s aimed at destroying the republic.[58] Last, Grimm claimed to have urged Hitler to pardon and release all of his political prisoners in September 1933 by issuing a general amnesty.[59] It was exactly this continuity from the Weimar to the Federal Republic that the Essen Amnesty Committee sought to exploit to establish its credibility. After all, Adenauer had belonged to the original Essen Amnesty Committee. It also urged Adenauer to press the Allies for a general amnesty for war criminals instead of being content with releases on a clemency basis since the chancellor had done this earlier for those who had tried to overthrow the government of the Weimar Republic. Grimm's self-proclaimed attempt to assist the first victims of the Nazis was most likely intended for Allied consumption to alleviate fears that the group consisted of right wing radicals.

Grimm's position on the war criminals question was relatively simple. For most of modern history, the professor stated, statesmen had applied the principle of a *tabula rasa* in the wake of wars. General amnesties were necessary to normalize the internal affairs of warworn countries during the reconstruction period. Only a pardon for all crimes connected with the military events could help achieve normalization and recovery. Any exceptions, such as punishing war criminals, violated the entire concept of a general amnesty. Grimm even came up with a catchy phrase to promote his views: "after total war, total amnesty (*Nach totalem Krieg, totale Amnestie*)."[60] He predicted hard times for the Federal Republic, should the Allies fail to enact a *tabula rasa*. Denazification and the war crimes trial program were bound to lead to a shortage of qualified personnel in administration, business and industry. This would destabilize the young German state and hamper its return to normalcy.[61]

In 1951 and 1952 Achenbach embarked on a public relations blitz to sell Grimm's views on the necessity of a general amnesty. The Essen lawyer insisted that the West could not expect a German defense contribution as long as imprisoned war criminals remained in Allied custody.[62] This position was identical to that initially held by Adenauer's rearmament negotiators, Generals Heusinger and Speidel. In February 1952 the Essen Committee organized a write-in campaign to pressure Adenauer into making the demand for a *tabula rasa* his official policy. According to Grimm, 150,000 responses had been received by September. Nonetheless, the Essen Committee failed to bring about a general amnesty for war criminals. In the end, its proposal was too radical to become a viable negotiating point in the Allied-German negotiations. Releases on the basis of clemency, the Allies and Adenauer were convinced, could best appease both Allied and German public opinion. In addition, the group's cause was not helped by choosing publicity over confidentiality, for Adenauer and the Allies insisted on a particularly careful treatment of the issue due to its controversial nature in Germany and abroad.

The call for a general amnesty, however, won widespread support from West Germany's numerous veterans and refugee groups. In May 1952 the *Auswärtiges Amt* counted no less than nine of these organizations as supporting a *tabula rasa* for war criminals. That year lobbyists for the veterans and refugees bombarded the foreign office with requests urging the chancellor to take a tougher stance on the issue during his talks with the Western Allies on the European Defense Community treaty and the Allied-German contractual agreements. These, the ultraconservative and right wing lobby felt, should be put to better use than mere sentence reviews with a view toward clemency. In the opinion of these organizations, the planned rearmament and political rehabilitation of the Federal Republic presented Adenauer with an excellent opportunity to play hardball and demand a general amnesty.[63] The veterans and refugee groups clearly equated the Landsberg, Werl and

Wittlich war criminals with regular POWs, a good indication that the lessons of the war crimes program had not been internalized. Officially, Adenauer assured the veterans that his government shared this view,[64] which contradicted Adenauer's earlier statements that the truly guilty must be punished. However, the chancellor most likely agreed with the POW theory in order to pacify his critics.

The former military men considered the release of the war criminals a prerequisite to a German contribution to the EDC.[65] The veterans condemned the Allied war crimes trials, and particularly those involving *Wehrmacht* officers, as a direct attack on the honor of the German soldier. One critic, Infantry General Schack, called this alleged defamation of Germany's military the *"Kulturschande"* (cultural disgrace) of the twentieth century. Thus, Schack wrote the foreign office, the Germans could not become the true partners of the Western Allies unless "this tragedy" came to an immediate end.[66]

The *Verband der Heimkehrer, Kriegsgefangenen und Vermißtenangehörigen* (Organization of Repatriated POWs, POWs and Relatives of Soldiers Missing in Action) blamed the continued imprisonment of the war criminals on Adenauer and his government. As a consequence, its leadership decided to pressure the chancellor to act. In April 1952, the organization used its publication *Der Heimkehrer* for a write-in campaign addressed to Adenauer with the title "Appeal in the Last Hour." The appeal demanded a general amnesty for all German "POWs," but was clearly aimed at the release of the war criminals only.[67] Adenauer did his best to ignore the demand, a reaction that angered the veterans group, which decried his inaction despite having received "hundreds of thousands" of petitions (Adenauer actually only received 40,000 postcards). As a result, it threatened to "enlighten" the public unless the government became more responsive to the idea of a *tabula rasa*.[68] The threat apparently worked. Only a few weeks later, Adenauer's security advisor, Theodor Blank, publicly proclaimed that no German should be asked to wear a uniform before the war criminals problem was satisfactorily resolved. For the Adenauer government, the Article 6 mixed clemency commission was such a solution. However, Blank wisely did not mention this and led the veterans to believe that the chancellor would now work for a general amnesty.

Most respectable German papers did not endorse the call for a general amnesty. However, much of the press was also clearly unhappy with the decision to review individual cases before the Article 6 mixed board. The majority of editorials displayed a cynical attitude toward this particular solution of the war criminals problem. The *Deutsche Zeitung und Wirtschaftszeitung* charged that the mixed commission did not represent a substantive change from current Allied clemency practices. The newspaper feared that the Adenauer government might be in violation of the West German constitution by assuming an Allied privilege, the granting of pardons. As a consequence, the war crimes program, which so far had caused many disagreements between the Allies and the Germans, might now drive a wedge between the German people and its administration.[69]

Conservative papers such as the *Bonner Rundschau* and the *Frankfurter Allgemeine* took an even more negative position. The *Bonner Rundschau* blamed many convictions on Allied political considerations, errors of justice and wrong investigative methods. Thus, the paper's editors thought it impossible to determine which of the prisoners were "true" war criminals.[70] The *Frankfurter Allgemeine* initially made similar allegations.[71] But in an editorial on July 2, 1952, the newspaper went even further. It argued that Hitler had largely destroyed the *Rechtsgefühl* (sense of justice) of the German people. The Allied war crimes trials had done away with what *Rechtsgefühl* was left after the surrender. The *Frankfurter Allgemeine* considered the idea of a mixed clemency commission as nothing more than a political measure to win the support of German soldiers for the EDC, not a restoration of justice.[72]

However, another conservative publication, *Die Welt*, favored the Allied-German agreement on the Article 6 board. The clemency commission, the editors contended, would provide a more favorable atmosphere for reviewing the remaining cases. In addition, the paper sensed a strong Allied desire to end the imprisonment of German war criminals, and predicted that the war crimes program would end quickly. This would also be in the interest of the Allies.[73]

While most papers focused on the political and legal arguments for and against the Article 6 mixed board, the *Abendpost* attempted to stir up German nationalistic sentiments. In November 1952 the Frankfurt newspaper suggested that its readers offer themselves as hostages to the Allies so that the imprisoned war criminals could spend Christmas at home. The West German government quickly distanced itself from the paper's action. However, the *Abendpost* claimed that the federal government had endorsed the idea.[74] The Allied High Commission reacted sharply to the hostage proposal. British High Commissioner Kirkpatrick, emphasizing that many prisoners had committed enormous crimes, wrote the *Abendpost* editors that the release of a large number of war criminals would hurt the Federal Republic's image in the world. Kirkpatrick was also convinced that already released prisoners with their allegations of Allied wrongdoing and injustice were now contributing to an increase of tensions between Germany and the Allies instead of a decrease, as had been hoped.[75]

The German response to the punishment of war criminals strongly points to a continuity in German nationalism. The surrender in 1945 evidently did not lead to a clean break and a completely new national identity, even though post-war German nationalism did not contain the militaristic and authoritarian features of its predecessor. Commentators inside and outside Germany continued to worry about a revival of right wing political extremism, although this threat never did become reality. Yet, the way the Germans felt about themselves and their country's history during the decade following their military defeat does not give cause for jubilation. For one, the Germans did not view their recent past as substantially different from what other nations had experienced and done. Wahl made this point very clear when blaming the brutalities of the war in the East on the actions of Soviet partisans. Second, encouraged by influential private lobbies, most Germans did not feel responsible for Nazi crimes and deemed it wiser not to accept any responsibility, as the reaction to the war crimes proceedings made abundantly clear. The historian Hajo Holborn, who was sent on a study mission to Germany by the U.S. State Department in the fall of 1947, reported that some Germans he encountered—according to Holborn, predominantly simple and non-intellectual people—were ashamed of their country's wartime deeds. Almost everyone, however, rejected the concept of collective guilt.[76] Since the writing of Holborn's report, several scholars have shown that the Germans should have felt more than shame during the first decade after the war. Lawrence D. Stokes charges that the German people knew enough about the Holocaust to be intimidated themselves. Yet, the Germans, Stokes writes, "were sufficiently undisturbed in their own security to remain overwhelmingly passive spectators to the most terrible outrage of their era."[77] Raoul Hilberg demonstrates that the annihilation of the European Jews required a vast administrative machinery. This machinery, Hilberg emphasizes, "was structurally no different from organized German society as a whole."[78] These scholars thus refute the often-heard claims of the immediate post-war years that the Holocaust were merely the work of a few, fanatical Nazis and remained largely hidden from the German people.

The war crimes program offered the Germans an opportunity to impress upon the Allies and world opinion the important lessons they had learned about their history from the trials. These proceedings revealed that Germany's militaristic and authoritarian tradition had created serious problems for German society, which needed to be addressed. Along with the Nazi organizations, the U.S. war crimes trials implicated several groups which had thus far been held in high esteem: the military officer corps, business and the civil service. However, most influential German circles, resenting American attempts to reeducate and restructure their society, chose to criticize the punishment of war criminals. The opponents of the operation made rather strange bedfellows, ranging from the Social Democrats to right wing fringe groups. Even Germany's bishops, as the country's highest moral authorities, strongly criticized the trials of war criminals. No other occupation program, except denazification, encountered such a united front in opposition. The Germans did not view the former as an education as to what abuses of power could accomplish, but instead interpreted it as the imposition of the victors' will on the vanquished. This was an important and disturbing aspect of the new German nationalism, one wherein Germans saw themselves as victims and not as perpetrators.

NOTES

1. "Current West German Views on the War Criminals Issue," HICOG, Office of Public Affairs, Research Analysis Staff, September 8, 1952, RG 338, USAREUR, Box 469, News Clippings File.

2. "Nationalism in Western Germany," HICOG, March 3, 1950, RG 466, Papers of John J. McCloy, Classified General Records 1949-1952, Box 10, D (50) 605.

3. See, Tauber, *Beyond Eagle and Swastika*, 985. For a more optimistic opinion, see Louis L. Snyder, *Roots of German Nationalism* (Bloomington: Indiana University Press, 1978), 290.

4. Erich J.C. Hahn, "Hajo Holborns Bericht zur deutschen Frage vom Herbst 1947," *Vierteljahrshefte für Zeitgeschichte* 35 (1987), 135-166.

5. Tauber, *Beyond Eagle and Swastika*, 984.

6. Brewster S. Chamberlin, "Todesmühlen. Ein Versuch zur Umerziehung," *Vierteljahrshefte für Zeitgeschichte* 29 (1981), 420-436.

7. Sarah Gordon, *Hitler, Germans and the "Jewish Question"* (Princeton: Princeton University Press, 1984), 197-206.

8. Cardinal Josef Frings' position is extensively quoted in Friedrich Wilhelm Rothenpieler, *Der Gedanke einer Kollektivschuld in juristischer Sicht* (Berlin: Duncker, 1982), 208-209.

9. *Report on Malmédy Massacre Investigation*, October 13, 1949, 81st Congress, 1st Session, 31-32.

10. Munich Auxiliary Bishop Johannes Neuhäusler to Congressmen Francis Case, John M. Vorys, Charles W. Vursell, Overton Brooks and E.E. Cox, March 25, 1948, RG 338, USAREUR, Box 464, Bishop Neuhäusler File.

11. Neuhäusler to OMGUS, August 27, 1948, ibid.

12. Neuhäusler to OMGUS, August 23, 1948; and Neuhäusler to Robert Murphy, Political Advisor, OMGUS, July 22, 1948, ibid.

13. "Clay Halts Execution of 45 Germans after Getting Appeal of Church Leaders," *New York Times*, October 26, 1948, 2.

14. Draper to Clay, December 16, 1948, RG 338, USAREUR, Box 490, General Clemency File.

15. Clay to Draper, December 21, 1948, in Smith, ed., *The Papers of General Lucius DuBignon Clay*, II, 962.

16. Wolfgang Löhr, ed., *Dokumente deutscher Bischöfe: Hirtenbriefe und Ansprachen zu Gesellschaft und Politik 1945-1949*, 2 vols. (Würzburg: Echter, 1985), I, 266-271.

17. Frings to McCloy, November 17, 1949, RG 466, Papers of John J. McCloy, Classified General Records 1949-1952, Box 5, 440d.

18. Draft letter: McCloy to Frings, December 9, 1949, ibid., D (49) 440b.

19. Internal memorandum, Federal Justice Ministry, January 30, 1950, *Bundeszwischenarchiv*, File B141-9576, 1.

20. Ibid.

21. Rev. A.J. Muench, Regent, Apostolic Nuntiature in Germany, to Handy, February 27, 1950, RG 338, USAREUR, Box 521, General Clemency File.

22. Neuhäusler to Gunn, September 9, 1950, ibid., Bishop Neuhäusler File.

23. Neuhäusler to McCloy, January 20, 1951, RG 466, Papers of John J. McCloy, Classified General Records 1949-1952, Box 24, D (51) 119.

24. U.S. *Land* Commissioner for Bavaria Oron J. Hale to McCloy, January 4, 1952, ibid., Box 35, D (52) 193.

25. Shuster, *The Ground I Walked On*, 208.

26. Donnelly to Acheson, August 11, 1952, RG 466, U.S. High Commission for Germany, Security-Segregated General Records 1949-1952, Box 28, 321.6, German War Criminals File.

27. John S. Conway agrees with this positive assessment of the Stuttgart declaration; see, John S. Conway, "How Shall the Nations Repent? The Stuttgard Declaration of Guilt, October 1945," *The Journal of Ecclesiastical History* 38 (1988), 596-622. Conway lauds the Stuttgart Declaration first and foremost for "its affirmation of individual responsibility" but admits that later criticisms of the document's failure to address the Holocaust and other Nazi atrocities were justified. Ibid., 620.

28. Verena Botzenhart-Viehe, "The German Reaction to the American Occupation, 1944-1947" (Diss., University of California-Santa Barbara, 1980), 158-159.

29. Protestant Bishop Theophil Wurm to Clay, June 1, 1948, RG 338, USAREUR, Box 462, Supreme Court File.

30. Clay to Wurm, June 2, 1948, ibid.

31. Protestant Bishops Wurm, Meiser, Wüstemann and Niemöller to Clay, May 20, 1948, ibid., Bishop Wurm File.

32. Clay to Wurm, June 18, 1948, ibid.

33. Memorandum by the Evangelical Church in Germany on the Question of War Crimes Trials before American Military Courts, 1949, RG 84, Foreign Service Posts of the Department of State, U.S. High Commission for Germany, Box 12, 321.6, German War Criminals 1949-1952 File, 18-23.

34. Harbaugh to Fleischer, September 25, 1948, RG 338, USAREUR, Box 462, Bishop Wurm File.

35. Internal Memorandum by Major James Haefele, War Crimes Branch, EUCOM, September 16, 1948, ibid.

36. Report of War Crimes Board of Review No. 2, January 5, 1949, ibid., Box 467, Bishop Meiser File.

37. "German Bishops on War Crimes Trials," *The Christian Century*, 1949, vol. 66, 725-726.

38. Wurm to McCloy, February 10, 1951, RG 466, Papers of John J. McCloy, Classified General Records 1949-1952, Box 24, D (51) 126.

39. Internal Route Slip by Theater Judge Advocate Edgar H. Snodgrass, October 22, 1952, RG 338, USAREUR, Box 523, Administrative File.

40. *Heidelberger Juristenkreis* to the subcommittee "Prisoners of War" of the *Bundestag* Committee for the Occupation Statute and Foreign Affairs, October 23, 1951, *Auswärtiges Amt*, File 515-00 h II, Document unnumbered/51.

41. *Heidelberger Juristenkreis* position paper *Einige Gedanken über die juristische, menschliche und politische Seite des Kriegsverbrecherproblems*, undated, ibid., Document 3299/53.

42. *Heidelberger Juristenkreis* member Freiherr von Hodenberg to Gunn, April 7, 1951, RG 338, USAREUR, Box 534, Organization 1951 File.

43. Hodenberg to Gunn, May 31, 1951, ibid.

44. Protocol of a meeting of the *Heidelberger Juristenkreis*, September 17, 1951, *Auswärtiges Amt*, File 515-00 h II, Document unnumbered/51.

45. Hodenberg to Gunn, September 24, 1951; and *Heidelberger Juristenkreis* member Rudolf Weeber to Gunn, September 28, 1951, RG 338, USAREUR, Box 518, War Crimes Modification Board 1951 File.

46. Gunn to Weeber, September 28, 1951, ibid.

47. War crimes defense lawyer Otto Kranzbühler to Hallstein, January 26, 1952, *Auswärtiges Amt*, File 515-00 h II, Document 1350/51.

48. Protocols of meetings of the *Heidelberger Juristenkreis*, February 26, 1952; and July 26, 1952, *Auswärtiges Amt*, File 515-11 II, Document 2508/52; and File 515-11/01, Document unnumbered/52.

49. Protocol of a meeting between the *Heidelberger Juristenkreis* and officials of EUCOM's Judge Advocate Division, October 18, 1952, RG 338, USAREUR, Box 523, Miscellaneous Administration File.

50. Internal Route Slip by Snodgrass, October 22, 1952, ibid.

51. Eddy to Wahl, December 11, 1952, *Auswärtiges Amt*, File 515-11 II, Document unnumbered/52.

52. War crimes lawyer Julius Fehsenbecker to the *Heidelberger Juristenkreis*, December 22, 1952, ibid.

53. Fehsenbecker to Bitter, November 11, 1952, ibid., Document 3299/53.

54. Friedrich, *Die kalte Amnestie*, 308.

55. Dr. Ernst Achenbach defended Fritz Gajewski in U.S. v. Krauch, *Trials of War Criminals*, VII-VIII; and Ernst Wilhelm Bohle in U.S. v. Weizsäcker, ibid., XII-XIV.

56. Baring, *Außenpolitik in Adenauers Kanzlerdemokratie*, 178.

57. Jörg Michael Gutscher, *Die Entwicklung der FDP von ihren Anfängen bis 1961* (Königstein: Hain, 1984), 157.

58. Professor Grimm is referring to a change in the *Reichsgesetz über Straffreiheit* of July 14, 1928. The law did not grant amnesty to those who had committed "crimes against life." The October 1930 amendment, of which Grimm appears to take a great deal of pride, even gave murderers immunity from prosecution as long as their crimes had been politically motivated, had occurred before September 1, 1924, and the victims had not been members of the Weimar government. See, *Gesetz über Straffreiheit*, July 16, 1928, *Reichsgesetzblatt, Teil I*, 195-196; and *Gesetz zur Ämderimg des Gesetzes über Straffreiheit vom 14. Juli 1928*, October 24, 1930, ibid., 467.

59. Grimm speech in Freiburg *Generalamnestie: Der einzige Weg zum Frieden*, September 17, 1952, *Arbeitsgemeinschaft Freiburg i. Br., zur Herbeiführung einer Generalamnestie*, 10-11; courtesy of Dr. Ernst Achenbach.

60. Ibid., 14-15. Grimm promoted these views on several occasions, e.g. in speeches on May 17, 1950 in Bad Boll and January 1, 1950, in Freiburg as well as in a *Denkschrift* published on September 3, 1949; courtesy of Dr. Achenbach.

61. *Denkschrift über die Notwendigkeit einer Generalamnestie*, September 3, 1949, 8.

62. Achenbach, "Generalamnestie!," *Zeitschrift für Geopolitik*, June 1952, 321-324.

63. Wilhelm Freiherr von Lersner, *Verband der Heimkehrer, Kriegsgefangenen und Vermißtenangehörigen*, to Adenauer, May 8, 1952, *Auswärtiges Amt*, File 515-11 II, Document 8105/52. Also, see "Ramcke drängt auf Amnestie," *Die Welt*, March 10, 1952.

64. Adenauer to August Fischer, chairman, *Verband der Heimkehrer*, May 23, 1952, *Auswärtiges Amt*, File 515-11 II, Document 6396/52.

65. Admiral Gottfried Hansen, *Verband Deutscher Soldaten*, to Adenauer and Hallstein, June 30, 1952, ibid., Document 8644/52.

66. Gen. Schack to the *Auswärtiges Amt*, June 30, 1952, ibid., Document 8729/52.

67. *Der Heimkehrer, Extrablatt*, April 1952.

68. *Verband der Heimkehrer* to Adenauer, May 27, 1952, *Auswärtiges Amt*, File 515-11 II, Document 8017/52.

69. "Die Mauern von Werl," *Die Deutsche Zeitung und Wirtschaftszeitung*, April 16, 1952.

70. "Peinliche Frage," *Bonner Rundschau*, June 19, 1952.

71. "Man kann sie nicht totschweigen," *Frankfurter Allgemeine*, June 21, 1952.

72. "Nicht das Ideal," *Frankfurter Allgemeine*, July 2, 1952.

73. "Keine Amnestie," *Die Welt*, September 18, 1952.

74. "Bundesregierung: Entschluß der Bürgen entspringt besonders hochherzigen Motiven," *Abendpost*, December 10, 1952.

75. Kirkpatrick to Emil Frotscher, editor, *Abendpost*, November 28, 1952, *Auswärtiges Amt*, File 515-11 II, unnumbered/52.

76. Hahn, "Hajo Holborn: Bericht zur deutschen Frage," *Vierteljahrshefte für Zeitgeschichte* 35 (1987), 150.

77. Lawrence D. Stokes, "The German People and the Destruction of the European Jews," *Central European History* 6 (1973), 167-191.

78. Raoul Hilberg, *The Destruction of the European Jews*, 3 vols. (New York: Holmes and Meier, 1985), III, 994.

6

Early Parliamentary Challenges to Allied War Crimes Authority, 1949-1950

The debate over the problem of convicted German war criminals changed dramatically in the fall of 1949 with the creation of the Federal Republic of Germany. This action added two significant participants, the *Bundesregierung* (the German federal government) and the *Bundestag* (the German legislature) to the dispute. Both immediately seized on the issue, attempting to use it to reduce Allied authority in Germany. The resolutions introduced in the *Bundestag* and the legislature's discourses on the subject also pointed to a second, much more disturbing aspect. Very few of the new German lawmakers actually believed that those Germans whom the Allies had imprisoned for the commission of war crimes were guilty of any crimes. Thus, the parliament perceived the continuation of the war crimes program as a threat to one of its favorite projects—burying the past without admitting guilt or assuming responsibility for it. The intensity of the *Bundestag*'s criticism of the Allies suggests that the legislature also intended to fire up a largely apathetic public. While the German people clearly did not support the trials of war criminals, they appeared to be more concerned with economic survival than with the fate of a few hundred German prisoners in Allied detention.

The evidence suggests that those Germans having a particular interest in Allied war crimes policy were members of the Federal Republic's elites. The U.S. High Commission found that the strongest opposition to the trials and imprisonment of war criminals came from individuals who were well educated and who belonged to the upper income brackets.[1] This assessment was on target. Recent studies indicate that the West German elites provided the most resistance to Allied occupation policies and reform efforts. Wolfgang Benz describes this phenomenon in his survey on Allied initiatives to reform the civil service.[2] Verena Botzenhart-Viehe also documents the role of German elites in instigating the opposition to American reeducation efforts.[3]

Clearly, the opponents to the American war crimes program—the bishops, law professors and other experts on international law, former officers of the armed forces, the press and the leadership of the veterans and refugee groups, discussed in the previous chapter—fell within this category. In 1949 these groups could turn to the *Bundestag* to express their dissatisfaction with this particular occupation policy and to rally public opinion against it.

This chapter will deal with the first phase of this process, when the *Bundestag* and the West German federal government emerged as strong voices in matters relating to war criminals. The parliament, however, was powerless in this area due to exclusive Allied jurisdiction, and, consequently, sought to change this arrangement. Because of its powerlessness, the importance of the *Bundestag*'s initial two years related to mostly anti-Allied rhetoric. That rhetoric showed that one of the parliament's priorities was to force the release of all German war criminals from Allied custody regardless of the nature of their offenses.

On August 14, 1949, the voters in the three Western zones of occupation elected the first central law-making body since the end of the Weimar era. The election campaign for the distribution of seats in the *Bundestag* provided Allied authorities with valuable insight into the problems that still lay ahead. The struggle for the German vote featured strong attacks against the Western Allies, a popular theme among all parties on the ballot. Nonetheless, Allied officials, particularly members of the U.S. High Commission for Germany, were extremely satisfied with the victory of the moderate and conservative parties, even though these had not abstained from criticizing the occupation policies. Konrad Adenauer's *Christlich Demokratische Union* (Christian Democratic Union: CDU) and its Bavarian sister party, the *Christlich Soziale Union* (Christian Social Union: CSU), received 139 seats and thus emerged as the strongest single faction. The good showing of the *Freie Demokratische Partei* (Free Democratic Party: FDP) with 52 and the *Deutsche Partei* (German Party: DP) with 17 future legislators bolstered the strength of the conservatives. The left-of-center *Sozialdemokratische Partei Deutschlands* (Social Democratic Party of Germany: SPD), which had not exactly endeared itself to U.S. officials during the occupation,[4] obtained 131 seats in the *Bundestag*. From HICOG's standpoint, the crushing defeat of the *Kommunistische Partei Deutschlands* (Communist Party of Germany: KPD) and the extreme right, each scoring less than 6 percent of the total vote, was the second most important outcome aside from Adenauer's victory.[5] As a result of the favorable election outcome, U.S. High Commissioner McCloy predicted that Washington would provide strong political and economic support to the new German government.[6]

Major American newspapers also welcomed the outcome of the West German election. The *New York Times* was relieved that the voters in the French, American and British zones had repudiated political extremism. The paper's editors, in a forgiving mood, declared the door open for full German integration in the West, despite the fact that many of Adenauer's supporters had joined in the "hue and cry" against the Western occupation. But Adenauer had at least conveyed his willingness to do business with the Allies, whereas the *New York Times* held strong suspicions about the willingness of the Social Democrats, the second strongest faction in the *Bundestag*, to cooperate with the Allied High Commission to shape a purely pro-Western Germany.[7]

The picture, however, was not quite as rosy as HICOG officials painted it in the late summer of 1949. The German electorate had endorsed Adenauer and thus political moderation, but, at the same time, had failed to give his CDU/CSU the absolute majority in the *Bundestag*. Consequently, Adenauer had to shop for coalition partners in order to become federal chancellor. He chose to build a government consisting of his own party, the DP and the FDP. Convinced he had a comfortable majority with 208 seats in the 402 member legislature, Adenauer confidently entered the *Bundestag's* election for chancellor on September 15, 1949. Adenauer won the chancellorship by merely one vote, receiving the support of 202 delegates.[8] Since the September 15 vote showed the chancellor's vulnerability, Allied observers quickly reassessed their initial optimism and admitted that the new German government was "off to a shaky start."[9]

At least one branch of the United States government also had misgivings about Adenauer's alliance with the conservative block. The outcome of the *Bundestag* vote appeared to support the substance of a report on the first West German election, which the Central Intelligence Agency (CIA) had prepared for President Truman in July 1949. The CIA interpreted Adenauer's alliance with the FDP and the DP as less than ideal for U.S. policy in Europe, stressing that U.S. interests would be best served by a CDU/CSU coalition with the Social Democrats. According to the report, a government consisting of the Christian Democrats and the Socialists having a 60 percent majority in the parliament would thus be able to fulfill its legislative program. Furthermore, the SPD would serve as a counterweight to the right wing of the CDU/CSU and ensure working class and organized labor support for the new Germany. This, the CIA felt, would help to prevent any West German designs to make a "deal" with the Soviets or a possible Communist East German state. The CIA was apprehensive about a coalition that did not include the SPD. Adenauer would have to align his party with the Free Democrats, the Center Party and possibly a rightist party, such as the DP, which actually did become one of the CDU/CSU's coalition partners. If the chancellor chose to govern without the Social Democrats, the influence of the CDU/CSU's reactionary wing would increase. The result would be a more rightist and nationalist German government, which the CIA regarded as a detriment to the Truman administration's German policy.[10]

The creation of the cabinet, completed on September 20, marked the official beginning of the Federal Republic of Germany since the occupation statute also became effective on that date. The new chancellor thereupon faced a variety of problems. The Allies continued to limit the government's authority and thereby ensured a continuous struggle with the opposition in the *Bundestag* over the German-Allied relationship as well as over social and economic issues. To add to Adenauer's problems, the fate of German war criminals, who had been convicted and sentenced by Allied courts and were now inmates at Wittlich (French zone), Werl (British zone) and Landsberg (American zone) prisons, would lead to friction within the government coalition itself. Many members of the parliament felt that these prisoners were now citizens of the Federal Republic and, as such, protected by the provisions of the Basic Law.[11] Thus, Allied war crimes policy, already portrayed as a source of strong discontent in Germany, quickly merged into the larger issue of German sovereignty and integration in the West. In addition, the majority of members of the *Bundestag* refused to believe that the prisoners were guilty of atrocities and war crimes. To that effect the representatives as well as cabinet members quickly adjusted their terminology from the word *Kriegsverbrecher* (war criminal) to *Kriegsverurteilter* (war sentenced or sentenced because of the war) whenever the *Bundestag* debated the issue. *Kriegsverurteilter* soon became a household word in the Federal Republic, only to be replaced by the term "political prisoner" when, in later years, the release of imprisoned war criminals appeared to take too much time. Adenauer shared the attitudes of many legislators, although the chancellor also realized that the Western Allies would have to move cautiously, due to public opinion at home, in answering German demands for the release of all "so-called war criminals" from Wittlich, Landsberg and Werl. Like many in the legislature, the chancellor was convinced that most German war criminals had merely followed orders from their superiors and were thus wrongly imprisoned.[12]

The importance which the *Bundestag* attached to the question of clemency for the imprisoned war criminals was evident from the very beginning. On September 15, 1949, five days before the Cold War officially gave birth to the new German state, the Center Party introduced a bill calling for an amnesty to celebrate the formation of the Federal Republic. The bill sounded harmless enough. The Center Party called for an amnesty of only those individuals who had committed crimes as a result of their opposition to National Socialism and their enthusiasm for the "democratic idea" after the German surrender on May 8, 1945. The bill specifically did not propose an amnesty for offenses that involved criminal intent, repeat offenders or convicted war criminals.[13]

The proposed legislation, a result of the *Bundestag's* obsession with drawing a *Schlußstrich* (final line) under the Nazi past and the occupation, did not satisfy some members of Adenauer's own faction. During the debate on the bill, CDU Deputy Eduard Wahl urged the government to ensure that convicted war criminals would also receive pardons. Wahl's ultimate goal was the abandonment of Control Council Law No. 10, which since 1945 had provided the legal foundation for war crimes trials and denazification proceedings.

To Wahl, the judgments handed down on the basis of that law, particularly its provision for guilt by association, indicated that the Allies were more interested in proving Germany's collective guilt than in helping the Germans to draw that elusive final line and to make a fresh start. Denazification and all its "sinister consequences" would have to be discontinued, in the opinion of the Christian Democratic lawmaker, because the spirit which gave utmost importance to the rights of the individual was again governing Germany's "justice conscience." Since the Allied trial and denazification programs (the latter was now under the control of the individual states, the *länder*, which constituted the Federal Republic) violated this principle, Wahl suggested that an amnesty including war criminals would be the only remedy.[14]

A more detailed version of the Center Party bill became the law of the land on December 31, 1949.[15] Amnesty was granted to those individuals whose offenses were committed after May 8, 1945, and who would have been punished under normal circumstances with up to six months in prison or fines with a maximum of 5,000 Marks. The law specifically excluded crimes involving murder, manslaughter, arson, kidnaping and violations of the explosives statute.[16] The amnesty law might have temporarily satisfied Adenauer and the majority of the representatives in the *Bundestag* by eliminating some of the pressure on the chancellor to push the Allies into the release of German war criminals, but it ran into serious trouble with the Allied High Commission.

High Commissioners McCloy, Kirkpatrick and François-Poncet feared that the 1949 amnesty law was a backdoor approach to eroding the exclusive Allied jurisdiction in war crimes cases. During their monthly Council of the Allied High Commission meeting in late December, the high commissioners questioned the intent of the law and criticized the ambiguity of its language, which was most likely intended. For the AHC, it was not at all clear that the legislation would not affect defendants who had been convicted by Allied courts and whose fates were thus off-limits to the German government. The high commissioners were particularly troubled by the section which excluded serious criminal offenses from the amnesty. That part of the law listed only specific infractions of the German penal code. The German government had never recognized the indictments and judgments of Allied war crimes courts. The war criminals in Allied custody had been convicted of crimes defined in Control Council Law No. 10, but not violations of German criminal statutes. Thus, the Germans considered the convictions invalid and the amnesty could have benefited those sentenced by Allied courts. To ensure that the Adenauer government and the *Bundestag* would not attempt to usurp the powers of the Allies, the AHC warned Adenauer that they would approve the law only if the chancellor could assure them that it would not apply to convictions by Allied tribunals.[17]

A concerned Adenauer quickly consulted with Justice Minister Thomas Dehler (FDP). Dehler, pretending to be surprised about the Allied reservations, assured the chancellor that the amnesty law was very precise on every point the AHC had listed and was not ambiguous at all.[18] Adenauer most likely believed his justice minister, but he did not intend to damage his relationship with the high commissioners over what he could still sell to the Allies as a seemingly genuine misunderstanding. Hoping that the AHC would cease to oppose the law if he gave in without a fight, the chancellor wrote François-Poncet that the West German federal government shared the opinion of the High Commission that parts of the legislation contained serious flaws.[19] The clever strategy paid off. The high commissioners were able to report to their governments that they had thwarted a German attempt to challenge Allied authority, but simultaneously the AHC dropped its objections to the amnesty law. Although suitably warned that the high commissioners did not wish to be presented with a similar dilemma in the future,[20] the chancellor was not prevented from declaring victory. In January 1950, Adenauer announced that the German-Allied exchange had not resulted in a change of the law and that altering the legislation had never even been under consideration.[21]

Everybody was not satisfied by the Allied-German settlement with regard to the amnesty law. Only a few weeks after the high commissioners and the German federal government had reached agreement, Adenauer's coalition partner, the FDP, introduced a new anti-denazification bill in the *Bundestag*. The Free Democrats were again trying to wrest the jurisdiction over war crimes out of Allied hands and to transfer denazification from the *länder* to the federal level. The FDP wanted to have such proceedings handled by ordinary German courts, which would show greater sympathy to the defendants due to the Nazi pasts of many judges and prosecutors.[22] As bait to the Allied High Commission, the bill specifically stated that it would not apply to major war criminals. That, however, was an ambiguous statement since the FDP conveniently failed to define whom it considered a major war criminal.[23]

The *Bundestag* engaged in a lengthy and heated discussion of the issue on February 23, 1950. The deliberations showed that, for different reasons, every party in the legislature opposed denazification. Furthermore, several speeches displayed a remarkable amount of anti-Allied, and particularly anti-American, sentiment. The Allies appeared to be the true villains, and not the Nazi party and those of its followers who now had to face the consequences of their deeds. For the right, denazification and war crimes trials were simply the results of an Allied lust for revenge and were symptomatic of the victors' mistreatment of post-war Germany in violation of international law. In contrast, the Social Democrats, Communists and the Economic Reconstruction Association condemned the programs as an exercise in unequal justice, claiming that the Allies had treated high-ranking Third Reich officials with kid gloves and had focused too much on the lower echelons of the Nazi organizations. Only one faction used the debate for purposes other than criticizing the Allies and emphasized what it considered to be the real goal of the FDP bill. The Center Party was convinced that the FDP bill aimed not simply at the end of denazification, but rather at a general amnesty for German war criminals.[24]

McCloy was not pleased with that turn of events or the tone of the *Bundestag* debate. But this time, the U.S. high commissioner adopted a different, more aggressive approach. Already infuriated by a highly nationalistic Dehler speech,[25] McCloy lashed out at German officials for attempting to make the Allies responsible for Germany's present troubles.[26] Furthermore, Dehler's Free Democrats did not fare well in a U.S. High Commission report on the nature and status of German nationalism. A summarized version of that document appeared in the *New York Times* on March 4, 1950. What the paper had to report about the Federal Republic now was not nearly as complimentary as the stories and editorials that had accompanied Adenauer's victory in the elections for the first *Bundestag* only six months earlier. The initial optimism about Germany's future potential as a European democracy without nationalistic ambitions had given way to a renewed fear of the dangers of German nationalism and its impact on the Federal Republic's politics.[27]

McCloy's decision to intervene more actively in German politics after he had given the Adenauer government several months to set up shop commanded the attention of the FDP, already nervous due to the U.S. high commissioner's suggestion to the chancellor that he fire the rebellious Dehler. When the *Frankfurter Rundschau* printed the *New York Times* article on the U.S. High Commission's nationalism report, *Bundestag* Vice President Hermann Schäfer (FDP) complained to McCloy that the American criticism of his party had caused "great excitement among our friends."[28] McCloy used the opportunity to warn the Free Democrats that their party and its nationalistic tendencies were under the scrutiny of the U.S. High Commission. McCloy left no doubt that he and the other high commissioners were aware of (and disturbed by) the increasingly rightist development of the FDP.[29]

The U.S. High Commission seemed to follow up McCloy's warning to the FDP with a sterner approach in at least one area of the war criminals problem. In the fall of 1950 the *Auswärtiges Amt* noticed that American authorities had again begun to process extradition requests from the British and French zones as well as other countries for suspected German war criminals and those sentenced *in absentia*. The extradition of those accused of war crimes and atrocities from other zones had not been unusual in the early post-war era. In the late 1940s the United States Military Government had developed a policy involving the participation of German officials in the *länder*.[30] Thus, the sending of war crimes suspects residing in the U.S. zone to other parts of Europe and to other zones for prosecution was, at least for a while, not controversial. Assuming jurisdiction in such cases in June 1950, the U.S. High Commission set up its own extradition board.[31] The HICOG extradition board ended the previous cooperation between the *länder* and the American authorities and completely excluded the Germans from the decision-making.[32] The procedure chosen by the U.S. High Commission did not make many friends in the Federal Republic. The HICOG board decided on extradition requests without *länder* input but then ordered German officials to arrest the accused.[33]

The U.S. High Commission's action was not merely a rebuff to German-Allied cooperation in an area to which the Germans attached a great deal of importance. It also put McCloy and his staff on a new collision course with the *Bundestag*, which saw the issue as a new opportunity to challenge U.S. officials and to harshly criticize the occupation. Adenauer predicted trouble in a carefully phrased letter to McCloy on October 25, 1950. Since Article 16, Section 2 of the Basic Law specified that the extradition of German citizens to foreign countries was unconstitutional,[34] Adenauer asked the U.S. High Commissioner to refrain from forcing German officials to participate in such violations of the Federal Republic's constitution. The chancellor used his, by now patented, "the-German-public-might-not-understand" approach in an attempt to convice McCloy to revise the policy. Arguing that the Federal Republic's populace would not be able to comprehend that an occupation power was ordering German authorities to commit clearly illegal official acts, Adenauer hinted at a possible increase in anti-American sentiment.[35]

The *Bundestag* echoed Adenauer's argument almost unanimously in an interpellation two days later. The factions of the CDU/CSU, FDP, DP, SPD, Bavarian Party and the Center went on record expressing the "German public's" (but most likely their own) concern with regard to renewed extraditions five years after the end of the war. The legislators grudgingly conceded that the number of extraditions had been decreasing overall during the past year and had not taken place at all in the American zone. Nonetheless, Deputy Franz Ott (Independent) urged the parliament to take the matter a step further. Realizing the issue's potential as a challenge to the AHC's authority, Ott demanded that the Allies respect "the laws of humanity" by recognizing and adhering to the Basic Law's provision prohibiting the extradition of German citizens.[36]

By the end of October the problem had developed into a full-fledged war between the U.S. High Commission on the one hand and the German government and legislature on the other. In one case the justice ministry of the *land* Württemberg-Baden in the American zone recommended not fulfilling a U.S. extradition order on the basis of flimsy evidence against the individual in question and Article 16, Section 2.[37] War crimes lawyer Julius Fehsenbecker, with two clients facing extradition, even employed the help of International League for Human Rights President and Honorary American Civil Liberties Union (ACLU) Chairman Roger N. Baldwin to force the HICOG extradition board to reconsider its decision. Fehsenbecker also tried to defeat the U.S. High Commission by submitting a complaint and request of *habeas corpus* on behalf of the defendants to the U.S. District Court at Mannheim.[38]

The degree of irritation in the Federal Republic over the issue of extradition also began to pose problems for Adenauer,[39] who now saw the *Bundestag's* support for his policies, particularly Germany's future contribution to the defense of the West, jeopardized. The Social Democrats had already used the term "Allied chancellor" to discredit Adenauer at the beginning of his term. The present HICOG-German feud had the even more dangerous potential of eroding Adenauer's position within the coalition itself. To contain the danger, the chancellor sent Heinz v. Trützschler of the chancellory's *Dienststelle für Auswärtige Angelegenheiten* (Office for Foreign Affairs), the predecessor to the *Auswärtiges Amt*, to talk to Bernard A. Gufler, an official at the U.S. High Commission. Trützschler pointed out that the resumption of extraditions from the American zone came at a rather inconvenient time for both the United States and the German chancellor. The U.S. High Commission had already reached the same conclusion. HICOG, however, found itself in an awkward situation. Former U.S. Military Governor Gen. Lucius D. Clay had previously contacted Washington asking for agreement to stop work on all extradition requests. The Truman administration had turned down the general's suggestion, but Clay had nevertheless stopped all ongoing extradition proceedings on his own authority. The U.S. High Commission, Trützschler was told, was about to submit a proposal, similar to Clay's, to the administration for a decision. Unfortunately, according to Gufler, the United States was now under great pressure to fulfill extradition requests which had been made years ago. But the HICOG official assured Trützschler that, once decisions were made in the pending cases, the problem would cease to exist.[40]

Fearing that such action would lead to increased verbal attacks against the Allies, Adenauer did not share with the parliament his knowledge that what many Germans considered to be the recent "rash" of extradition proceedings was the result of an inconsistent U.S. policy in that area.[41] Instead, the chancellor decided to find a counterweight to the pressures that had compelled McCloy to resume turning suspected and convicted German war criminals over to foreign countries and the other two Western zones. The chancellor suspected that HICOG viewed Article 16, Section 2 of the Basic Law as an attempt to prevent the Allies from extraditing Nazi perpetrators and thus to limit Allied authority. Using language which the experienced attorney McCloy could appreciate, Adenauer explained that permitting the extradition of one's own citizens was a unique aspect of Anglo-Saxon, but not Continental, law. Consequently, history was the reason for that part of the Federal Republic's constitution, nothing else.[42]

Adenauer's fear that the *Bundestag* would continue to challenge the Allies, and thereby endanger the chancellor's own foreign political program, was more than justified. On November 10, 1950, the major parties in the parliament introduced *Drucksache Nr. 1599*, an expanded version of their interpellation two weeks earlier. The new resolution focused not only on the Basic

Law's provision prohibiting the extradition of German citizens, but also on the constitution's short and clear statement in Article 102 that "the death penalty has been abolished."[43] The problem was, however, that over twenty convicted war criminals were still waiting on death row at Landsberg prison, despite the fact that the Basic Law had replaced capital punishment with lifelong imprisonment as the Federal Republic's most severe form of penalizing its criminal offenders. The *Bundestag* almost unanimously believed that HICOG's plans to carry out the executions infringed on the Basic Law and consequently harmed U.S. interests in Germany. There was little the legislature could do, however, since U.S. military courts had tried and sentenced these defendants on the basis of Control Council Law No. 10. Consequently, the U.S. High Commission and the Army's European Command retained exclusive jurisdiction over the fate of the condemned. Still, the *Bundestag* urged the Adenauer government to persuade the Americans to promise not to stage executions in the future.[44]

There was more to the resolution, however, than the mere interest of the *Bundestag* to gain Allied respect for the Federal Republic's constitution. CDU Deputy Heinrich Höfler's justification of *Drucksache Nr. 1599* before the legislature made it abundantly clear that many representatives did not share the opinions of those U.S. courts that had sentenced the German war criminals—among them Oswald Pohl and the leaders of the mobile killing squads—to death in the first place. In spite of the solid criminal credentials of the prisoners, Höfler argued that in these cases the condemned deserved a humane gesture on the part of the U.S. High Commission since they appeared to have been law-abiding citizens who somehow ended up on the "path of illegality." This stunning assessment of the crimes committed by the Landsberg prisoners was coupled with a warning to the Allies. With the applause of the *Bundestag*, Höfler stated that the German people were deeply disenchanted with HICOG's war criminals policies, which now bore significance for both the German and the European future. It was hardly comforting that, according to Höfler, the *Bundestag* had no interest in preventing the punishment of those crimes truly worthy of death, which, in the usual fashion, were not defined.[45]

The Adenauer government's response to *Drucksache Nr. 1599* was more temperate, although the chancellor left little doubt that he agreed with much of what Höfler had said. The government did not address the thorny issue of the planned executions and instead focused on the extradition problem. Adenauer told the legislature that the Allies, "to the anguish of all good democrats," did not recognize Article 16 as binding for themselves and continued to operate on the basis of the Control Council law. But the Chancellor remained optimistic, believing that the high commissioners would soon end the practice of extraditing German citizens because it was incompatible with the future integration of the Federal Republic into the European "family of peoples."[46]

McCloy had apparently concluded the same, but he was not yet willing to surrender all of his prerogatives in this area. Instead, the high commissioner limited extradition proceedings to cases of murder only. U.S. officials also thought the time was ripe to remind the Germans of the risks involved in causing a public furor of this magnitude over the fate of individuals accused of very serious crimes. McCloy's deputy, General G.P. Hays, issued a stern warning to the German government and the *Bundestag* that the American public would react very negatively in light of the caliber of persons on whose behalf German officials and legislators had challenged the Allied High Commission.[47]

The extradition problem was laid to rest in February 1951. The Allied High Commission made German authorities responsible for most extraditions in and out of the Federal Republic. That left the Adenauer government in charge of requests from other countries, which the Germans could now turn down on their own authority by implementing Article 16, Section 2 of the Basic Law. The new procedure enabled Adenauer to eliminate one especially bothersome aspect—his irritation with extraditions to the East Bloc. The AHC, however, did not completely surrender control over the matter and retained jurisdiction in some cases. Without Allied permission, the Federal Republic could not meddle with extraditions of German citizens to Britain, France and the United States. The same applied to war criminals.[48] But even these last vestiges of Allied control could be circumvented. In 1952 the AHC received an extradition request from a Western country for an *SS*-man, sentenced *in absentia* to twenty years in prison for shooting several prisoners during the war. The suspect was promptly located in Germany, but the AHC had no intention of reopening the Pandora's box. Finding the evidence in this particular case very convincing, the AHC felt that the accused should be penalized for his crimes. The Allied High Commission designed a solution which would satisfy all the countries involved by trying the individual without extraditing him. For that purpose, the AHC contacted the Federal Justice Ministry and inquired whether a German court could try the accused if the request for his extradition was denied.[49] That, the Germans assured the AHC, was possible.[50]

Although the Adenauer government and the Allies had apparently solved the problem amicably, the *Bundestag's* attacks on the Americans in the process had left a bitter taste in McCloy's mouth. When three right wing deputies wanted to visit the last seven death row inmates at Landsberg in early 1951 and thereby stir up anti-American sentiment, McCloy shared his anger and frustration with General Handy:

We just received a telegram from three members of the Bundestag, asking to visit the prison and the condemned. Two of them are very bad _____ and the third is none too good.

This one fellow has just made a terrible speech about the American soldier—this fellow Richter [Deputy Franz Richter of the *Nationale Rechte* (National Right: NR)].

He is the fellow I talked about—the gum-chewing gangster who constantly uses the American soldier.[51]

While McCloy's irritation with some members of the *Bundestag* was understandable, the U.S. High Commissioner faced much harder times with the legislature in the months ahead. Until the fall of 1951 the Federal Repbulic's parliament was largely limited to harassing and criticizing the Allies on the issue of convicted war criminals. The *Bundestag* perceived the problem as one of great importance to the general population and thus sought to exploit it for its own benefits. However, during most of the first two years of the parliament's existence the lawmakers could do little else but verbally denounce the continued Allied detention of a small number of Germans. During this period, the *Bundestag* as yet lacked the leverage to seriously challenge Allied authority in such areas as denazification, extradition and imprisoned war criminals, as the experience with Articles 16 and 102 of the Basic Law proved.

Adenauer shared the legislature's determination to stop Allied domination of German affairs and certainly did not object to the *Bundestag* playing its role toward the achievement of this end. But when the *Bundestag's* rhetoric caused more damage than good, Adenauer preferred to work confidentially through his excellent contacts at the U.S. High Commission.[52] For the chancellor, it was certainly beneficial to be able to point to the pressure from the *Bundestag* to obtain further concessions. Nevertheless, Adenauer knew that excessive anti-American talk in the legislature could increase suspicions at the U.S. High Commission that the Federal Republic was not yet ready to be left to operate on its own. Thus, the chancellor appreciated the sensitivity of the emotional war criminals problem. The *Bundestag* was useful in demonstrating the great importance that the German public allegedly attached to this problem, but it could also damage Adenauer's good relationship with the AHC. There was an additional hazard for the chancellor. During the first two years of his government Adenauer could show only little progress, at least in the opinion of the parliament, with regard to imprisoned war criminals. This provided the opposition with another opportunity to question the chancellor's competence. In addition, members of the cabinet and the coalition parties were also clearly dissatisfied with Adenauer's failure, and that of the Allies, to quickly resolve the issue.

The debate, however, involved more than pure power politics. The philosophy of the *Bundestag* was that the inmates of Landsberg, Werl and Wittlich were almost exclusively honorable soldiers, who had merely followed orders. The parliament, including the cabinet, did not share the Allied opinion that these prisoners were truly guilty of horrendous crimes. Such views, held by the Federal Republic's political elites, were bound to influence the thinking of the general public sooner or later. This was additional evidence that the occupation had failed to reeducate the Germans. The confusing coexistence of the Basic Law and the occupation statute created a constitutional gray zone that made it possible for the lawmakers to couch their obvious biases in legalistic terms. As a result, they could freely attack the Allies for allegedly violating the provisions of the Federal Republic's constitution when extraditing and executing German citizens. Only a handful of legislators dared to admit that some of the inmates deserved their destinies. Even when doing so, these statements were obscured by their failure to mention specific names and offenses. For the legislature the drawing of the final line under the Nazi past did not translate into assuming responsibility for the human misery which Nazi Germany had caused. The *Bundestag* made this abundantly clear by attempting to portray the imprisoned German war criminals as the victims of a giant Allied injustice. As McCloy had already observed, the Germans, particularly the elite, found it easier to blame the country's problems on the Allies instead of themselves. Judging from the debates in the *Bundestag*, it is evident that this strategy was also applied to those guilty of war crimes and atrocities. For these Germans, the perpetrators were in effect an Allied, and not a German, problem.

NOTES

1. "Current West German Views on the War Criminals Issue," HICOG, Office of Public Affairs, Research Analysis Staff, September 8, 1952, RG 338, USAREUR, Box 469, News Clippings File.

2. Wolfgang Benz, "Versuche zur Reform des öffentlichen Dienstes in Deutschland 1945-1952: Deutsche Opposition gegen alliierte Initiativen," *Vierteljahrshefte für Zeitgeschichte* 29 (1981), 216-245.

3. Botzenhart-Viehe, "The German Reaction to the American Occupation, 1944-1947," 135-168.

4. For example, see Smith, ed., *The Papers of General Lucius DuBignon Clay*, II, 1114.

5. The first *Bundestag*, following the tradition of the Weimar legislature, was fractured into a number of political groupings. In addition to the major parties, several minor ones managed to climb the five percent hurdle required by the Federal Republic's constitution, the Basic Law, to be represented in the federal legislature. Of these, the *Wiederaufbauverein* (Economic Reconstruction Association: WAV) received twelve, the *Zentrum* (Center: Z) ten, the *Südschleswigsche Wählerverein* (South Schleswig Voters Association: SSW) one and the independents three seats. Thilo Vogelsang, *Das geteilte Deutschland* (München: dtv, 1966), 107.

6. "U.S. Help Pledged to German Regime of Conservatives," *New York Times*, August 16, 1949, 1.

7. "Germans for Democracy," *New York Times*, August 16, 1949, 22.

8. The one vote that made him chancellor came from Adenauer himself. Konrad Adenauer, *Memoirs 1945-53* (Chicago: Regnery, 1966), 182.

9. "Adenauer Elected by a Single Vote," *New York Times*, September 16, 1949, 5.

10. "Probable Consequences of the Forthcoming West German Elections," Central Intelligence Agency, ORE 67-49, July 19, 1949, Truman Library.

11. The Basic Law went into effect on May 23, 1949, several months before the official creation of the Federal Republic.

12. Adenauer summed up his personal views in a letter to Pope Pius XII. The document shows that the chancellor viewed most of the convicted war criminals as *subalterne* (subordinates) but not as former high-ranking Nazi officials. Adenauer to Pope Pius XII, April 10, 1951, *Bundeszwischenarchiv*, File B141-3576, 35-37. Adenauer preferred to speak of the war criminals problem in general terms and often pointed out that the "truly guilty" deserved punishment. Unfortunately, the chancellor never named names or specified the nature of offenses of "truly guilty" war criminals, thus leaving the impression that he was insincere on this point.

13. *Drucksache Nr. 17*, September 15, 1949, *Verhandlungen des deutschen Bundestages, 1. Wahlperiode.*

14. *19. Sitzung*, December 2, 1949, *Verhandlungen des deutschen Bundestages, 1. Wahlperiode*, 581. Ending denazification was particularly popular during the first months of the Federal Republic's existence, probably due to the fact that it was easier to persuade the *ministerpräsidenten* of the *länder* to stop denazification than to convince the Allies to release all war criminals in their custody. Hans-Christoph Seebohm (DP), who became Adenauer's Minister of Transportation, introduced a resolution urging the end of denazification on September 13, 1949. The Economic Reconstruction Association made a similar demand, but its resolution called for the continued imprisonment of "proven war criminals." See *Drucksache Nr. 13*, September 13, 1949, and *Drucksache Nr. 27*, September 21, 1949, *Verhandlungen des deutschen Bundestages, 1. Wahlperiode*. To make sure the Allies and the *Länder* got the message, the FDP introduced a third anti-denazification resolution in September. *Drucksache Nr. 97*, September 28, 1949, ibid.

15. *Gesetz über die Gewährung von Straffreiheit*, December 31, 1949, *Bundesgesetzblatt, 1949, Teil I*, 37-38.

16. Excluded from the amnesty were Articles 168, 211, 212, 213, 234, 249, 250, 251, 252, 306, 307 of the German penal code.

17. Council of the Allied High Commission to Adenauer, December 29, 1949, *Bundeszwischenarchiv*, File B141-4282, 2-3.

18. Dehler to Adenauer, December 30, 1949, ibid., 5-6.

19. Adenauer to François-Poncet, December 30, 1949, ibid., 4.

20. McCloy to Acheson, January 2, 1950, RG 466, U.S. High Commission in Germany, Papers of John J. McCloy, Classified General Records 1949-1952, Box 6, D (50) 15a.

21. Press Statement of the *Bundesregierung*, January 9, 1950, *Bundeszwischenarchiv*, File B141-4282, 12-14.

22. Friedrich, *Die kalte Amnestie*, 364.

23. *Drucksache 482*, January 31, 1950, *Verhandlungen des deutschen Bundestages, 1. Wahlperiode.*

24. *40. Sitzung*, February 23, 1950, *Verhandlungen des deutschen Bundestages, 1. Wahlperiode*, 1340-1355.

25. At the FDP party congress in Hamburg on January 2, 1950, Dehler had proclaimed that Germany was no more responsible for the outbreak of World War I than France. The justice minister went on to say that Hitler had been the result of the Treaty of Versailles and the timidity of France. François-Poncet strongly protested Dehler's statements in a letter to Adenauer. Three weeks later, Dehler claimed that his remarks had been misinterpreted. Dehler argued that it was "not true that I burdened France with responsibility of [sic] World War I." Files on the Dehler case,

HICOG, January 1950, RG 466, Papers of John J. McCloy, Classified General Records 1949-1952, Box 7, D (50) 196c-e.

26. "McCloy Warns the Germans against a Revival of Nazism," *New York Times*, February 7, 1950, 1.

27. "U.S. Fears Nationalist Rise in Germany despite Curbs," *New York Times*, March 4, 1950, 1.

28. Hermann Schäfer, vice president of the *Bundestag*, to McCloy, March 16, 1950, RG 466, Papers of John J. McCloy, Classified General Records 1949-1952, Box 10, D (50) 752.

29. McCloy to Schäfer, March 28, 1950, ibid., Box 11, D (50) 1000.

30. G.H. Garde, Adjutant General Department, EUCOM, to the Military Governments of Bavaria, Hesse, Württemberg-Baden and the U.S. sector of Berlin, June 22, 1948, *Bundeszwischenarchiv*, File B141-9559, 118.

31. HICOG directive *Verfahren bei Auslieferungsersuchen von angeblichen Kriegsverbrechern aus der amerikanischen Besatzungszone und dem amerikanischen Sektor von Berlin. Umbenennung des Auslieferungsausschusses*, June 28, 1950, ibid., 100-102.

32. v. Trützscher to Professor Ophüls, Federal Justice Ministry, September 4, 1950, ibid., 16.

33. *Bayrisches Staatsministerium der Justiz* to the Federal Justice Ministry, September 4, 1950, ibid., 19-20. The new policy was first applied during the extradition board's meetings on July 14 and July 26 when it decided to send three Germans to France and one to Austria for prosecution.

34. See Friedrich Giese and Egon Schunck, eds., *Grundgesetz für die Bundesrepublik Deutschland* (Frankfurt: Kommentator, 1960), 42.

35. Adenauer to McCloy, October 25, 1950, *Bundeszwischenarchiv*, File B141-9559, 30-31.

36. *Drucksache Nr. 1527*, October 27, 1950, *Verhandlungen des deutschen Bundestages, 1. Wahlperiode*.

37. Richard Schmid, Justice Ministry of Württemberg-Baden, to the State Ministry of Württemberg-Baden, October 28, 1950, *Bundeszwischenarchiv*, File B141-9559, 38.

38. Fehsenbecker to Dehler, November 4, 1950, *Bundeszwischenarchiv*, File B141-9558, 22.

39. Internal memorandum, Federal Justice Ministry, November 9, 1950, *Bundeszwischenarchiv*, File B141-9559, 51.

40. Trützschler to Adenauer advisor Herbert Blankenhorn, November 8, 1950, ibid., 45-46.

41. In 1950/51 there were twenty-three requests in the American, six in the French and eight in the British zone. *Aufstellung*, undated, ibid., 126-135.

42. Adenauer to McCloy, November 9, 1950, ibid., 90-91.

43. See Giese and Schunck, eds., *Grundgesetz für die Bundesrepublik Deutschland*, 188.

44. *Drucksache Nr. 1599*, November 10, 1950, *Verhandlungen des deutschen Bundestages, 1. Wahlperiode*.

45. *101. Sitzung*, November 14, 1950, *Verhandlungen des deutschen Bundestages, 1. Wahlperiode*, 3691.

46. Ibid., 3691-3692.

47. v. Trützschler to Wilhelm v. Grolmann, Federal Justice Ministry, November 24, 1950, *Bundeszwischenarchiv*, File B141-9559, 96-97.

48. *Bundesanzeiger, Nr. 26*, February 7, 1951.

49. State Secretary Walter Strauß, Federal Justice Ministry, to Heinrich Grützner, Extradition Department, Federal Justice Ministry, July 23, 1952, *Bundeszwischenarchiv*, File B141-9560, 59.

50. Internal memorandum by Grützner, July 29, 1952, ibid., 67.

51. Transcript of telephone conversation between McCloy and Handy, February 2, 1951, RG 338, USAREUR, Box 461, Administrative File. Adenauer himself made several attempts to prevent the executions. In April 1950 he asked McCloy to commute the remaining death sentences of prisoners under HICOG jurisdiction because of the Basic Law's prohibition of the death penalty and the long period of time which had elapsed since the announcement of the sentences; McCloy to Adenauer, April 24, 1950, RG 466, Papers of John J. McCloy, Classified General Records 1949-1952, Box 13, D (50) 1228. On January 8, 1951, the chancellor sent Deputy Justice Minister Walter Strauß to Handy, asking the latter not to carry out the remaining executions of prisoners under EUCOM jurisdiction; memorandum for the record by Handy, January 8, 1951, RG 338, USAREUR, Box 537, Execution File.

52. The chancellor's good relationship with HICOG is very evident in an exchange of letters between Adenauer and James W. Riddleberger, director of political affairs, Office of Political Affairs at HICOG in Frankfurt, in the summer of 1950. Riddleberger feared that the State Department would give him a different post and that he might not return to Germany. After congratulating the chancellor on the occasion of his daughter's wedding and expressing concern for his health, Riddleberger wished "to express to you my great satisfaction and pleasure which I have always had in both our official and personal relationship and the hope that this will continue in the future." Riddleberger to Adenauer, June 22, 1950, *Auswärtiges Amt*, File 240.01, Document 3152/50. Adenauer seemed heavyhearted over the prospect that Riddleberger might have to leave the Federal Republic and assured the latter that the German government appreciated the HICOG official's "great love of work and understanding for things German [für die deutschen Dinge]." Adenauer to Riddleberger, June 30, 1950, ibid.

7

Adenauer, the **Bundestag** *and the Resolution of the War Criminals Issue, 1951-1955*

The *Bundestag's* political leverage in matters relating to convicted German war criminals increased greatly during 1951. Although McCloy and Gen. Handy had announced reprieves for twenty-one condemned Landsberg inmates and had significantly reduced the sentences of numerous others at the beginning of the year, the parliament by no means regarded the issue as solved. Time was on the legislature's side. The Western Allies and the Adenauer government had already agreed that the Federal Republic would contribute to the defense of the West in some form or another in the near future. In return, the Allies promised to abolish the occupation statute and to restore German sovereignty. The rearmament-for-sovereignty trade ended the short period wherein the *Bundestag's* role had been limited to verbal attacks against Allied policy in Germany. Any treaty specifying the nature of West Germany's participation in a Western defense force, the deputies knew, required ratification. Thus, the *Bundestag* soon found the opportunity to engage in a new strategy, which could be appropriately termed "legislative blackmail," to end once and for all the war criminals problem.

A number of new, and at times surprising, developments accompanied the parliament's new approach. The Free Democrats appeared willing to risk the dissolution of Adenauer's coalition over the issue of convicted war criminals. In 1952 the FDP faction in the *Bundestag* threatened to vote against ratification of the European Defense Community treaty and the contractual agreements, an action that jeopardized Adenauer's foreign political agenda. The party's ranks included a good number of former Nazi officials and it constantly attempted to appeal to right wing voters.[1] For this group, there were three important reasons to oppose the chancellor's foreign policy: (1) Allied-controlled rearmament; (2) the continued existence of some Allied rights even after the restoration of German sovereignty; and (3) the war criminals issue. With regard to war criminals, the rightists within the FDP appeared to have the full support of more moderate party members.

The development of the Social Democrats' attitude was even more amazing. Since many of its members had suffered greatly during the Third Reich, the SPD, quite understandably, did not at first consider the fate of Nazi war criminals in Allied custody a top political priority. However, the SPD used the context of the debate over the rearmament of Germany to join in the general chorus, demanding that the Allies and the German chancellor solve the problem. For the Social Democrats, the prisoners were valuable for two reasons. First, the party's post-war leadership decided that the SPD had not been nationalistic enough in the opinion of Weimar voters, contributing to its defeat by Hitler. To avoid a recurrence, the Social Democrats formulated a foreign policy agenda with an appeal for the more national-minded voter. As part of this program, the SPD opposed the Federal Republic's integration into the West, fearing that such an action would lead to the permanent division of Germany.[2] Social Democratic opposition to the war crimes program was also meant to enhance the party's new image as fighting solely for West Germany's national interest. Second, the imprisoned war criminals posed a continuing embarrassment to Adenauer by demonstrating the limits of the latter's rapport with the Allies. With the September 1953 federal elections approaching, the party increased its rhetoric on the issue to win additional votes. McCloy's successor as U.S. High Commissioner, Walter Donnelly, was surprised by the strong SPD attacks against the Allies during a debate on the handling of the war criminals problem in September 1952. Donnelly, however, dismissed the SPD's action as political opportunism, based on the party's conviction that the German electorate was keenly interested in the prisoners.[3] The high commissioner's assessment of the SPD's motivation indicates that the *Bundestag* might have succeeded in its efforts to rally public opinion on this point. Because the legislature had dwelled on the war criminals question since the inception of the Federal Republic, it was only a matter of time until the average German came to share the political leadership's belief that those imprisoned for war crimes were the victims of Allied injustices.

A third development concerned the Committee for the Occupation Statute and Foreign Affairs of the *Bundestag*. The committee, chaired by Carlo Schmid (SPD), formed a subcommittee *"Kriegsgefangene"* (prisoners of war). That title sounded innocent enough. In reality, the subcommittee's name was a misnomer. In addition, the name "Prisoners of War" inferred that the *Bundestag* had decided that war criminals deserved the same status as those who were legitimate POWs. Consequently, the parliament gave yet another indication of its conviction that the former had merely acted as soldiers who had followed orders.

The parliament already had a regular committee in charge of looking after the thousands of German POWs still in the East bloc. The Foreign Affairs subcommittee "Prisoners of War" dealt almost exclusively with convicted German war criminals who were serving their sentences in the Allied prisons in Germany as well as in individual European countries. The subcommittee as such became yet another device to pressure the Allies into quickly resolving the problem. Adenauer employed the subcommittee to keep a limited number of influential lawmakers informed and to clear some of the government's war criminals policy with the opposition. In return, Schmid agreed with Adenauer advisor Herbert Blankenhorn not to discuss aspects of the issue in the *Bundestag* that had the potential to turn Allied public opinion against the Federal Republic.[4]

In the fall of 1951 the *Heidelberger Juristenkreis* approached the subcommittee with a list of proposals aimed at eliminating the problem. Commanding excellent connections with the parliament and the government through CDU/CSU Deputy Eduard Wahl, the *Juristenkreis* recommended that the Federal Republic attempt to assume jurisdiction in two vital areas: clemency and the execution of the sentences of all Allied prisoners in West Germany. If the Adenauer government could not persuade the Allies to surrender their exclusive rights with regard to these points, the Federal Republic should at least obtain permission to make proposals for clemency. A mixed commission, consisting of Allied and German representatives, would then decide on their merits. For defendants tried and sentenced by the International Military Tribunal, the *Juristenkreis* proposed what it termed a "Japanese solution." Convicted war criminals in the Far East could receive clemency if the majority of the Allied countries, which had participated in the trials, agreed. The *Juristenkreis* desired that the same procedure become effective in Germany, where the granting of a pardon still required Allied unanimity.[5]

The subcommittee heard a similar argument during its meeting on October 26, 1951, when the deputies listened to a presentation by Otto Kranzbühler, a prominent German defense lawyer in war crimes cases.[6] Kranzbühler urged the Adenauer government to demand from the Allies reviews of all cases by mixed commissions with neutral chairmen. But Kranzbühler, obviously well-informed by the *Heidelberger Juristenkreis*, went beyond the previous proposal. He suggested that all defendants still awaiting sentencing and those who had not received a life sentence be released until the final decisions of the review commissions were made. Kranzbühler's plan won the overwhelming approval of the subcommittee, although some disagreement existed on the question of whether such releases should be preliminary or final. Some members feared that prisoners whose offenses were also punishable by German law would receive an automatic amnesty from prosecution in the Federal Republic if the releases from Allied prisons were final.[7]

This meeting of the subcommittee brought into the open its differences with the Adenauer government. The majority of its members suspected that the chancellor was not working hard enough to solve the war criminals problem. Thus, the SPD deputies on the subcommittee asked the government's representative, the *Auswärtiges Amt's* expert for war crimes issues, Heinz von Trützschler, if Adenauer had covered the subject in his talks with the Allies. The secrecy with which the chancellor had treated the war criminals issue of late not only annoyed the Social Democrats, but also the other parties. Thus, the subcommittee as a whole ordered an irritated v. Trützschler to appear with a complete explanation of the government's policy and efforts at the next meeting of the full Foreign Affairs Committee.[8]

The *Bundestag* Foreign Affairs Committee as a whole shared the sentiment of its prisoners of war subcommittee. Durings its November 15, 1951, meeting, the committee concluded that the Allies had convicted many innocent individuals of war crimes. In other cases, the deputies alleged, Allied courts had been unable to prove the guilt of the defendants. The committee did admit that the war crimes tribunals had also dealt with a number of obviously guilty Germans. That admission, however, was rather halfhearted and suffered from the usual lack of names or detail as to what offenses qualified the accused for the "obviously guilty" label. The committee complained to Adenauer about the Allied refusal to consider questions of guilt or innocence in sentence reviews, which had so far only been conducted to consider the granting of clemency. In the opinion of the legislators, such an approach was unsatisfactory. Thus, chairman Schmid informed the chancellor that the Foreign Affairs Committee, in the interest of "justice," wished to see Allied authorities quickly and convincingly reexamine the sentences on the basis of the defendant's guilt. In reality, the committee's demand constituted another assault on the war crimes trial procedure of not allowing a reevaluation of the verdict. Schmid also passed Kranzbühler's plan for mixed boards on to Adenauer, coupled with a call for the release of all German prisoners who had served one-third of their sentences. To emphasize the deputies' discontent with the Allied handling of the problem in the past, the chairman pointed out that the committee viewed its recommendations as the minimum.[9]

Schmid, however, failed to supply Adenauer with all the information regarding the Foreign Affairs Committee's meeting. The deputies had also discussed whether to demand a general amnesty from the Allies as well as a transfer of the Landsberg, Wittlich and Werl prisoners into German custody. The majority of committee members voted against pressing these points, for good reasons. Insisting on a general amnesty would, in all likelihood, have led to an unfavorable response from the Allies with regard to the sentence review process as a whole. The result could have been fewer releases. The question of a custody transfer had an even greater danger potential. The deputies feared that the execution of Allied sentences against war criminals by German authorities would constitute a tacit admission that the Federal Republic now recognized the war crimes program as valid in international law. As yet unwilling to jeopardize their political careers by suggesting the implementation of such a policy, the legislators instead decided to pressure the Allies and Adenauer to ensure the fulfillment of their "minimum" demands during the rearmament negotiations.[10]

The perceived lack of progress on the war criminals issue during Adenauer's talks with the Allies also irritated the chancellor's coalition partners. The government had officially accepted only one of the Foreign Affairs Committee's recommendations, the mixed clemency board, and had adopted it as the German position. The cabinet had also agreed to seek a solution within the context of the Allied-German contractual agreements by incorporating the committee's suggestion for a mixed board in the treaties. This failed to satisfy the chancellor's own political allies. On November 19, 1951, the coalition parties discarded the concerns of the Foreign Affairs Committee regarding the demands for a large-scale amnesty and a custody transfer for imprisoned war criminals by introducing a resolution calling for both.[11]

The *Auswärtiges Amt* viewed this development with concern. The resolution greatly exceeded the chancellor's policy. As a result, the foreign office worried about the resolution's possible negative impact on Allied-German negotiations. In language reminiscent of the Nazi era, the *Auswärtiges Amt* expressed its fear that the coalition itself might hamper progress toward a "final solution" of the war criminals problem.[12]

To quiet the dissatisfaction within his coalition, Adenauer addressed the call for a custody transfer during Allied-German talks in London in December 1951. The chancellor's visit to Britain demonstrated how plans for rearming the Federal Republic had boosted German assertiveness. In his conversations with British politicians, Adenauer announced that West Germany would not recognize the Allied verdicts. In addition, the chancellor demanded the creation of a mixed commission to reexamine the sentences. But Adenauer also enhanced his reputation as a skillful negotiator by attempting to find a viable middle ground between the Foreign Affairs Committee's recommendations, the more radical coalition resolution calling for a large-scale amnesty and Allied willingness to compromise. Adenauer, in contrast to the Foreign Affairs Committee, saw the mixed commission as a clemency granting function, but not as an appellate court empowered to review the verdicts. Furthermore, the chancellor did not ask for the release of all prisoners who had received sentences of up to twenty years, for fear that the Allies would not agree to such a demand. Adenauer actually had no reason to bring up this particular point. These cases would soon be reviewed by the envisaged mixed clemency board.[13] Since this group had received relatively light sentences, it seemed likely that the review board would deal with such cases first and show the most leniency.

Despite Adenauer's apparent success in finding a solution to the war criminals problem in return for German rearmament, a number of *Bundestag* deputies remained unwilling to let the issue die. To sound out if the parliament's obsession with the by now dwindling number of prisoners might lead some legislators to resist rearmament,[14] McCloy talked to FDP lawmakers August Euler, Hans Wellhausen and Martin Blank in early 1952. What the three had to say to the U.S. high commissioner seemed reassuring. While the deputies emphasized that West Germany could not recognize the Allied verdicts, they agreed with the idea of a mixed clemency board. Euler, Wellhausen and Blank urged McCloy to show greater clemency for the German generals imprisoned for war crimes, arguing for the release of those generals who had established a reputation as "good soldiers" in Germany. Such an action would greatly improve the odds for obtaining the public's approval of the planned German participation in the defense of the West.[15]

McCloy probably did not pay too much attention to the last argument, which seemed sufficiently harmless at the time. However, the FDP deputies' statement signaled the beginning of a new line of reasoning in the *Bundestag*. Suddenly, the release of imprisoned war criminals became the "psychological requirement" (allegedly on the part of the German public) for the rearmament of Germany. Most parties in the *Bundestag* and the Adenauer government eventually adopted this theme. The Allied war crimes program stood accused of having dirtied the reputation of the German soldier. The only remedy, and thus the only chance to ensure the German public's agreement with the country's defense contribution, was, as the legislators claimed, the release of the *"Kriegsverurteilte."*[16]

Only a few days before Adenauer was to embark on his historic journey to London in February 1952 to meet with Acheson, Eden and Schuman, the coalition parties voiced their disappointment with what they saw as the too slow pace of progress. The Allies had not heeded the coalition's call for a generous Christmas amnesty and a change of custody for those unnamed prisoners who had, in the words of the November 19, 1951, resolution, committed "serious crimes." Now the CDU/CSU, the DP and the FDP introduced an additional resolution urging the Allies to release all convicted war criminals and those in detention for investigative purposes. Furthermore, the parties insisted on "objective" investigations of each case. That sounded suspiciously like a call for an appellate court, which was a far cry from the mixed sentence review commission now on the drawing board. The Social Democrats disagreed with such sweeping demands. The resolution, however, carried despite SPD opposition.[17]

The new coalition resolution had its intended effect. Adenauer had earlier indicated to the *Heidelberger Juristenkreis* that he might attempt to solve the problem on the basis of a quiet gentlemen's agreement with the Allies. Such procedure, in violation of the government's official policy to include a solution of the nagging issue in the contractuals, would help to avoid the impression that the Federal Republic was indeed swapping rearmament for war criminals. The resolution, however, convinced Adenauer that the coalition itself thought little of a possible oral agreement between the chancellor and the Allies. As a result, the *Auswärtiges Amt* urged Adenauer to insist on a solution within the context of the treaties in order to pacify the coalition partners. The foreign office regarded the recent CDU/CSU, FDP and DP demands as a negative development, but one that Adenauer could still defuse. Elevating the subject of war criminals officially to the treaty level, the *Auswärtiges Amt* recommended, would ensure the DP and FDP's support of Adenauer's foreign policy. It would also provide for smoother sailing in the Foreign Affairs Committee.[18]

Adenauer's meetings with the three Western foreign ministers appeared to give the West German government the upper hand in the ongoing struggle over how to deal with the imprisoned war criminals. The *Auswärtiges Amt* felt it was time to end the secrecy, which the chancellor preferred for fear of alienating Allied public opinion, and to announce publicly that negotiations on the subject were now under way in London at the highest level. Since the Allies themselves had become extremely interested in the problem during the past months, the time was right to drop the precautions and make a public statement. In the opinion of the *Auswärtiges Amt*, pointing to the chancellor's talks with the foreign ministers would counter the tendency of some coalition lawmakers to make the solution of the war criminals problem a prerequisite for their support of a German defense contribution.[19]

Adenauer followed the foreign office's recommendations and held a press conference on the results of the London negotiations on February 20, 1952. The chancellor, now portrayed as an equal to Acheson, Schuman and Eden, had good news to report with regard to the *"Kriegsverurteiltenproblem."* Adenauer emphasized the strong interest of West Germans in the treatment of the war criminals "due to psychological reasons and sympathy for those among the convicted who, in our opinion, had not committed any war crimes." The Allies and the Federal Republic, the chancellor stated, had agreed on the creation of a mixed commission with authority to grant clemency. The West German government now hoped that the "wrongly convicted" prisoners could expect major sentence reductions or release once the EDC treaty and the contractual agreements were signed.[20]

Unfortunately for Adenauer, his trimphant return to Bonn only temporarily quieted the opposition to his foreign policy in general and his handling of the war criminals issue in particular. The criticism of Adenauer and the Allies cut, in the usual fashion, across party lines. For one, the Social Democrats were keenly interested in the problem, viewing it as an opportunity to embarrass the chancellor. Thus, SPD Deputy Alfred Gleisner was one of the first to inquire whether Adenauer had any actual sentence reductions to show for the London negotiations. Gleisner was also interested in the fate of those convicted before the International Military Tribunal, who were serving their sentences at Spandau prison in Berlin. The London agreement, as Gleisner well knew, did not apply to these prisoners since any clemency decisions for them automatically required the consent of the Soviet Union. Nonetheless, Gleisner brought up this point.[21]

Even more disturbing than SPD challenges was talk around the Federal Republic in the spring of 1952 that the German government had secretly and successfully mobilized French legal scholarship against that country's guilt-by-association war crimes statute. That law, the *Lex Oradour*, had led to a number of convictions in trials of German war criminals on French soil. The revelation that the Federal Republic had worked through the French military justice apparatus to strike down the *Lex Oradour* was acutely embarrassing to Adenauer.[22] The chancellor viewed Franco-German reconciliation as one of his foreign political priorities.[23] As a result, Adenauer had to be concerned that the news of the Federal Republic's intervention in French judicial affairs would have a negative impact on French public opinion. In addition, the discovery could pose severe problems for the chancellor's personal friend, French Foreign Minister Robert Schuman, who had not been informed of the German operation.

Surprisingly, the *Lex Oradour* debacle had no immediate impact on releases of prisoners from the war crimes prison at Wittlich in the French zone of occupation. In fact, French High Commissioner François-Poncet told the chancellor that he intended to release nineteen war criminals and to reduce the sentences of twenty-seven others on July 14, 1952, the anniversary of the French national holiday celebrating the storming of the Bastille. The developments in the British zone were also relatively positive. High Commissioner Kirkpatrick promised Adenauer a further reexamination of all cases at Werl, but he cautioned that he would not take any extraordinary action such as granting a large-scale amnesty on behalf of the war criminals.[24]

Meanwhile, the Bonn government was not at all pleased with the American High Commissioner. McCloy, perhaps still mulling over the largely negative German reaction to his January 1951 mass sentence commutation, had, in the *Auswärtiges Amt's* assessment, developed "attitude problems" in the area of clemency for war criminals. The U.S. high commissioner did not regard the London agreement of February 1952 on the mixed clemency board as binding since the treaties had yet to be signed. Instead, McCloy stubbornly refused to conduct a general reexamination of the sentences. In fact, the *Auswärtiges Amt* thought McCloy had made it more difficult for the war criminals and their lawyers to obtain releases from Landsberg. The U.S. High Commission now insisted on the introduction of new evidence for reviews of individual sentences. HICOG, the foreign office lamented, was definitely not making the desired progress on this issue.[25]

McCloy soon discovered that the days had passed when he could show the *Bundestag* the limits of its power, as he had done in the case of the 1949 amnesty law. By the beginning of May 1952 it was evident that the leaders of the coalition parties had considerable doubts about the contractual agreements. The DP argued that the agreements resembled the Treaty of Versailles. For the FDP leadership, as usual, the war criminals problem ranked very high on the list of complaints. Article 6 of the contractuals also called for an eventual custody transfer to German authorities without demanding Germany's recognition of the verdicts and judgments. FDP politicians Reinhold Maier and Ernst Achenbach strongly objected to this particular part of the treaty. For Maier and Achenbach, such an arrangement was tantamount to forcing German authorities to execute the Allied sentences and thus to violate the provisions of the Basic Law.[26]

McCloy's approach to the war criminals problem changed somewhat in the spring of 1952. To appease the Germans, the U.S. high commissioner visited the Spandau prisoners, allegedly out of concern for their health and to inspect the general conditions at the prison.[27] Furthermore, McCloy reassured Adenauer that, despite German comments to the contrary, neither he nor Gen. Handy had ceased altogether to conduct sentence reviews. According to McCloy, he and Handy only considered a general reexamination of all cases inappropriate. That did not mean, however, that they were unwilling to review individual sentences.[28]

The signing of the EDC treaty and the contractuals in late May 1952 finally gave the *Bundestag* the opportunity to force the Allies to make concessions with regard to the war criminals problem. For the United States and the German government the crucial question became whether the man whom the parliament had elected as chancellor with a margin of one vote could muster enough loyalty among the coalition deputies to obtain ratification of the treaties despite the continued Allied imprisonment of German war criminals. The initial outlook was not good. Hans-Christoph Seebohm, transport minister and deputy chairman of the DP, warned that the SPD would use the issue against the government. More importantly, Seebohm feared that the opposition on the right would exploit the "war criminals question." He predicted that both groups would attempt to excite public opinion and to radicalize the population in order to kill the treaties. The transport minister, whose own party had done its share of criticizing the war crimes program and denazification, reminded Adenauer of another danger. If the opposition succeeded in turning public sentiment against the German-Allied agreements, this could cause problems for the coalition in the upcoming federal elections.[29]

Seebohm's bleak predictions concerning the opposition's probable actions were not that farfetched. Regardless, the main threat to ratification came from inside the coalition. FDP Deputy Erich Mende publicly announced in June 1952 that several coalition lawmakers intended to reject the treaties as long as "former soldiers" were in the prisons of the Western Allies. Mende termed the contractual agreement's provision for the mixed clemency commission an unsatisfactory solution, warning that "even a defeated nation can only go so far before it reaches the limits of its self-respect." Mende's other comments demonstrated clearly that the war crimes program as an educational function had failed. The FDP legislator accused Allied troops now fighting in Korea of acting no differently from their German counterparts in the Second World War. In fact, in Mende's opinion, the German soldiers had only answered the brutal and mean fighting methods of others with appropriate measures.[30]

The war criminals problem continued to haunt the coalition throughout the summer of 1952. For the opposition on both the left and the right the *"Kriegsverurteilte"* offered a welcome opportunity to hammer away at Adenauer's foreign policy and to display patriotism in the hope of gaining additional votes in the next *Bundestag* election. On July 10, 1952, the parliament again debated the issue and its relationship to the Federal Republic's rearmament and integration into the West. Margarete Hütter (FDP), who, together with Mende, had developed into one of the *Bundestag's* self-proclaimed experts on the legality of the war crimes program, attacked both the Allies and the German government. Hütter was particularly perturbed with the Americans. The Free Democratic lawmaker accused the United States of stopping clemency proceedings for its prisoners in order to force the German legislature into quick ratification of the EDC treaty and the contractuals. In addition, Hütter urged her colleagues not to be content with the mixed clemency commission and to push for a solution outside the treaties, meaning a general amnesty. Hütter, emphasizing the board's function as sentence but not verdict review, suspected that each Allied country would use the commission to show the validity of its war crimes trials. This, according to Hütter, would lead the Allies to deny clemency to a substantial number of the "so-called war criminals" to create a reservoir of "definite criminals" in order to prove the correctness of the proceedings.[31]

The Social Democrats remained opposed to a general amnesty. The SPD, however, was also convinced that the Allies had convicted many innocent individuals who should be given the right to appeal their verdicts. The mixed commission, the SPD argued, was an objectionable political payoff on the part of the Allies in exchange for German participation in the EDC. Fortunately, as the party pointed out, neither the fact that the Allied trials had violated the fundamental rights of some defendants nor the obviously politically motivated solution of the war criminals problem had destroyed the honor of the German soldier and the wrongly convicted. Thus, the Germans should not beg for a general amnesty for reasons of self-respect. The decision to solve the problem by way of an amnesty or clemency was in the Allied realm. For its part, the *Bundestag*, the Social Democrats urged, should ensure that justice had been accorded even to the last "prisoner of war."[32]

The day after the debate Adenauer received further suggestions from Schmid and the Foreign Affairs Committee. It appeared that the committee, after realistically considering the issue, had finally given up on the idea of creating an appellate procedure and had begun to regard a mixed commission as the best solution the Federal Republic could hope to receive. Consequently, Schmid recommended that Adenauer more fully exploit the idea of the clemency board by attempting to persuade the Allies to release a large number of prisoners before the first meeting of this body. This would greatly lighten the work load of the commission once the treaties went into effect.[33]

To the annoyance of the German government, the United States was the least willing of the Western Allied governments to agree to Schmid's suggested solution. McCloy, during his final press conference as U.S. high commissioner for Germany, made it clear that the United States would not grant clemency to a large group of Landsberg prisoners simply to ensure German ratification of the treaties.[34] These were hardly encouraging words for the foreign office, which was now gearing up for yet another battle with the subcommittee "Prisoners of War." The *Auswärtiges Amt* concluded that the Adenauer government should not expect a generous settlement from the United States. However, the foreign office shrugged off McCloy's statement as having been highly influenced by the upcoming U.S. presidential elections in November 1952. Thus, the present HICOG no-release policy might only be a temporary phenomenon. For the *Auswärtiges Amt*, Gen. Handy was the real source of concern. The commander of EUCOM, who had jurisdiction over the Army's war crimes program, had virtually shut the door on clemency requests. In the opinion of the *Auswärtiges Amt*, Handy's attitude was very dissatisfying. The Army had granted only three pardons since April 1, 1951. Despite McCloy's comments and Handy's slow progress, the foreign office hoped that the subcommittee would remain silent on the issue. In a reversal of its May policy, when it urged Adenauer to advertise his successes with the Allies before the German public, the *Auswärtiges Amt* now thought that the government could best deal with the problem through constant (and secret) contact with the Allies. Furthermore, the summer of 1952 was an inopportune time for the government to press for a general amnesty, as the subcommittee had demanded earlier. Such a request, the *Auswärtiges Amt* felt, would only lead to a harsher war crimes policy.[35]

The subcommittee agreed only partly with the *Auswärtiges Amt's* position. At its July 18, 1952, meeting the members rejected a proposal calling for a general amnesty. The lawmakers, however, added another potentially damaging demand. The subcommittee voted to propose that the Adenauer government inform the imprisoned war criminals about any progress made during the Allied-German negotiations. The rationale was that such information would lead to a "positive attitude" on the part of the prisoners and their relatives. The foreign office objected to this suggestion for fear that it might endanger the secrecy of the talks. As a result, the subcommittee "Prisoners of War" reduced its proposal to allow the foreign office to formulate such information in a very general manner in order to avoid negative consequences for the negotiations.[36]

The *Auswärtiges Amt* accordingly decided to circumvent the subcommittee's order. The foreign office had first discussed this proposal with the justice ministry's division in charge of imprisoned war criminals, the Central

Legal Protection Office, before concluding that the government could not fulfill this particular demand. Noting the confidential nature of the negotiations as well as the Allies' preference for secrecy on the subject of clemency, the *Auswärtiges Amt* opted for deceptive methods to make it appear that the Adenauer government was complying with the subcommittee's request. The foreign office thought it best to impose a news blackout on almost everything relating to the war criminals problem. This also included refusing to provide a public prognosis on the future activities of the mixed clemency board. Instead, the foreign office recommended that any information for the prisoners be formulated in such a manner that it in no way corresponded with the actual German efforts to secure their releases. By choosing deception, Adenauer could publicly portray the government's role in negotiating on behalf of the imprisoned war criminals as much less intensive than it was in reality. Such a strategy was deemed necessary to avoid a negative public reaction in the Allied countries.[37]

The government's refusal to supply information to the war criminals did not prevent individual members of the coalition from violating this policy. Mende continued constant and close contact with the prisoners and their kin. The FDP legislator was very disillusioned with recent statements by U.S. officials. Since he did not expect McCloy to grant clemency generously in the near future, Mende urged Adenauer to try another avenue. The lawmaker submitted a list of thirty-seven Landsberg prisoners whom the United States should release for "humanitarian reasons." These inmates, Mende claimed, were either ill, sixty-five years of age or older or had not legally been adults at the time of their trial. The German government was not at all enthusiastic about creating categories of prisoners to be targeted for an early release owing to special considerations. Adenauer and his cabinet feared that knowledge about the existence of such a list would only lead to discontent among the war criminals at Landsberg, Werl and Wittlich. In contrast, Mende held the general disappointment that the signing of the EDC treaty and the contractuals had not resulted in a major clemency action responsible for the alleged "uneasiness" among the detainees.[38]

If the Germans had thought that McCloy's departure might lead to a change in the U.S. position, the latter's successor, Donnelly, quickly dashed such hopes. Donnelly, who began his short tenure as U.S. high commissioner on August 1, 1952, announced during his first press conference his full support of McCloy's clemency policy. Donnelly rejected the pleas of FDP politicians for a general amnesty. The new high commissioner stated that he would continue McCloy's method of examining cases and granting pardons on an individual basis. Although promising to carefully weigh each new piece of evidence in his sentence reviews, Donnelly also felt it was time to remind the Germans that those still imprisoned for war crimes had committed offenses "which speak for themselves."[39]

Donnelly's words immediately alientated the Free Democrats. In the party's opinion, the new U.S. high commissioner had tarnished the reputation of the German military. If Donnelly could find the time to examine the files of some of the high-ranking *Wehrmacht* oficers still in prison, the FDP noted sarcastically, he would soon discover that the word "crime" was hardly appropriate to describe their deeds. Donnelly would come to similar conclusions with regard to the Malmédy trial, where a short examination of the records would prove the *SS* soldiers "were victims of misunderstandings, but not criminals."[40]

By the end of August 1952 the FDP's relentless attacks against Allied war crimes policy appeared to show some results with at least one Western Ally. The British were planning to release those classes of war criminals which Mende had outlined for Adenauer in July. The United States Ambassador to France David Bruce viewed this development with great concern. Bruce thought that a possible adoption of the Mende proposals by the British posed a number of dangers. Giving in to the Free Democrats at this stage would hurt the Allied reputation and undermine the entire war crimes program. In addition, the pardoning of entire categories of prisoners would seriously damage the concept of the mixed clemency board and violate U.S. policy, which stipulated that sentence reviews take place on a non-political and individual merit basis.[41]

In the late summer of 1952, the U.S. High Commission realized that the Allied-German clash over war crimes policy was moving into a new phase. Donnelly cautiously hinted at the necessity of changing the U.S. position and making concessions to the *Bundestag* after all. The German press and prominent politicians were continuing their efforts to whip up public opinion. As a consequence, Donnelly predicted problems for the interests of the United States in Germany and in Europe as a whole. The campaign against the war crimes program was leading German officials and the media to create much anti-Allied and anti-rearmament sentiment in the Federal Republic. The Germans, Donnelly emphasized, were doing so "in convenient ignorance of the facts" established by the war crimes trials.[42]

Ironically, the West Germans heated up the war of words at the same time as the number of imprisoned war criminals continued to decline. Figures circulating in the *Auswärtiges Amt* in September 1952 indicated that the problem was diminishing, at least numerically. The total number of Germans in the custody of foreign countries for war crimes had fallen from 1,650 on December 15, 1951, to 1,017 on September 13, 1952. The statistic also showed that the Allies had granted clemency quite generously to those prisoners inside the Federal Republic. The United States had reduced its prison population at Landsberg from 448 to 338. Britain had released 88 of 210 from Werl and France 80 of 185 from Wittlich during this period.[43]

The Allies soon discovered the real reason behind the stepped-up propaganda activities of German politicians and the Federal Republic's press. On

June 21 the German party had introduced a grand inquiry (*Große Anfrage*) in the *Bundestag* demanding that the government clarify the probable consequences of Article 6 of the contractuals. This section of the treaty dealt with the composition and authority of the mixed clemency commission. The DP's grand inquiry clearly stated that, aside from considerations of "justice and political prudence," the party viewed the release of German war criminals as a prerequisite to West Germany's rearmament.[44] Adenauer, who had decided to address this particular challenge during a debate scheduled for September 17, 1952, sought last-minute help from the Allies. The chancellor asked the Allied High Commission for permission to declare before the legislature that the Allies were considering convening the clemency board even before the treaties went into effect. The AHC, however, denied Adenauer's request.[45]

On September 17, 1952, the *Bundestag* engaged in a two and a half hour, at times bitter, debate on the issue of imprisoned war criminals. The chancellor largely avoided becoming the victim of his own secretive policies by emphasizing his government's achievements in that area. The main targets of parliamentary criticism, in any event, were the Allies. Donnelly later cabled the State Department that "all parties, except Commies, attacked [the] judgments as having served 'political ends rather than justice' and demanded that the question be resolved in the near future." The U.S. high commissioner regarded the debate as the climax of German-Allied tension which had built up throughout the spring and summer. Thus, a somewhat relieved Donnelly described the *Bundestag's* discourses on the subject as generally moderate in tone. Most importantly, Adenauer seemed to have controlled the situation and the war criminals issue appeared unlikely to jeopardize the German legislature's ratification of the EDC treaty and the contractuals.[46]

Donnelly's cable to Acheson underscored how the United States now regarded passage of the treaties in the *Bundestag*, and not the continuation of its war crimes program, as its top priority. Consequently, the U.S. High Commission was pleased to note that the coalition, although its speakers insisted that the war crimes program had violated international law, stood behind Adenauer's policy to obtain the gradual release of the prisoners within the context of the contractuals, via the mixed board.[47] Donnelly's enthusiasm over the apparently certain success of the Allied-German agreements led him to miss the finer nuances of the coalition speeches. The FDP and DP's support for the mixed board was lukewarm and only the result of these parties' realization that the United States would not agree to any other arrangement, particularly not a general amnesty. Mende emphasized this when he conceded his preference for applying the principle of a *tabula rasa* for the war criminals. The FDP lawmaker considered it more desirable to release some "unworthy individuals" during an amnesty than to continue the imprisonment of a "large number of innocent [*einen großen Teil Unschuldiger*]" inmates. For the time being, Mende agreed to solving the problem on an individual clemency rather than an amnesty basis. At the same time, he made it abundantly clear that his vote in favor of ratification depended on "settlement of the war criminals question."[48]

It was exactly this political connection between the treaties and the release of the imprisoned war criminals to which the SPD objected. SPD lawmaker Hans Merten, a former Protestant pastor, accused the Adenauer government of having destroyed the once united German front by tying the fate of the war criminals to the EDC and the contractual agreements. The Social Democrats thus used the debate to demonstrate their own patriotism to the German public. Merten harshly denounced the Allied war crimes program because it had, in his opinion, victimized many innocent individuals. Consequently, the Social Democrat believed that the imprisoned war criminals in Western custody deserved the same status as the remaining German POWs in the East.[49] Merten, who was to deliver similarly inflammatory speeches in 1955 and 1956, showed that the SPD's interest in the war criminals was by no means a "one-time derailment," as the Social Democratic Swiss paper *Volksrecht* put it while commenting on a later Merten speech.[50] Instead, it was part of a calculated Social Democratic campaign to capture additional votes by portraying the SPD as more nationalistic than the coalition and its "Allied chancellor." Assuming that the majority of Germans cared deeply about the war criminals question, the SPD decided to jump on the anti-Allied bandwagon on this issue, just in time for the September 1953 election.

The press reaction to the lengthy debate largely corresponded with Donnelly's general optimism about the *Bundestag.* However, the editorials also emphasized the need to be content with minute changes in attitude and not to expect expressions of guilt or responsibility for the past on the part of German lawmakers. For the *Hessischer Rundfunk,* the debate was already a true success merely because all parties recognized the difference between innocent and guilty prisoners. The radio network lauded the speakers of the FDP and the DP for admitting the existence of "asocial elements" among the inmates. The commentary viewed such an admission as a great leap forward, considering the often heard demand that the Allies should release all prisoners because they were all innocent.[51]

The American-sponsored *Neue Zeitung* also expressed its satisfaction with the legislature. The paper contended that the *Bundestag* and the Adenauer government had gained respect abroad for rejecting a general amnesty and for refusing to make the release of the war criminals a prerequisite to the German ratification of the treaties. The manner in which the *Bundestag* had defused this extremely nationalistic issue would reassure both the French and German public.[52] These conclusions were erroneous. Mende had reaffirmed that the Federal Republic saw nothing morally wrong with trading war criminals for rearmament. In addition, the tone of the debate had been clearly nationalistic. The French, in particular, could surely not have been pleased with German complaints about their war crimes program, voiced both by the lawmakers and high-ranking government officials like Hallstein, Adenauer's deputy foreign minister.[53]

In the weeks before the second and third readings of the EDC treaty and the contractuals, it became clear that the generally positive assessment of the *Bundestag's* "new attitude" toward the war crimes program had been premature. The Adenauer government was planning to press the Allied high commissioners to release a large number of prisoners. Renewed contact with the Allies was necessary, according to the *Auswärtiges Amt*, since both the coalition and opposition still expected the release of a substantial portion of the Allied prison populations before the final vote on the treaties.[54]

The government, well aware that the war criminals question still posed a serious threat to the treaties, again decided to end some of the secrecy regarding its negotiations with the Allies to gain additional support. In November 1952 the executive distributed a memorandum on the status of the war criminals problem to the minister presidents of the *länder* as well as leading members of the *Bundestag*. The *Auswärtiges Amt*, in charge of preparing the memorandum, was careful not to reveal the more sensitive aspects of the issue. Since the document had originally been written to supply information to the minister presidents only, the foreign office chose to alter it now that its readership had expanded to include less trustworthy key legislators. Thus, the revised document no longer contained the section dealing with the activities of the Central Legal Protection Office on behalf of German war criminals in France. In addition, to avoid having to list the number of executed prisoners for fear of a nationalistic backlash, the *Auswärtiges Amt* limited its statistics to the total numbers of prisoners on a given date. By not creating single categories such as "released," the government thus did not have to account for numerical discrepancies, that is the numbers of prisoners who died of natural causes during imprisonment or those who were actually executed for war crimes. The foreign office also emphasized that the larger part of the 971 Germans still imprisoned had not served as members of the regular armed forces, the *Wehrmacht*.[55] The government evidently assumed that the *Bundestag* would be less willing to lobby on behalf of inmates who had once belonged to Nazi organizations like the *Gestapo*, the *SD* or the *SS*, instead of the still "reputable" *Wehrmacht*.

The German government, which by now prided itself on its "courage to be unpopular" by continuing to support the concept of the mixed commission, was not alone in its public relations effort to ensure passage of the treaties even among the greatest foes of the war crimes program. On November 28, 1952, Donnelly met with Hütter and Mende to discuss the war criminals problem. With less than a week to go before the second reading of the treaties in the *Bundestag*, Donnelly informed the lawmakers of a new HICOG medical parole policy aimed at securing the release of high-ranking army officers at Christmas time. Mende repeated his call for the release of prisoners over sixty-five years of age as well as sick inmates. In addition, he again urged the Americans to grant clemency to those who had not legally been adults at the time of their war crimes trials. Hütter demanded that the U.S. High Commission release all former soldiers before any Germans would begin to serve as conscripts or volunteers in the EDC. The two Free Democrats wished to avoid the impression that they were attempting to blackmail the United States into concessions in exchange for their votes for the treaties. Thus, Hütter and Mende pretended to show some understanding of the U.S. position and conceded that the mixed board would have to convene before the Americans could meet these demands.[56] Donnelly was not yet prepared to completely repudiate the U.S. war crimes program, at least publicly. He agreed with Mende and Hütter to issue a press release that mentioned none of the details the three had discussed. Consequently, on the following day the *Neue Zeitung* only reported that the three had discussed the possibility of some releases before Christmas.[57]

If Donnelly had assumed that his policy of appeasement toward the FDP would lead Mende and Hütter to vote for the treaties after the second reading, he was badly mistaken. On December 4 the two were among eight FDP deputies who voted "no" in an intraparty trial vote. The deputies blamed the unsolved war criminals problem for their opposition to the Allied-German agreements.[58]

The Social Democrats also continued to use the imprisoned war criminals in their attempts to defeat the EDC treaty and the contractuals. On December 3, 1952, the beginning of the second reading in the *Bundestag*, the Social Democrats introduced a resolution calling for a treaty between the Federal Republic and France on the treatment of convicted war criminals and those who were still under investigation. The SPD had apparently given up hope that the majority of the *Bundestag* would vote against the agreements. Consequently, the resolution aimed at blocking the deposition of the ratification documents, the diplomatic procedure referring to the exchange of the treaties after the heads of state had signed them. The Social Democrats wanted to prevent this exchange as long as a separate Franco-German treaty covering the war criminals in France did not exist.[59]

In spite of the SPD resolution and the negative outcome of the FDP trial vote, Adenauer was able to produce a majority in favor of the treaties after the second reading on December 5, 1952. However, due to a challenge of the treaties' constitutionality before the Federal Republic's Constitutional Court, the legislature also voted on that day to postpone the third and final reading. Five days after the vote the government admitted that Mende had voted against the treaties, even though, as the executive claimed, he approved of their foreign political concept. Adenauer decided to side with the renegade FDP legislator and blamed the Western Allies for Mende's refusal to endorse the treaties. The government found it discouraging that the Allies had not followed up on Mende's "humble suggestion" to release the sick, the old and the very young prisoners.[60]

Adenauer should have known better than to expect the release of 146 prisoners at one time. In fact, the chancellor was already aware of Allied plans to grant a Christmas amnesty and medical parole to some war criminals.[61] The Allies had agreed to release those whose sentences would "expire shortly before or soon after Christmas."[62] That was not quite true. Among the prisoners slated for release were twelve war criminals under Army jurisdiction. According to State Department records, there were no remaining Army prisoners whose sentences expired as early as December 1952 and before January 31, 1953, the U.S. cutoff date for its Christmas amnesty. Consequently, none of these inmates was truly eligible to be included in the amnesty, an indication that their release was intended as a concession to the Germans.[63]

The U.S. High Commission for Germany concluded after the second vote that attempts to deal with the problem would have to go far beyond Christmas amnesties and the current pace of individual clemency releases. The *Bundestag* had used its December 5 approval of the treaties to fire another warning shot by reminding the Allies of this "psychological prerequisite" to German rearmament.[64] Consequently, HICOG's Political Affairs Division, in a lengthy memorandum on the war criminals question and possible solutions, outlined for Acheson the grave danger for U.S. policy in Europe and Germany. Noting that every party, with the exception of the Communists, had attacked the war crimes trials, HICOG viewed the imprisoned war criminals as a problem which would adversely affect the EDC, German-Allied relations and Adenauer's pro-Western foreign policy. In addition, U.S. officials wanted Adenauer to win the September 1953 federal elections. But the war criminals problem had put the chancellor in the very awkward position of appearing to be more pro-Allied than pro-German. According to the memorandum, it was time to act since

if some progress in solving the question is not made well before the elections, the CDU will have to choose between maintaining its present moderation on the subject, thus running the risk of losing some of its more national-minded voters, and itself adopting a more nationalistic, demanding attitude. Either course would be unfortunate in the light of present American policy.[65]

To solve the problem and thus eliminate this perceived irritant in American-German relations, HICOG proposed a liberal clemency policy for all but two categories of prisoners even before the mixed board went into action. Having concluded that the mixed commission would be too slow in its establishment and operation, the U.S. High Commission suggested that the board only deal with the following cases: prisoners who had been ringleaders or active participants in the murder or torture of POWs and those defendants who had been convicted for their involvement in concentration camps, euthanasia, medical experiments and mobile killing squads. For all other war criminals, including the High Command generals and the Malmédy trial defendants, U.S. authorities should be more lenient in applying sentence reductions and parole in the coming months. As a result, the mixed board would only have to deal with the most serious of war criminals, for whom the *Bundestag* and the German public might have only little sympathy. Emphasizing its belief that time was running out, HICOG estimated that the United States would have six to nine months to rid itself of the second category. This would prevent a dangerously intensive revival of German nationalism and a further drift to the right in the *Bundestag.* The result would be a sincere German commitment to the EDC and to the chancellor's pro-Western policies.[66]

Acheson fully agreed with HICOG's assessment. In one of his last cables to the U.S. High Commission, the secretary voiced concern with the way in which the war criminals question had emerged as a "highly emotional and political problem of considerable proportions." He also expressed doubts about the use of the mixed board to improve the German attitude toward the Allies. The delay and uncertainties in the ratification process in Germany and France did not inspire confidence that the mixed board, as part of the contractual agreements, would ever come into existence. Acheson accordingly thanked HICOG for submitting proposals for alternative solutions of the war criminals problem. The Truman administration had hoped that the treaties and the mixed commission would quiet German protests against the continuation of the war crimes program. It had failed to anticipate the extent to which the *Bundestag* would exploit the issue and had neglected to draw up plans for emergencies such as the possibility of non-ratification.[67]

On March 19, 1953, the *Bundestag* ratified the EDC treaty and the contractuals. In the end, the German legislature was unwilling to defeat the chancellor's foreign political program because of the war criminals question. It had done its part to set in motion the mechanism to eliminate the problem—the mixed clemency and parole board. However, the French Chamber of Deputies had yet to approve the treaties. Despite the delay in France, the *Bundestag* did not dwell on the issue with the same intensity it had displayed earlier, particularly in 1952. The Allies and Adenauer prevented another outbreak of anti-Allied hostility by establishing interim mixed boards on a zonal basis, while the treaties were still pending in the French parliament. This arrangement helped avoid the impression of a complete end to clemency and parole releases from Landsberg, Wittlich and Werl. But the government was also careful to point out to the *Bundestag* that the number of prisoners had continued to decrease even before the agreement on the interim mixed boards was reached. On June 25, 1953, Hallstein reported to the legislature that 811 Germans were still imprisoned for war crimes as of June 1. Two weeks later that number had been cut to 788.[68]

The chancellor himself made sure that the German electorate would credit his government with solving the war criminals problem. Only three days before the September 6, 1953, election, the government-published *Bulletin* offered a lengthy explanation of the new German-Allied arrangement. By then, the number of war criminals in Landsberg, Werl and Wittlich alone had shrunk to 449, with the majority, 292 inmates, held by the United States. All three interim commissions had authority to review sentences, to grant clemency and to consider eligibility for parole. Far more important, from Adenauer's perspective, was the plan to put Germans on the interim boards.[69] This ensured participation in the last domain from which the Allies had so far excluded the Germans, the war crimes program. The presence of German members on the review commission was also expected to lead to greater leniency.

In any event, Adenauer's coalition won the 1953 election. Sensitive to political realities, the chancellor used the swearing-in of his cabinet on October 20 to prevent the war criminals problem from again emerging as a serious source of friction between the *Bundestag* and the Allies during his second term in office. In his speech, Adenauer emphasized his government's hope for a speedy examination of all cases "so that those who have not committed any real crimes will soon be released and experience a reduction of their sentences without delay."[70]

The government reassured the *Bundestag's* Foreign Affairs Committee that it remained committed to a speedy resolution of the war criminals problem. Since the three interim boards did not begin their work until late October and November 1953, the foreign office was justifiably worried that the committee might become impatient. Thus, on December 9 the Foreign Affairs Committee ordered the *Auswärtiges Amt* to submit a report on the activities of the mixed boards. The foreign office did not yet have much progress to report and limited its response to outlining the government's efforts to secure the creation of these commissions and their functioning. The foreign office was careful to point out that the current arrangement might actually be more desirable than the Article 6 mixed board, which was part of the still not ratified (by France) treaties. The work of three commissions in the Western zones of occupation was more likely to produce quick results than only one German-Allied board.[71]

By January 1954 the *Auswärtiges Amt* finally possessed some statistics on the board's work. The mixed commissions were functioning very well from the German standpoint. Since mid-December, the Allies had released sixty-eight prisoners. Of these, fifty-nine were paroled due to the boards' recommendations. Again, the development in the French zone was most gratifying. The French High Commission had fulfilled thirty-two clemency requests. Half of those were parole decisions.[72]

Some delays existed in the British and American zones. Clemency requests to British authorities consumed more time since the board's recommendations were sent directly to the London government instead of the British High Commission. In the U.S. zone, the volume of paperwork seemed to hamper the German-American commission's work. A total of 182 Landsberg prisoners had fulfilled the requirements for parole by having served one-third of their sentences. The great majority of these war criminals actually filed for parole, thus flooding the board with requests. To avoid potential problems, particularly with the *Bundestag,* the foreign office urged HICOG to cut through the red tape and quickly conclude formalities.[73]

On August 30, 1954, the French parliament voted against ratification of the EDC treaty and the contractual agreements. This action, for the time being, also sounded the death knell for the German-Allied mixed sentence review commission on a treaty basis. However, the Allies and the Federal Republic quickly signed a new set of agreements in Paris in the fall of that year. These documents also called for the end of the occupation. In addition, West Germany was admitted to NATO with its own national army. Although a potentially more negative development for France than the concept of the supranational EDC, the French legislature approved this arrangement with surprising speed.[74] The mixed board now became part of the German-Allied *Convention on the Settlement of Matters Arising out of the War and the Occupation.* As soon as the new treaties went into effect, the commission was to become active.[75]

The debate concerning the ratification of the Paris treaties offered the *Bundestag* a renewed opportunity to express its misgivings about the war criminals problem. Many legislators again called for a general amnesty as the "psychological prerequisite" for German participation in Western defense. Dissatisfaction with the Allied war crimes program continued to cut across party lines. The war criminals issue appeared to remain a threat to Adenauer's foreign policy, even among the coalition parties. The chancellor had added another rightist element, the All-German Block/Federation of Expellees and Dispossessed (*Gesamtdeutscher Block/Bund der Heimatvertriebenen und Entrechteten: GB/BHE*), to his coalition. This party also opposed Adenauer's pro-European policy. However, by making it part of the government, the chancellor was in the end able to control the dangerous nationalist forces in the Federal Republic.[76]

This did not mean, however, that the right wing of the government coalition did not attempt to push Adenauer himself into a more nationalistic direction. On November 12, 1954, the DP and the All-German Block introduced a grand inquiry regarding the fate of the remaining German war criminals in Allied prisons. The two parties wanted to know if Adenauer was prepared to press the Allies for a general amnesty before the ratification of the Paris treaties.[77] The grand inquiry was potentially damaging to the chancellor. The rules of procedure required an answer in the *Bundestag,* whereas the government could respond to a little inquiry (*Kleine Anfrage*) in writing to the concerned parties. The foreign office, as usual afraid of publicity, attempted to persuade the coalition partners to alter their motion to a little inquiry, thus preventing a renewed public debate on the war criminals issue.[78]

Neither the BG/BHE nor the DP agreed to withdraw the grand inquiry, even after the *Auswärtiges Amt* had informed the parties' leadership about the motion's inherent risks. The All-German Block thought that the release of all prisoners could only be achieved by giving up secrecy and informing the public.[79] The DP was also unwilling to abandon the grand inquiry, but it at least suggested a number of alternatives such as referring the problem to committee or delaying the debate until after Christmas. Postponement of the debate would avoid endangering the upcoming Christmas releases of imprisoned war criminals, which the *Bundestag* anticipated. Neither solution was popular with the U.S. High Commission. HICOG insisted on dealing with the issue in a highly confidential manner. The Americans feared the prospect of becoming targets of the U.S. press as a result of the numerous releases of Landsberg prisoners after the convening of the German-American interim board.[80]

In early December 1954 Adenauer responded in writing to the grand inquiry of the DP and the All-German Block. The chancellor hoped that this precautionary gesture might lead to the scrapping of the motion. Adenauer warned of the possible negative consequences for the fate of the prisoners in Western custody, should the *Bundestag* decide to proceed with its plans for a public discussion. The government reiterated its opposition to the call for a general amnesty as only leading to negative public reaction abroad. Fortunately, the legislature itself had provided the chancellor with another valuable argument against this demand. The first *Bundestag* itself had rejected the concept of a *tabula rasa* during its debates on the ratification of the EDC treaty and the contractuals.[81]

The second *Bundestag* heeded neither Adenauer nor HICOG's wishes and used the time prior to the ratification of the Paris conventions on February 27, 1955, to attack anew the Allies and their war crimes policy. The legislature had precious few new arguments to make. Mende, who only grudgingly supported the concept of the sentence review commission in favor of a general amnesty, suggested forming mixed boards for each country still holding German war criminals, and not just the three major Western Allies.[82] The DP and the All-German Block, as expected, pleaded for the application of a *tabula rasa.*[83] The Social Democrats continued to portray their party as respectfully nationalistic. SDP Deputy Merten repeated his opposition to the entire concept of a mixed review and clemency commission and expressed his party's hope that the new board, contained in the Paris conventions, would never have to convene because the Allies might release all "prisoners of war" before the German-Allied agreements became effective. The Social Democrats refused to commit themselves to demanding a general amnesty, but left it up to the Allies to solve the war criminals problem, as long as this was done quickly.[84]

The February debate was the last time that the *Bundestag* discussed the war criminals problem before the Federal Republic gained its sovereignty on May 5, 1955. The legislature clearly emerged as the victor in the war of words with the Allies, for in the end the Allied governments succumbed to the pressure by the German legislature and agreed to dismantle the war crimes program. The Allies themselves provided the parliament with the opportunity to demand a solution of the war criminals problem to its liking. By conveying the impression that the defense of the West would not be possible without Germany's participation, the Western Allies set the stage for ever-increasing German assertiveness. The experience with Mende and other FDP deputies showed that many in the *Bundestag* were perfectly willing to blackmail the Allies into solving the problem prior to any German commitments to Western defense. Similarly, the Social Democrats did not hesitate to use the imprisoned war criminals to endear themselves to the German electorate, a rather shady tactic to gain votes. It is truly ironic, particularly from the American standpoint, that the Communists were the only faction supporting the Allied trials and the continued imprisonment of convicted German war criminals. Even that support was suspect, however, stemming from the KPD's desire to prevent the release of former military officers.[85] The Communists apparently thought that such a tactic would delay West German rearmament and integration.

Adenauer himself is responsible for much of the criticism he received from the legislature. From the very beginning, the *Bundestag* had made known its interest in the fate of the Wittlich, Landsberg and Werl prisoners. Adenauer, who at times made important foreign policy decisions without even informing his cabinet, preferred to solve the war criminals problem in secrecy. This aspect of his management style, coupled with his adoption of only one of the Foreign Affairs Committee's proposals as official German policy, invited complications. Such a procedure allowed the opposition and the conservative coalition partners to exploit the issue even further and to increase their demands.

It would be a mistake, however, to attribute the *Bundestag's* attitude solely to a feeling of exclusion from the foreign policy-making process. Almost all of the legislators regarded the war crimes program as unjust and a violation of international law. In addition, many were convinced that the prisoners in Allied custody had not committed any crimes. Some, like the chancellor himself, modified this argument by admitting that terrible offenses had taken place, but on orders from above. This, they felt, exonerated individual offenders. Most importantly, during the period between the creation of the Federal Republic and the attainment of its sovereignty, the parliament stubbornly refused to accept any responsibility for Nazi Germany's atrocities and war crimes. Instead, legislators of almost all parties portrayed the Allies as the villains and the violators of the law.

NOTES

1. Friedrich, *Die kalte Amnestie*, 305-312.

2. Henry Ashby Turner, *The Two Germanies since 1945* (New Haven: Yale University Press, 1987), 68-69.

3. Donnelly to Acheson, September 17, 1952, RG 338, USAREUR, Box 466, Cables File.

4. Hoppe to Hallstein, June 4, 1951, *Auswärtiges Amt*, File 515-00 g II, Document 4797/51.

5. *Heidelberger Juristenkreis* to the subcommittee "Prisoners of War," October 23, 1951, *Auswärtiges Amt*, File 515-00 h II, unnumbered/51.

6. Kranzbühler defended Admiral Karl Doenitz before the International Military Tribunal. His other clients were Odilo Burkhart in U.S. v. Flick, *Trials of War Criminals*, VI; and Hermann Schmitz in U.S. v. Krauch, ibid., VII-VIII.

7. v. Trützschler to Hallstein, October 29, 1951, *Auswärtiges Amt*, File 515-00 h II, Document 12515/51.

8. Ibid. Von Trützschler had good reason to be annoyed. In addition to having to defend the chancellor, who liked to go it alone in foreign policy matters, v. Trützschler was facing a much more serious challenge in the fall of 1951. The foreign officer in charge of convicted German war criminals was now himself under investigation by a *Bundestag* committee for his Nazi past. The committee, brought into existence as the result of an SPD motion, examined allegations against v. Trützschler, Adenauer's close friend Blankenhorn and nineteen other members of the *Auswärtiges Amt*, who had previously served in Hitler's foreign office. The charges had been made by the *Frankfurter Rundschau* in a series of articles, in which the paper accused v. Trützschler of having authored several white books on Nazi foreign policy. Although the *Bundestag* investigation ended with a slap on the wrist for v. Trützschler, it came at a rather inopportune time for Adenauer, who wanted to demonstrate to the Allies that the Federal Republic had matured enough to take its rightful place in the community of free and honorable nations. See, *Drucksache Nr. 2680*, October 12, 1951, *Verhandlungen des deutschen Bundestages, 1. Wahlperiode*; and *Drucksache Nr. 3465*, June 18, 1952, ibid.

9. Schmid to Adenauer, November 15, 1951, *Auswärtiges Amt*, File 515-00 h II, Document 14296/51.

10. v. Trützschler to Hallstein, November 19, 1951, ibid., Document 13644/51.

11. *Drucksache Nr. 2845*, November 19, 1951, *Verhandlungen des deutschen Bundestages, 1. Wahlperiode*.

12. Hoppe to Hallstein, December 4, 1951, *Auswärtiges Amt*, File 515-00 h II, Document 14184/51.

13. v. Trützschler to CDU Deputy Heinrich Höfler, December 24, 1951, ibid., Document 15405/51.

14. On April 1, 1950, a total of 3,643 Germans were imprisoned for war crimes by the Allies and other European countries. Of these, 1,315 were inmates at Landsberg, Werl and Wittlich. By December 15, 1951, these figures had shrunk significantly. The total had been reduced to 1,650 and the number of Allied prisoners on German soil was now 853. The United States held 458 (down from 663) war criminals at Landsberg, Britain 210 (down from 379) at Werl and France 185 (down from 273) at Wittlich. *Auswärtiges Amt*, File 515-11 II, Document 8105/52.

15. McCloy to Acheson, February 4, 1952, RG 466, Papers of John J. McCloy, Classified General Records 1949-1952, Box 36, D (52) 300.

16. For examples of this argument, see *230. Sitzung*, September 17, 1952, *Verhandlungen des deutschen Bundestages, 1. Wahlperiode*; and Adenauer to Schuman, June 14, 1952, *Auswärtiges Amt*, File 515-11 II, Document 6404/52. McCloy had earlier heard similar statements from Schmid and the Foreign Affairs Committee.

"Bonn Legislators Press McCloy for Amnesty for War Criminals," *New York Times,* January 10, 1951, 10.

17. *Drucksache Nr. 3078,* February 8, 1952, *Verhandlungen des deutschen Bundestages, 1. Wahlperiode.*

18. Hoppe to Hallstein, February 12, 1952, *Auswärtiges Amt,* File 515-00 h II, Document 1956/52.

19. Hoppe to Hallstein, February 18, 1952, ibid., Document 2281/52.

20. *Presse- und Informationsamt der Bundesregierung, Bulletin,* February 23, 1952, 217.

21. SPD Deputy Alfred Gleisner to Adenauer, April 4, 1952, *Auswärtiges Amt,* File 515-11 II, Document 6020/52.

22. Hoppe to Hallstein, April 25, 1952, *Auswärtiges Amt,* File 515-00 h II, Document 8822/52.

23. Baring, *Außenpolitik in Adenauers Kanzlerdemokratie,* 57.

24. Hoppe to Hallstein, April 25, 1952, *Auswärtiges Amt,* File 515-00 h II, Document 8822/52.

25. Ibid.

26. McCloy to Acheson, May 2, 1952, RG 466, Papers of John J. McCloy, Classified General Records 1949-1952, Box 41, D (52) 1096.

27. Blankenhorn to Gleisner, May 23, 1952, *Auswärtiges Amt,* File 515-11 II, Document 6020/52.

28. McCloy to Adenauer, July 3, 1952, ibid., 10401 Spr. 586/52.

29. Transport Minister Hans-Christoph Seebohm to Adenauer, June 5, 1952, *Auswärtiges Amt,* File 515-11 E II, Document 9517/52.

30. "Kriegsverbrecherfrage gefährdet die Verträge," *Die Welt,* June 20, 1952, 1.

31. *222. Sitzung,* July 10, 1952, *Verhandlungen des deutschen Bundestages, 1. Wahlperiode,* 9888-9891.

32. Ibid., 9891-9892.

33. Schmid to Adenauer, July 11, 1952, *Auswärtiges Amt,* File 515-11 II, Document 9642/52.

34. "M'Cloy Confident on West Germany," *New York Times,* July 17, 1952, 4.

35. Dr. Karl-Hans Born to Dr. Gottfried Kaumann, German foreign officers, July 17, 1952, *Auswärtiges Amt,* File 515-00 h II, Document 9472/52.

36. Kaumann to Hallstein, July 19, 1952, ibid., Document 9596/52.

37. Kaumann to Hallstein, August 2, 1952, ibid.

38. Mende to Adenauer, July 19, 1952, *Auswärtiges Amt,* File 515-11 II, Document 9706/52.

39. "Absage an Kriegsverbrecher," *Die Welt,* August 5, 1952, 1.

40. "Donnelly 'schlecht beraten," *Die Welt,* August 7, 1952, 1.

41. David Bruce, U.S. ambassador to France, to Acheson, August 28, 1952, RG 466, U.S. High Commission for Germany, Security-Segregated General Records 1949-1952, Box 28, 321.6, German War Criminals File.

42. Donnelly to Acheson, September 10, 1952, RG 338, USAREUR, Box 466, Cables File.

43. v. Trützschler to Hallstein, September 14, 1952, *Auswärtiges Amt,* File 515-11 II, Document 12102/52, Anlage 2.

44. *Drucksache Nr. 3477,* June 21, 1952, *Verhandlungen des deutschen Bundestages, 1. Wahlperiode.*

45. François-Poncet to Adenauer, September 16, 1952, *Bundeszwischenarchiv*, File B141-9577, 80-81.

46. Donnelly to Acheson, September 17, 1952, RG 338, USAREUR, Box 466, Cables File.

47. See the speeches of Wahl and Mende, *230. Sitzung*, September 17, 1952, *Verhandlungen des deutschen Bundestages, 1. Wahlperiode*, 10496-10498, 10502-10505.

48. Ibid., 10503-10504.

49. Ibid., 10498-10502.

50. "Nur eine einmalige Entgleisung," *Volksrecht*, March 3, 1955.

51. Presse- und Funkbericht, September 18, 1952, 1.

52. "Respektgewinn," *Neue Zeitung*, September 19, 1952.

53. *230. Sitzung*, September 17, 1952, *Verhandlungen des deutschen Bundestages, 1. Wahlperiode*, 10504.

54. *Referat XIIa, Auswärtiges Amt*, to Hallstein, October 14, 1952, *Auswärtiges Amt*, File 515-11 II, Document 9642/52.

55. Born to Blankenhorn, November 17, 1952, ibid., Document 14652/52.

56. Donnelly to Acheson, November 28, 1952, RG 466, U.S. High Commission for Germany, Security-Segregated General Records 1949-1952, Box 28, 321.6, German War Criminals File.

57. "Donnelly empfängt Bundestagsabgeordnete," *Neue Zeitung*, November 29, 1952.

58. *Presse- und Informationsamt der Bundesregierung, Schnellinformation*, December 4, 1952, 1.

59. *Umdruck Nr. 713*, December 3, 1952, *Verhandlungen des deutschen Bundestages, 1. Wahlperiode*.

60. *Presse- und Informationsamt der Bundesregierung, Schnellinformation*, December 10, 1952.

61. Donnelly to Acheson, December 9, 1952, RG 466, U.S. High Commission for Germany, Security-Segregated General Records 1949-1952, Box 28, 321.6, German War Criminals File.

62. Donnelly to Acheson, December 9, 1952, ibid.

63. Acheson to Donnelly, December 11, 1952, ibid.

64. Internal memorandum, *Auswärtiges Amt*, December 30, 1952, File 515-11 h II, Document 20108/52.

65. HICOG to State Department, December 11, 1952, RG 466, U.S. High Commission for Germany, Security-Segregated General Records 1949-1952, Box 28, 321.6, German War Criminals File.

66. Ibid.

67. Acheson to Acting High Commissioner Samuel Reber, January 7, 1953, RG 466, U.S. High Commission for Germany, Security-Segregated General Records 1953-1955, Box 164, 321.6, War Criminals—Mixed Board File.

68. *276. Sitzung*, June 25, 1953, *Verhandlungen des deutschen Bundestages, 1. Wahlperiode*.

69. *Presse- und Informationsamt der Bundesregierung, Bulletin*, September 3, 1953, 1397-1398.

70. *3. Sitzung*, October 20, 1953, *Verhandlungen des deutschen Bundestages, 2. Wahlperiode*.

71. *Auswärtiges Amt* memorandum *Zwischenbericht über die Tätigkeit der Gemischten Beratungsausschüße und über den Stand des sogenannten Kriegsverbrecherproblems allgemein*, December 17, 1953, ibid., Document 22250/53.

72. v. Trützschler to Hallstein, January 7, 1954, File 515-00 h, Document 204-54 56/A.

73. Ibid.

74. Baring, *Außenpolitik in Adenauers Kanzlerdemokratie*, 333-334.

75. *Vertrag zur Regelung aus Krieg und Besatzung entstandener Fragen*, March 31, 1955, *Bundesgesetzblatt, Teil II*, 411-413.

76. Richard Hiscocks, *The Adenauer Era* (New York: Lippincott, 1966), 100-102.

77. *Drucksache Nr. 979*, November 12, 1954, *Verhandlungen des deutschen Bundestages, 2. Wahlperiode*.

78. Brückner to Blankenhorn, November 24, 1954, *Auswärtiges Amt*, File 204-515-00 h, Document 4515/54.

79. Dr. Jansen, German foreign officer, to Blankenhorn, December 3, 1954, ibid., Document 4826/54.

80. Brückner to Blankenhorn, December 6, 1954, ibid., Document 4579/54.

81. Adenauer to Joachim v. Merkatz, chairman of the DP faction; and Horst Hasler, chairman of the DP faction; December 7, 1954, ibid.

82. *62. Sitzung*, December 16, 1954, *Verhandlungen des deutschen Bundestages, 2. Wahlperiode*, 3218-3220.

83. Ibid., 3240-3243; and *66. Sitzung*, February 17, 1955, 3382-3383.

84. *71. Sitzung*, February 26, 1955, ibid., 3841-3844.

85. *230. Sitzung*, September 17, 1952, *Verhandlungen des deutschen Bundestages, 1. Wahlperiode*, 10506-10507.

Conclusion

The war crimes program failed to achieve the two major goals of American occupation authorities. It did not adequately punish convicted war criminals. In addition, it did not convince the Germans that their society with its authoritarian and militaristic traditions needed reform. These failures cannot be attributed to one single factor but were the consequence of a variety of reasons. Trials of war criminals were, as this study has shown, controversial on both sides of the Atlantic Ocean. Nonetheless, public controversy alone did not bring down the program. As important, the planning and the execution of this particular occupation policy as well as the negative German response were the reasons for its demise. I shall begin with the planning for the war crimes program.

American officials' first serious mistake involved their failure to define a general long-term punishment policy for post-surrender Germany. The treatment of convicted war criminals became detached from other American operations. Were the war crimes program to succeed, it would require a firm foundation in the overall goals of the United States. Such a foundation did not exist. By the late 1940s U.S. occupation officials were concerned with setting the groundwork for the inclusion of Germany in the Western front against Soviet communism. Punishment of war criminals, which had been part of almost every American proposal with regard to the treatment of post-war Germany, ceased to be a priority, and became instead a political burden in the 1950s.

In addition, as the files of the EUCOM Judge Advocate Division and the opinions of U.S. civil courts in war crimes cases document, constitutional and legal considerations during the 1940s were extremely important. Many American officials were troubled by the procedure for the trials of war criminals, based on the London Agreement of 1945, and the absence of an appellate court in particular. Not only was this a departure from the Anglo-

American legal tradition, it also mandated that other remedies had to be found to allow defendants to challenge at least their sentences, if not the verdicts. Furthermore, war crimes courts were not always consistent. In fact, time appears to have played a major role in sentencing. During the immediate post-war years defendants could rarely expect leniency. By 1947, however, the tribunals had begun to hand down milder sentences. Consequently, U.S. authorities became increasingly concerned with what they called "sentence equalization," stressing that comparable offenses should receive equal punishment. Since civil courts refused to assume jurisdiction over the Landsberg prisoners, Generals Clay and Handy decided to go beyond the normal review process to which defendants before courts-martial are normally entitled. This resulted in the creation of the Boards of Review and the War Crimes Modification Board. Clemency and sentence modification effectively substituted for an appellate procedure.

McCloy had similar motivations when he first came to Germany, although some historians have accused him of granting clemency to the war criminals under his jurisdiction in order to establish a good relationship with the Germans. While there may be an element of truth in this contention, McCloy's primary interest in setting up his Advisory Board on Clemency was to ensure sentence equalization. The German reaction to McCloy's January 1951 commutation shows that the high commissioner's decisions regarding the HICOG prisoners were not viewed as a gesture of friendship. McCloy apparently learned his lesson and resisted the increasing German pressure for additional large-scale releases.

The U.S. war crimes program posed other problems. For one, prosecutors tended to rely excessively on conspiracy or common design indictments instead of focusing on specific criminal acts. The fact that the sentence review process focused on evidence of individual crimes made such a prosecutorial strategy particularly risky, as the Ilse Koch case made abundantly clear. One can argue that the American prosecutors had to rely on this tactic in order to obtain convictions in the first place. In fact, it is questionable if Col. Peiper would have ever been found guilty of murder in the Malmédy case since, as Gen. Handy later stated in a memorandum, there was no evidence that Peiper actually shot a POW. The Ferguson subcommittee rightly criticized the Army for failing to adjust the indictments before its war crimes courts to the priorities of reviewing authorities. Similar shortcomings of the program involved the appearances of conflicts of interest, which Theater Judge Advocate Damon Gunn brought to the attention of the commander in chief in the late 1940s. It was clearly improper for the deputy theater judge advocate for war crimes to serve as prosecutor and as the first reviewing instance. The same can be said about the theater judge advocate's presence on the EUCOM War Crimes Modification Board. These mistakes highlighted the inadequacies of the planning process. American officials had not paid much attention to the post-trial treatment of convicted war criminals. They also had not given much thought to the possibility that the desire to punish the perpetrators might weaken considerably the more the war faded into distant memory. This led to a confusing array of *ad hoc* measures to address questions of legality and propriety that should have been dealt with long before they arose.

Another serious mistake was the decision to split the jurisdiction over the Landsberg prisoners, which led to considerable in-fighting between the Army's European Command and the U.S. High Commission. The clearest indication of distrust between the two bureaucracies was Gen. Handy's refusal to agree to the creation of one clemency board for both HICOG and EUCOM prisoners in 1950. There were numerous other instances of disagreement between U.S. military and civilian occupation authorities, notably the dispute over the availability of trial records and the amount of good conduct time. The Army, which held a tougher attitude toward war criminals, viewed HICOG as too lenient. In return, the High Commission worried that the unwillingness to take a softer stance on the part of EUCOM commanders would adversely affect Allied-German relations. In addition, the U.S. decision to divide its prisoners into two groups allowed German critics of the war crimes operation to charge that all inmates did not receive equal treatment. The Protestant and Catholic bishops, for example, alleged that the more prominent defendants from the Nuremberg program had many advantages over prisoners under Army jurisdiction. The Nuremberg defendants, they argued, were benefiting from sentence reviews conducted by independent jurists, complete trial records and competent American judges, who had held positions on the highest state and federal courts before coming to Germany.

Despite these criticisms, it is important to recognize that U.S. war crimes authorities acted in good faith during the 1940s. These officials did their best to carry out their mission in an environment which was becoming increasingly hostile to the concept of punishment for war criminals. Unfortunately, the same does not hold true for the period from 1951 to 1955. After Handy and McCloy's January 1951 clemency decisions, the imprisoned war criminals became a purely political problem. This development was the result of the Allied decision to seek a German contribution to the defense of the West against a possible Soviet attack. For obvious reasons, the Allies could not dictate such a move, having come to realize that rearmament would require the abolition of the occupation regime and the restoration of full German sovereignty in the near future. Thus, the war crimes program was doomed as soon as the Adenauer government and the Allies began negotiations on German rearmament and the establishment of contractual relations. By January 1953 the continued imprisonment of convicted war criminals had become such an uncomfortable burden for the Truman administration that Acheson ordered HICOG to rid the Allied-German relationship of this "serious irritant." This position did not change with the advent of the Eisenhower administration. The British and French held similar views. As a consequence, Britain and France closed their prisons for war criminals, Werl and Wittlich, in 1957. The United States followed suit in 1958.

The emergence of the war criminals question as a major problem in Allied-German, and particularly U.S.-German relations in early 1951, led to a frantic search for a solution which would be acceptable to all sides. The United States still had to consider domestic public opinion which, for the most part, backed the punishment of war criminals. A second obstacle was the need to find a formula that conveyed the impression that the integrity and the credibility of the war crimes program had been preserved, and that the U.S. had not traded the Landsberg prisoners for German rearmament. Thus, occupation officials ruled out a general amnesty as well as any reexamination of the original verdicts and judgments. In the fall of 1951 the concept of a mixed clemency board became the best possible solution. This offered several important advantages. The United States had ample experience with clemency and sentence review commissions as a result of the earlier programs in the late 1940s. The mixed board, because removed from public scrutiny, could effectively limit criticism of individual clemency decisions. This arrangement enabled the Allied and German governments to hide the fact that they were actually dismantling the war crimes program.

Although U.S. war crimes officials had made several mistakes in planning and executing the program, its failure to reorient the German public was due to more complex reasons. The German surrender of 1945 contained elements of both continuity and discontinuity. The experiences of the war and the disastrous defeat did not lead the Germans to feel a sense of guilt. Instead, the immediate post-war years saw the emergence of a national identity consisting of both old and new features. The Germans often viewed themselves as victims of arbitrary Allied policies, but not as a people which had stood passively by while the Nazi government unleashed a world war, executed the annihilation of European Jewry and ordered the commission of numerous other crimes and atrocities. *"Schlußstrich ziehen"* (drawing the final line) became the motto of the post-war years, especially after the founding of the Federal Republic. This call for complete discontinuity, culminating in the demand for a general amnesty for war criminals in the 1950s, constituted a powerful, unifying force. It became part of the repertoires of almost every influential group in West Germany, from the Social Democrats to the churches to right wing fringe groups.

The Allied trials and imprisonment of war criminals did not permit the drawing of the final line just yet. The evidence and testimonies that were presented at these proceedings were constant and grim reminders of Germany's most recent past. Many Germans felt that the trials implied the collective guilt of the German people. But the Germans had no desire to assume final responsibility for the Nazi crimes. Instead, they chose to vigorously attack this particular Allied policy. The United States became the main target because its war crimes program was the largest and because American officials, thinking this would be educational, allowed themselves to become involved in the debate over the legality and propriety of the operation. United States authorities apparently underestimated the program's potential as a highly emotional issue, a failure which proved to be ideal to challenge the occupation as a whole. Nonetheless, the attitude of the Germans explains why the program's underlying premise that only a reform of German society would prevent similar tragedies in the future was never popularly accepted.

As Hajo Holborn discovered, his former countrymen were insensitive in discussing the past. Many Germans saw no significant differences between Nazi Germany's deeds and the actions of other powers during their occupations of foreign countries. A similar attitude prevailed with regard to war criminals. The churches, newspapers and politicians portrayed the Landsberg prisoners, particularly the generals and the defendants sentenced by Army courts, as honorable soldiers whose only crime was that they had fulfilled their orders. This view was frequently coupled with statements that the Germans wanted punishment for the "truly guilty." Unfortunately, even the admission that some of the prisoners deserved their destinies seemed insincere. The Germans conveniently failed to identify "truly guilty" individuals and the crimes they had committed. The fact that the Adenauer government, members of the *Bundestag* and bishops of both churches attempted to prevent the June 1951 executions of Pohl, Ohlendorf and the five other condemned further indicates that the use of this phrase was often insincere. If the head of the *SS* Economic and Administrative Main Office and the commanders of the mobile killing squads did not fit the "truly guilty" category, who did?

German elites attacked the war crimes program with pseudo-legal arguments during its entire existence. Many charged that the Allied trials of war criminals violated the principle of *nulla poena sine lege*. When the Basic Law went into effect in the summer of 1949, the situation became increasingly awkward. The Federal Republic's constitution outlawed the use of the death penalty, the extradition of German citizens and reliance on *ex post facto* law. None of these provisions actually affected the convicted war criminals since the Allies retained exclusive war crimes authority on the basis of the Occupation Statute. However, the program's foes could now claim that the three major Western democracies were acting against their own interests by continuing a policy which appeared to violate the provisions of the Basic Law. They charged that the German people would lose faith in their new democracy and its laws since U.S. authorities were executing prisoners as late as June 1951 and forcing German officials to commit unconstitutional acts.

Nonetheless, the failure of the American war crimes program to achieve its major goals in Germany does not negate the concept of bringing war criminals to justice. Instead, it teaches important lessons for future planners of such policies. It is likely that war crimes trials will always be perceived as expressions of victor's justice and desire for revenge. However, the controversy, which will undoubtedly surround such proceedings, should be held to a minimum. The most important aspect is proper and careful planning to prevent abuses, inconsistencies and bureaucratic in-fighting. In addition, future war crimes programs should be limited to punishing the perpetrators only and should not be used as a policy to reform and reeducate an entire people. It is questionable if the occupation as a whole convinced the Germans that their society needed to undergo significant change, or if later events such as the economic miracle actually achieved what the occupation tried to accomplish—a Federal Republic which shared the values of the West. The war crimes program, criticized because of its procedural rules and lack of legal precedent, was hardly suited for another controversial undertaking, the reform of post-war German society.

APPENDIX *A*
Individual Examples

For the most part, this study has focused on the history of the U.S. war crimes program as a whole. American occupation policies, including the trial and clemency operations, affected large numbers of Germans. All in all, the United States prosecuted over 1,800 offenders. As a consequence, individual cases cannot be presented as representative of all defendants and of every Landsberg prisoner. Less than 10 percent of these belonged to the second string of prominent former Nazi officials, tried before the twelve subsequent tribunals at Nuremberg. Among this particular group of perpetrators were many high-ranking bureaucrats, who had organized, administered and executed Nazi crimes such as the Holocaust, the use of slave labor, the mistreatment of civilian populations in the occupied territories and countless other offenses. The 1,672 defendants before U.S. Army courts at Dachau constitute an even more diverse group. The majority of war criminals convicted by the Army had murdered or mistreated American military personnel. Others had committed crimes in concentration camps now located in the U.S. zone of occupation. The Buchenwald and Malmédy trials as well as the controversies they generated have shown the weaknesses of many indictments, which relied excessively on charges of conspiracy rather than individual criminal acts. Such prosecution strategies prevent the historian from pointing to one specific case as typical of the Dachau program, not to mention the operation as a whole.

I have referred to individual cases and defendants—e.g., those charged at the Malmédy trial, Lothar Eisenträger, Ilse Koch, Otto Ohlendorf, Oswald Pohl and others in previous chapters—because of their significance to the entire war crimes program. Here, I will follow the fate of three convicted war criminals from their indictments to their releases from Landsberg. For this purpose, I have selected Martin Sandberger from the *Einsatzgruppen* trial, Georg Lörner from the *SS* Economic and Administrative Main office trial and Joachim Peiper, the commanding *SS* officer at Malmédy. While not representative of the entire trial and clemency operation, these individual cases nonetheless provide the reader with insight into the treatment of convicted war criminals in the U.S. zone.

Martin Sandberger studied law at the universities of Munich, Cologne, Tübingen and Freiburg. After graduation, he worked as an assistant judge in the Interior Administration of Württemberg. Sandberger held two more civilian positions in the Nazi government in the late 1930s before his appointment as chief of *Einsatzkommando 1a* of *Einsatzgruppe A* in June 1941. Six months later he was promoted to commander of the security police and the *Sicherheitsdienst* (*SD*) in Esthonia. His function was to execute Hitler's directive to rid the area under his control of Jews, Communists, members of the intelligentsia and others. Sandberger spent approximately two years in the Soviet Union.[1] During this time Sandberger, whose *SS* rank was *Standartenführer* (colonel), received glowing reviews for his work and political reliability, which, in the opinion of his superiors, "far exceed the average."[2]

In September 1947 a U.S. military tribunal at Nuremberg indicted Sandberger and the other *Einsatzgruppen* leaders for crimes against humanity, war crimes and membership in criminal organizations. Sandberger admitted that large numbers of Esthonian Jews and Communists had been shot under his command. However, the defendant attempted to evade responsibility by stating that he was absent during most of the killings.[3] The American judges rejected this argument and determined that Sandberger was criminally responsible for the murders since they occurred under his command. Consequently, it found the accused guilty of all three counts of the indictment.[4] Unfortunately for Sandberger, the U.S. tribunal in the *Einsatzgruppen* case did not follow the examples of other American military courts which, due to the passage of time, were becoming increasingly lenient. The proceedings against the commanders of the mobile killing squads, which had murdered approximately two million innocent victims, did not permit leniency. As a result, the *Einsatzgruppen* case ended with the largest number of death sentences ever pronounced during the subsequent Nuremberg trials. Sandberger, as a former high-ranking police and *SS* officer, was among those sentenced to die for their war crimes.[5]

The initial EUCOM review of Sandberger's sentence did not lead to a commutation to a life term. U.S. Military Governor Clay confirmed the court-assessed punishment in March 1949. Two months later the Supreme Court denied Sandberger's petition for a writ of *habeas corpus*.[6] The Army soon discovered that the defendant had influential friends in the United States. Senator William Langer sent EUCOM affidavits on Sandberger's behalf, which Langer had received from one Rev. T.W. Strieter of Chicago, on at least three occasions.[7] In return, the Army promised to delay the execution until "after thorough consideration has been given to these matters."[8] But Sandberger's fortunes changed considerably in June 1949, when McCloy became U.S. high commissioner for Germany and assumed jurisdiction over the war criminals convicted during the Nuremberg program. Essentially, this development nullified Clay's confirmation of the sentence and provided Sandberger with another opportunity for a review and a possible reduction by the U.S. High Commission.

On January 31, 1951, McCloy commuted Sandberger's sentence from death to life imprisonment. In fact, the U.S. high commissioner upheld only four of the original fourteen death sentences in the *Einsatzgruppen* case.[9] Sandberger soon benefited from an additional clemency action on the part of the U.S. High Commission. In January 1953, exactly two years after the commutation of his death sentence, the United States released Sandberger from Landsberg.[10] One can only speculate as to why McCloy decided to reduce the court-assessed punishment to such an extent. The U.S. high commissioner may have been influenced by Senator Langer's efforts on

Sandberger's behalf. A second possibility is that the desire of U.S. officials to ensure sentence equalization led to the commutation in this case. Perhaps McCloy felt that Sandberger's crimes were less severe than those of the four mobile killing squad commanders whose death sentences he reaffirmed that same month.

A similarly drastic sentence reduction occurred in the case of Georg Lörner, a former high-ranking official in the *SS* Economic and Administrative Main Office. Lörner served as a deputy chief to Oswald Pohl and was in charge of providing clothing and food for all *SS* troops (except those fighting in the field) and concentration camp inmates. In addition, Lörner was the deputy chief of Division W, controlling the economic enterprises of the *SS*. His ranks were *Gruppenführer* (major general) in the *SS* and *Generalleutnant* (major general) in the *Waffen SS*. In March 1947, Lörner, Pohl and thirteen other defendants were indicted before a U.S. military tribunal for conspiracy to commit war crimes and crimes against humanity, and membership in criminal organizations.[11]

In its November 1947 judgment the court found that Lörner had actively participated in the use of slave labor and had failed to supply adequate food and clothing to camp inmates. However, the judges did not find sufficient evidence to determine that Lörner "took a consenting part in or was actually connected with" *Aktion Reinhardt*, the code name for the systematic pillage of the Nazis' Jewish victims. The tribunal pronounced Lörner guilty of war crimes, crimes against humanity and membership in criminal organizations, after it had dropped the conspiracy charge.[12] Lörner, like his superior Pohl, received the death sentence.

Whereas the Sandberger sentence went to the Theater Judge Advocate Division for review, in Lörner's case the court itself decided to undertake reductions on its own authority before sending the trial record to EUCOM. The tribunal convened again in July 1948 to reconsider and to modify the sentences of several defendants. Lörner's punishment was commuted to life imprisonment. The court cited its inability to prove that Lörner had ever functioned officially as deputy chief of the *SS* Economic and Administrative Main Office since the prosecution had failed to present documents which the defendant had signed as deputy.[13] Clay confirmed the reduced sentence on April 30, 1949.[14] Lörner, like Sandberger, greatly benefited from McCloy's January 1951 mass sentence reduction. The U.S. high commissioner cut the life term to fifteen years.[15] The U.S. High Commission released Lörner in March 1954 after increasing good conduct time.[16]

Joachim Peiper's case was quite different from those of Sandberger and Lörner. Col. Peiper's *SS* unit had been responsible for the Malmédy massacre of American POWs and Belgian civilians. Since many victims had been American servicemen, Peiper and his co-defendants were prosecuted by the EUCOM theater judge advocate before a U.S. Army court at Dachau. News of the massacre had outraged many in the United States. In addition, the Army generally tended to react sharply to the mistreatment and murder of G.I.s. The accused soon learned that EUCOM judges were less lenient than their counterparts who presided over the subsequent Nuremberg trials. The Dachau court sentenced Peiper and forty-two others to death, even though, as Gen. Handy later admitted, no proof existed at the time that Peiper had actually shot any of the victims himself.[17]

Peiper remained on death row for the remainder of the decade. On March 20, 1948, the Theater Judge Advocate Division confirmed the sentence. In May the U.S. Supreme Court denied the prisoner's petition for writ of *habeas corpus*. A year later

Clay, as the final reviewing authority, also held that Peiper should be executed. Fortunately for Peiper, the Americans had suspended executions until after the controversy surrounding the Dachau war crimes program, and particularly the Malmédy trial, had ended. In August 1950 Peiper's case came before EUCOM's War Crimes Modification Board. Three of its five members voted to reaffirm the original sentence; the others recommended commuting it to a life term.[18]

Handy commuted Peiper's sentence on January 31, 1951, as part of his clemency decisions. Peiper was indeed fortunate. Handy had concluded that the acts of Peiper's *SS* unit were different from the "deliberate" murders in concentration camps and had occurred during a "desperate combat action."[19] During 1954 and 1955, Peiper applied for clemency with the Interim Mixed Parole and Clemency Board with varying results. In May 1954, IMPAC finally reduced his life sentence to a prison term of thirty-five years, but it rejected a second application for further modification seven months later.[20]

On March 22, 1955, IMPAC recommended that Peiper's current sentence be reduced by three years because the prisoner would then be eligible for parole in February 1956. That proposal drew protests from the Theater Judge Advocate Brig. Gen. George W. Gardes. Gardes took issue with the board's, and thus Handy's, claim that Peiper's action had been the result of a desperate combat situation. Instead, the theater judge advocate found that Peiper had abetted and encouraged his troops to kill American POWs in clear violation of the laws of war. In Gardes's opinion, this was "conclusive evidence of the criminal intent" of Peiper's order to shoot the prisoners. Gardes accused IMPAC of having paid too much attention to Peiper's good prison behavior and neglecting the nature of the crimes for which he was imprisoned at Landsberg. As a result, Gardes urged the Article 6 mixed board, which considered the case after May 5, 1955, not to reduce the sentence to thirty-two years.[21] The mixed board heeded Gardes's plea. However, a sentence of thirty-five years made Peiper eligible for parole in December, instead of February, 1956. On December 19 the Army issued Peiper's parole orders and released him from Landsberg.[22]

These three cases point to several disturbing aspects of the American war crimes program. In his final report to the State Department, IMPAC board member Plitt emphasized that excessive sentence reductions had made the operation less credible. The post-trial treatment of Sandberger, Lörner, Peiper and others strongly support Plitt's criticism. The commutations of death sentences to fifteen-year prison terms, for example, quickly led to German suspicions that the original punishment was too harsh and that the Americans themselves had lost faith in the trials. Second, the war crimes program appeared to punish perpetrators with relatively low ranks to a greater extent than the defendants of the Nuremberg program. This was particularly true when the victims had been U.S. servicemen. The March 1, 1952, prison roster shows that of 372 Landsberg war criminals 33 percent had been convicted in "flier" cases and eleven percent, including Peiper, for their involvement in the Malmédy massacre. In contrast, ten percent were from the subsequent Nuremberg tribunals. This inevitably created the impression that the lower ranks of the German army and the *SS* were subject to greater punishment than the policy-makers of Nazi atrocities. Many German critics of the war crimes operation regarded those convicted during the Army's Dachau program as common soldiers whose crimes had occurred in battle. Although largely incorrect, this view nonetheless became the rallying cry of veterans and refugee organizations, political parties and the government of the Federal Republic.

NOTES

1. U.S. v. Ohlendorf et al., *Trials of War Criminals*, IV, 532.

2. Ibid., 536.

3. Ibid., 534-535.

4. Ibid., 535.

5. Ibid., 588.

6. Ibid., 590.

7. Langer to Huebner, May 25, June 1 and June 24, 1949, RG 338, USAREUR, Box 464, Petition of Martin Sandberger File.

8. Huebner to Langer, June 27, 1949, ibid.

9. "Landsberg: A Documentary Report," January 31, 1951, RG 466, Papers of John J. McCloy, Classified General Records 1949-1952, D (51) 123.

10. Rückerl, *NS-Verbrechen vor Gericht*, 131.

11. U.S. v. Pohl et al., *Trials of War Criminals*, V, 201-208.

12. Ibid., 1004-1010.

13. Ibid., 1183-1184.

14. Ibid., 1252-1254.

15. "Landsberg: A Documentary Report," January 31, 1951, RG 466, Papers of John J. McCloy, General Classified Records 1949-1952, D (51) 123.

16. *Auswärtiges Amt*, File 204/515-11-02, Document 1781/54.

17. "43 Germans Doomed, 22 Get Life for 'Bulge' Killing of Americans," *New York Times*, July 17, 1946, 1.

18. Brig. Gen. George W. Gardes, theater judge advocate, USAREUR, to chairman, Mixed Board, August 3, 1955, RG 338, USAREUR, Box 487, Cases Tried-Miscellaneous Administration File.

19. EUCOM Release No. 51-91, January 31, 1951, ibid., Box 461, Executions of War Criminals File.

20. Gardes to chairman, Mixed Board, August 3, 1955, ibid., Box 487, Cases Tried-Miscellaneous Administration File.

21. Gardes to Commander in Chief, USAREUR, June 23, 1955, ibid.

22. Order of Parole for Joachim Peiper, December 19, 1956, ibid., Box 507, Cases Tried-Miscellaneous Orders of Parole.

The Numerical Development of the War Criminals Problem, 1950-1955

Table 1[1]

Country/ Prison	Prisoners 4-1-1950	Prisoners 12-15-1951	Prisoners 8-25-1952	Released between 4-1-1950 and 8-25-1952
Landsberg	663	458	338	325
Werl	379	210	132	247
Wittlich	273	185	105	168
France	864	376	291	573
Netherlands	218	83	72	148
Belgium	126	30	6	126
Denmark	53	14	9	44
Norway	51	26	21	30
Luxembourg	23	14	6	17
Switzerland	25	17	15	10
Italy	11	2	2	9
Greece	3	2	1	2
Yugoslavia	947	226	34	913
Brazil	7	7	1	6
Totals	**3,643**	**1,650**	**1,033**	**2,610**

---

[1] Auswärtiges Amt, File 515–11 II, Document 8105/52.

Table 2[2]

Convicted War Criminals in Western Custody	
Country/ Prison	*Prisoners 11-15-1953*
Landsberg	290
Werl	79
Wittlich	74
France	169
Holland	63
Belgium	4
Denmark	4
Norway	–
Luxembourg	6
Italy	1
Greece	–
Yugoslavia	1
Brazil	–

[2] Zentrale Rechtsschutzstelle, Statistik, November 17, 1953, Auswärtiges Amt, File 515–00 k, Document 21707/53. Of the 169 prisoners in France, 67 had not yet been convicted.

Table 3[3]

Releases between December 1, 1952 and December 18, 1953.

Country/ Prison	Total	Early	After two-thirds	After one-third	Served Full Sentence	Liberté Provis.	Found Not Guilty
Landsberg	43	27	16	–	–	–	–
Werl	30	12	18	–	–	–	–
Wittlich	29	28	–	–	1	–	–
France	80	44	–	–	14	12	10
Belgium	2	1	–	1	–	–	–
Denmark	9	9	–	–	–	..	–
Greece	1	1	–	–	–	–	–
Holland	8	7	1	–	–	–	–
Norway	14	14	–	–	–	–	–
Totals	216	143	35	1	15	12	10

[3] Ibid., December 19, 1953, Document 22350/53.

Table 4[4]

**Effects of the Work of the Interim Mixed Boards
on the Number of Imprisoned War Criminals**

Prison	*11-1-1953*	*11-1-1954*	*7-1-1955*
Landsberg	288	112	50
Werl	79	39	25
Wittlich	75	47	20
Totals	442	198	95

---

[4] Ibid., October 1, 1955, Document 3734/55.

The Effects of McCloy's January 1951 Decisions on Prisoners under HICOG Jurisdiction[1]

Trial/ Name	Original Sentence	Modified Sentence
Krupp (United States v. Krupp et al)		
Alfred Krupp	12 years	time served
F. v. Bülow	12	time served
Erich Müller	12	time served
E. Houdremont	10	time served
F. Janssen	10	time served
K. Eberhardt	9	time served
M. Ihn	9	time served
H. Korschan	6	time served
H. Lehmann	6	time served
Ministries (United States v. von Weizsäcker et al)		
G. Berger	25	10 years
E. Vessemayer	20	10
H. Kehrl	15	time served
P. Körner	15	10
P. Pleiger	15	9
W. Keppler	10	time served
v . Schwerin–Krosigk	10	time served
Hostages (United States v. List et al)		
W. List	life	no change
W. Kuntze	life	no change
L. Rendulic	20	10
W. Speidel	20	time served
H. Felmy	15	10
E. Leyser	10	time served
H. Lanz	12	time served

---

[1] "Landsberg: A Documentary Report," January 31, 1951, RG 466, Papers of John J. McCloy, Classified General Records 1949–1952, Box 24, D (51) 123.

Trial/ Name	Original Sentence	Modified Sentence
E. Dehner	7	time served
Justice Ministry (United States v. Altstötter et al)		
H. Klemm	life	20
G. Joel	10	time served
R. Öschey	life	20
O. Rothaug	life	20
E. Lautz	10	time served
W. v. Ammon	10	time served
F. Schlegelberger	life	medical parole
High Command (United States v. von Leeb et al)		
H. Reinecke	life	no change
W. Warlimont	life	18
G. v. Küchler	20	12
H. Hoth	15	no change
H.–G. Reinhardt	15	no change
Medical (United States v. Brandt et al)		
F. Fischer	life	15
K. Genzken	life	20
S. Handloser	life	20
G. Rose	life	15
H. Becker–Freysing	20	10
W. Beigelböck	15	10
H. Oberheuser	20	10
H. Poppendick	10	time served
Milch (United States v. Milch)		
E. Milch	life	15
RuSHa (United States v. Greifelt et al)		
R. Creutz	15	10
W. Lorenz	20	15
H. Brückner	15	time served
O. Hoffmann	25	15
F. Schwalm	10	time served
H. Hübner	10	time served

Trial/ Name	Original Sentence	Modified Sentence
SS Economic and Administrative Main Office (United States v. Pohl et al)		
O. Pohl	death	no change
F. Eirenschmalz	death	9
K. Sommer	life	20
K. Mummenthey	life	20
A. Frank	life	15
H.-K. Fanslaw	20	15
G. Lörner	life	15
H. Lörner	10	time served
H. Baier	15	time served
H. Pook	10	time served
L. Volk	10	8
E. Tschentscher	10	time served
M. Kiefer	20	time served
H. Hohberg	10	time served
Einsatzgruppen (United States v. Ohlendorf et al)		
P. Blobel	death	no change
E. Biberstein	death	life
W. Blume	death	25
W. Braune	death	no change
W. Hänsch	death	15
W. Klinghöfer	death	life
E. Naumann	death	no change
O. Ohlendorf	death	no change
A. Ott	death	life
M. Sandberger	death	life
H. Schubert	death	10
W. Seibert	death	15
E. Steimle	death	20
H. Jost	life	10
G. Noßke	life	10
W. v. Radetzky	20	time served
E. Schulz	20	15

Trial/ Name	Original Sentence	Modified Sentence
F. Six	20	10
L. Fendler	20	8
F. Rühl	10	time served

Flick (United States v. Flick et al)

The High Commissioner's decisions did not affect convicted war criminals from the Flick trial. These individuals either had been released or were already scheduled for release.

I.G. Farben (United States v. Krauch et al)

The High Commissioner's decisions did not affect convicted war criminals from this trial. They also had either been released or were already scheduled for release.

Totals

Number of cases	Result
10	no clemency (including 5 death sentences)
10	changed from death to life or less
15	changed from life to 15–20 years
21	changed from longterm to shortterm sentences
31	changed to time served
1	medical parole

Glossary of Names and Abbreviations

AHC	Allied High Commission
Article 6 board	mixed Allied-German clemency board; part of the contractuals
Auswärtiges Amt	German foreign office
Awtry, Lt.Col. J. H.	Assistant Chief, EUCOM War Crimes Branch
Baldwin, Raymond	U.S. Senator, chairman of Armed Services subcommittee investigation into the Malmédy trial
Bitter, Margarete	Official of the Central Legal Protection Office
Bolte, Gen. Charles L.	Commander in Chief, USAREUR
Bowie, Robert R.	General Counsel, HICOG
CCC	Civilian Conservation Corps
CDU	*Christlich-Demokratische Union* (Christian Democratic Union)
Clay, Gen. Lucius D.	U.S. Military Governor 1947-1949, Commander in Chief, EUCOM, until 1949
Conant, James B.	U.S. High Commissioner, January 1953-May 1955
CSU	*Christlich-Soziale Union* (Christian Social Union)
Dehler, Thomas	Federal Justice Minister
Donnelly, Walter J.	U.S. High Commissioner, August 1952-December 1952
DP	*Deutsche Partei* (German Party)
EDC	European Defense Community
Eddy, Gen. M.S.	Commander in Chief, USAREUR
Essener Amnestieausschuß	Essen Amnesty Committee; a private interest group
EUCOM	European Command, United States Army
FDP	*Freie Demokratische Partei* (Free Democratic Party)

Ferguson, Homer	U.S. Senator, chairman of the Investigative Subcommittee probe into the Ilse Koch trial
Fleischer, Col. Wade M.	Chief, EUCOM War Crimes Branch
François-Poncet, André	French High Commissioner
Gunn, Col. Damon M.	EUCOM Theater Judge Advocate 1949-1952
Hallstein, Walter	Deputy Foreign Minister
Handy, Gen. Thomas T.	Commander in Chief, EUCOM, after 1949
Harbaugh, Col. James L.	EUCOM Theater Judge Advocate 1947-1949
Heidelberger Juristenkreis	Heidelberg Circle of Jurists; a private interest group
Heusinger, Gen. Adolf	German rearmament negotiator
HICOG	U.S. High Commission for Germany
Hoppe, Wilhelm	foreign officer in charge of war criminals
Hütter, Margarete	FDP member of the *Bundestag*
IMPAC	Interim Parole and Clemency Board, 1953-1955 (U.S. zone)
JAD	Judge Advocate Division
Kirkpatrick, Ivonne	British High Commissioner
KPD	*Kommunistische Partei Deutschlands* (Communist Pary)
Landsberg	U.S. prison for German war criminals
McCloy, John J.	U.S. High Commissioner, June 1949-July 1952
McClure, Mark	Chairman, EUCOM War Crimes Modification Board
McNarney, Gen. Joseph	U.S. Military Governor 1945-1947
Mende, Erich	FDP member of the *Bundestag*
Merten, Hans	SPD member of the *Bundestag*
Mickelwait, Col. C.B.	EUCOM Theater Judge Advocate 1946-1947
Moran, Frederick	Member of HICOG Advisory Board on Clemency
OGPU	Soviet secret police agency under Stalin
OMGUS	Office of United States Military Government
Peck, David	Member of HICOG Advisory Board on Clemency
PWA	Public Works Administration
Reber, Samuel	Deputy U.S. High Commissioner
Schmid, Carlo	Chairman, *Bundestag* Committee for the Occupation Statute and Foreign Affairs
Snow, Conrad E.	Member of HICOG Advisory Board on Clemency
SPD	*Sozialdemokratische Partei Deutschlands* (Social Democratic Party)
Speidel, Gen. Hans	German rearmament negotiator
Strauβ, Walter	Deputy Federal Justice Minister
Trützschler, Heinz v.	foreign officer in charge of war criminals

USAREUR	United States Army, Europe
Wahl, Alfons	Federal Justice Ministry official in charge of war criminals
Wahl, Eduard	CDU member of the *Bundestag* and professor for international law
Werl	British prison for German war criminals
Wittlich	French prison for German war criminals
WPA	Works Progress Administration
Zentrale Rechtsschutzstelle	Central Legal Protection Office, justice ministry division, provided the defense of war criminals before foreign courts

References

A. UNPUBLISHED PRIMARY SOURCES

Bundesarchiv, Koblenz, West Germany

Files of the *Deutsches Friedensbüro*

Politisches Archiv, Auswärtiges Amt, Bonn, West Germany

Files of *Abteilung II des Auswärtigen Amtes* on the war criminals problem, the Article 6 mixed board, the *Bundestag* subcommittee "Prisoners of War," and United States-West German relations. File series: 515-11 II, 515-00 e II, 515-00 g II, 515-h II, and 210.01/80.

Bundeszwischenarchiv, St. Augustin/Hangelar, West Germany

Files of the Federal Justice Ministry. File series: B141.

Parlamentsarchiv, Bonn, West Germany

Debates and *Drucksachen* of the *Bundestag*, protocols of the *Rechtsausschuß, 1. Wahlperiode* and *2. Wahlperiode*.

General Branch, Civil Archives Branch, NARA

Record Group 84: Foreign Service Posts of the Department of State, Office of the United States High Commission for Germany.

Record Group 466: The United States High Commission for Germany, Papers of John J. McCloy, Classified General Records 1949-1952, Security-Segregated General Records, 1949-1952, Eyes Only File, Top Secret File; The United States High Commission for Germany, Classified General Records 1953-1955, Security-Segregated General Records 1953-1955.

Military Field Branch, Military Archives Division, NARA

Record Group 338: The United States Army in World War II, United States Army, Europe (USAREUR), files of the Theater Judge Advocate Division.

Harry S. Truman Library, Independence, Missouri

Naval Aide Files, State Department Briefs, Truman Papers; President's Secretary's File (PSF), Subject File, Foreign Affairs; PSF-Intelligence Files; Memoranda of Conversations, Acheson Papers; White House Central File, State Department Correspondence; Records of the NSC; Notes on Cabinet Meetings, Papers of Matthew J. Connelly; PSF-NSC.

Dwight D. Eisenhower Library, Abilene, Kansas

Official File, White House Central File; NSC Series, Ann Whitman File; Ann Whitman Diary Series.

B. PUBLISHED PRIMARY SOURCES

Bulletin des Presse- und Informationsamtes der Bundesregierung
Bundesanzeiger
Bundesgesetzblatt
Conduct of Ilse Koch War Crimes Trial. Interim Report of the Investigations Subcommittee of the Committee on Expenditures in the Executive Departments Pursuant to S. Res. 189. *Senate Reports*, December 27, 1948, Report No. 1775, Part 3, 80th Congress, 2nd Session.
Conduct of Ilse Koch War Crimes Trial. Hearings before the Investigations Subcommittee of the Committee on Expenditures in the Executive Departments Pursuant to S. Res. 189. 80th Congress, 2nd Session.
Congressional Record
Diplomatische Korrespondenz
Federal Register
Federal Reporter
Giese, Friedrich and Egon Schunck, eds. *Brundgesetz für die Bundesrepublik Deutschland.* Frankfurt: Kommentator, 1960.
Goodrich, Leland M. and Marie J. Carroll, eds. *Documents on American Foreign Relations, 1943-1944.* Boston: World Peace Foundation, 1945.
Hearings before a Subcommittee of the Committee on Armed Services, United States Senate. 81st Congress, 1st Session, Pursuant to S. Res. 42. Investigation of Action of Army With Respect to Trial of Persons Responsible for the Massacre of American Soldiers, Battle of Bulge, Near Malmédy, Belgium, December 1944.
International Military Tribunal. *Trial of the Major War Criminals.* 42 vols. Nuremberg: IMT, 1947.
Internationale Diplomatische Information
Löhr, Wolfgang, ed. *Dokumente deutscher Bischöfe: Hirtenbriefe und Ansprachen zu Gesellschaft und Politik 1945-1949.* 2 vols. Würzburg: Echter, 1985.
Mendelsohn, John, ed. *The Holocaust.* 18 vols. New York: Garland, 1982.
Merritt, Anna J. and Richard L. Merritt, eds. *Public Opinion in Occupied Germany: The OMGUS Surveys, 1945-1949.* Urbana: University of Illinois Press, 1970.
_____. *Public Opinion in Semi-Sovereign Germany: The HICOG Surveys, 1949-1955.* Urbana: University of Illinois Press, 1980.
Nuremberg Military Tribunals. *Trials of War Criminals.* 15 vols. Washington, D.C.: Government Printing Office, 1953.

Report of the Subcommittee of the Committee on Armed Services, United States Senate, 81st Congress, 1st Session, Pursuant to S. Res. 42, October 13, 1949.

Schnellinformation des Presse- und Informationsamtes der Bundesregierung

Smith, Bradley F., ed. *The American Road to Nuremberg: A Documentary Record.* Palo Alto: Hoover Institution Press, 1982.

Smith, Jean Edward, ed. *The Papers of General Lucius DuBignon Clay.* 2 vols. Bloomington: Indiana University Press, 1974.

United States Department of State *Bulletin*

United States Department of State. *Foreign Relations of the United States: The Conference at Malta and Yalta 1945.* Washington, D.C.: Government Printing Office, 1950.

_____. *Germany 1947-1949: The Story in Documents.* Washington, D.C.: Government Printing Office, 1953.

_____. *Foreign Relations of the United States, 1943.* 6 vols. Washington, D.C.: Government Printing Office, 1964.

_____. *Foreign Relations of the United States: The Conferences at Cairo and Tehran 1943.* Washington, D.C.: Government Printing Office, 1966.

_____. *Foreign Relations of the United States, 1944.* 7 vols. Washington, D.C.: Government Printing Office, 1966.

_____. *Foreign Relations of the United States: The Conference at Quebec 1944.* Washington, D.C.: Government Printing Office, 1972.

_____. *Foreign Relations of the United States, 1952-1954.* 16 vols. Washington, D.C.: Government Printing Office, 1983.

USAREUR Releases

U.S. Reports

Verhandlungen des deutschen Bundestages

C. SECONDARY SOURCES—BOOKS

Adenauer, Konrad. *Memoirs 1945-1953.* Chicago: Regnery, 1966.

Baring, Arnulf. *Außenpolitik in Adenauers Kanzlerdemokratie.* Munich: Oldenbourg, 1965.

Benton, Wilbourn E., ed. *Nuremberg: German Views of the War Trials.* Dallas: Southern Methodist University Press, 1955.

Blum, John Morton. *From the Morgenthau Diaries.* 3 vols. Boston: Houghton Mifflin, 1967.

Bosch, William J. *Judgment on Nuremberg.* Chapel Hill: University of North Carolina Press, 1970.

Botzenhart-Viehe, Verena. "The German Reaction to the American Occupation, 1944-1947." Ph.D. diss., University of California-Santa Barbara, 1980.

Bower, Tom. *The Pledge Betrayed: America and Britain and the Denazification of Germany.* New York: Doubleday, 1982.

Campbell, Thomas M. and George C. Herring. *The Diaries of Edward R. Stettinius, 1943-1946.* New York: New Viewpoints, 1975.

Central Commission for the Investigation of German War Crimes in Poland. *German Crimes in Poland.* New York: Fertig, 1982.

Dallek, Robert. *Franklin D. Roosevelt and American Foreign Policy, 1932-1945.* New York: Oxford University Press, 1979.

Eisenhower, Dwight D. *Crusade in Europe.* New York: Doubleday, 1948.

Feingold, Henry L. *The Politics of Rescue: The Roosevelt Administration and the Holocaust, 1938-1945.* New Brunswick: Rutgers University Press, 1970.

Frederiksen, Oliver J. *The American Military Occupation of Germany, 1945-1953.* Karlsruhe: USAREUR, 1953.

Friedrich, Jörg. *Die kalte Amnestie.* Frankfurt: Fischer, 1984.

Gatzke, Hans Wilhelm. *Germany and the United States: A Special Relationship?* Cambridge, Mass.: Harvard University Press, 1980.

Gilbert, Martin. *Auschwitz and the Allies.* New York: Holt, Rinehart, and Winston, 1981.

Gimbel, John. *The American Occupation of Germany: Politics and the Military, 1945-1949.* Palo Alto: Stanford University Press, 1968.

Gimbel, John and John Hennessey, eds. *From Coalition to Confrontation: Readings on Cold War Origins.* Belmont, Calif.: Wadsworth, 1972.

Gordon, Sarah. *Hitler, Germans and the "Jewish Question."* Princeton: Princeton University Press, 1984.

Grabbe, Hans-Jürgen. *Unionsparteien, Sozialdemokratie, und Vereinigte Staaten von Amerika, 1945-1966.* (Beiträge zur Geschichte des Parlamentarismus und der politischen Parteien, Nr. 71.) Düsseldorf: Droste, 1983.

Gutscher, Jörg Michael. *Die Entwicklung der FDP von ihren Anfängen bis 1961.* Königstein: Hain, 1984.

Hanrieder, Wolfram. *West German Foreign Policy, 1949-1963: International Pressure and Domestic Response.* Palo Alto: Stanford University Press, 1967.

Hilberg, Raoul. *The Destruction of the European Jews.* 3 vols. New York: Holmes and Meier, 1985.

Hiscocks, Richard. *The Adenauer Era.* New York: Lippincott, 1966.

Hull, Cordell. *The Memoirs of Cordell Hull.* 2 vols. New York: Macmillan, 1948.

Jackson, Robert H. *The Nürnberg Case.* New York: Knopf, 1947.

Jacobsen, Hans A., ed. *Deutschland und die Welt; zur Außenpolitik der Bundesrepublik 1949-1963.* Munich: dtv, 1966.

Kelly, Alfred H., Winfred A. Harbison, and Herman Belz. *The American Constitution: Its Origins and Development.* New York: Norton, 1983.

Kimball, Warren F. *Swords or Ploughshares? The Morgenthau Plan for a Defeated Germany, 1943-1945.* New York: Lippincott, 1976.

Kirkpatrick, Ivonne. *The Inner Circle: Memoirs.* London: Macmillan, 1959.

Lerner, Daniel and Raymond Aron. *France Defeats EDC.* New York: Praeger, 1957.

McGeehan, Robert. *The German Rearmament Question: American Diplomacy and European Defense after World War II.* Urbana: University of Illinois Press, 1971.

Merkl, Peter H., ed. *Germany: Yesterday and Tomorrow.* New York: Oxford University Press, 1965.

————. *West German Foreign Policy: Dilemmas and Directions.* Chicago: Chicago Council on Foreign Relations, 1982.

Montgomery, John D. *Forced To Be Free: The Artificial Revolution in Germany and Japan.* Chicago: University of Chicago Press, 1957.

Morgenthau, Henry, Jr. *Germany Is Our Problem.* New York: Harper, 1945.

Nobleman, Eli E. *American Military Courts in Germany: With a Special Reference to Historic Practice and Their Role in the Democratization of the German People.* Fort Gordon, Ga.: U.S. Army, Civil Affairs School, 1961.

Peterson, Edward N. *The American Occupation of Germany: Retreat to Victory.* Detroit: Wayne State University Press, 1977.

Plischke, Elmer. *Allied High Commission Relations with the West German Government.* Bad Godesberg: HICOG Historical Division, 1952.

_____. *Revision of the Occupation Statute for Germany.* Bad Godesberg: HICOG Historical Division, 1952.

_____. *The Allied High Commission for Germany.* Bad Godesberg: HICOG Historical Division, 1953.

Pogue, Forrest C. *The Supreme Command,* in the official Army history, *The United States Army in World War II: The European Theater of Operations.* Washington, D.C.: Government Printing Office, 1954.

Prittie, Terence C. *Konrad Adenauer, 1876-1967.* Chicago: Cowles, 1971.

Reeves, Thomas C. *The Life and Times of Joe McCarthy: A Biography.* New York: Stein and Day, 1982.

Rothenpieler, Friedrich Wilhelm. *Der Gedanke einer Kollektivschuld in juristischer Sicht.* Berlin: Duncker, 1982.

Rückerl, Adalbert. *NS-Verbrechen vor Gericht.* Heidelberg: Müller, 1982.

Schmitt, Hans A., ed. *U.S. Occupation of Europe after World War II.* Lawrence: Regents Press of Kansas, 1978.

Schuster, George N. *The Ground I Walked On.* Notre Dame: Notre Dame University Press, 1969.

Schwartz, Thomas A. "From Occupation to Alliance: John J. McCloy and the Allied High Commission in the Federal Republic of Germany 1949-1952." Ph.D. diss., Harvard University, 1985.

Schwarz, Hans-Peter. *Vom Reich zur Bundesrepublik. Deutschland im Widerstreit der außenpolitischen Konzeption in den Jahren der Besatzungsherrschaft 1945-1949.* Neuwied: Luchterhand, 1966.

Smith, Bradley F. *Reaching Judgment at Nuremberg.* New York: Basic Books, 1977.

_____. *The Road to Nuremberg.* New York: Basic Books, 1981.

Smith, Glenn H. *Langer of North Dakota: A Study in Isolationism 1940-1959.* New York: Garland, 1979.

Stimson, Henry L. and McGeorge Bundy. *On Active Service in Peace and War.* New York: Harper, 1947.

Snyder, Louis L. *Roots of German Nationalism.* Bloomington: Indiana University Press, 1978.

Tauber, Kurt P. *Beyond Eagle and Swastika: German Nationalism since 1945.* 2 vols. Middletown, Conn.: Wesleyan University Press, 1967.

Tent, James F. *Mission on the Rhine: Reeducation and Denazification in American-Occupied Germany.* Chicago: University of Chicago Press, 1982.

Thayer, Charles W. *The Unquiet Germans.* New York: Harper, 1957.

Turner, Henry Ashby. *The Two Germanies since 1945.* New Haven: Yale University Press, 1987.

Vogelsang, Thilo. *Das geteilte Deutschland.* Munich: dtv, 1966.

Weingartner, James F. *Crossroads of Death: The Story of the Malmédy Massacre and Trial.* Berkeley: University of California Press, 1979.

Wettig, Gerhard. *Entmilitarisierung und Wiederbewaffnung in Deutschland 1943-1955. Internationale Auseinandersetzung um die Rolle der Deutschen in Europa.* Munich: Oldenbourg, 1967.

Willis, F. Roy. *France, Germany and the New Europe, 1945-1967.* Palo Alto: Stanford University Press, 1968.

Wolfe, Robert, ed. *Americans as Proconsuls: United States Military Government in Germany and Japan, 1944-1952.* Carbondale: Southern Illinois University Press, 1984.

Ziemke, Earl F. *The U.S. Army in the Occupation of Germany, 1944-1946.* Washington, D.C.: Government Printing Office, 1975.

Zink, Harold. *The United States in Germany, 1944-1955.* Princeton: Nostrand, 1957.

D. SECONDARY SOURCES—ARTICLES

Benz, Wolfgang. "Versuche zur Reform des öffentlichen Dienstes in Deutschland 1945-1952: Deutsche Opposition gegen alliierte Initiativen." *Vierteljahrshefte für Zeitgeschichte* 29 (1981), 216-245.

Boyens, Armin. "Das Stuttgarter Schuldbekenntnis vom 19. Oktober 1945—Entstehung und Bedeutung." *Vierteljahrshefte für Zeitgeschichte* 19 (1971), 374-397.

Chamberlin, Brewster S. "Todesmühlen. Ein Versuch zur Umerziehung." *Vierteljahrshefte für Zeitgeschichte* 29 (1981), 420-436.

Connor, Ian. "The Churches and the Refugee Problem in Bavaria 1945-49." *Journal of Contemporary History* 20 (1985), 399-421.

Conway, John S. "How Shall the Nations Repent? The Stuttgart Declaration of Guilt, October 1945." *The Journal of Ecclesiastical History* 38 (1988), 596-622.

Diehl, James M. "Change and Continuity in the Treatment of the German *Kriegsopfer.*" *Central European History* 18 (1985), 170-187.

Doenecke, Justus D. "Protest over Malmédy: A Case of Clemency." *Peace and Change* 4 (1977), 28-33.

Dorn, Walter L. "Die Debatte über die amerikanische Besatzungspolitik für Deutschland (1944-1945)." *Vierteljahrshefte für Zeitgeschichte* 20 (1972), 39-62.

Gimbel, John. "Byrnes' Stuttgarter Rede und die amerikanische Nachkriegspolitik in Deutschland." *Vierteljahrshefte für Zeitgeschichte* 20 (1972), 39-62.

―――. "The American Reparations Stop in Germany. An Essay on the Political Uses of History." *Historian* 37 (1974/75), 276-296.

Hahn, Erich J.C. "Hajo Holborn: Bericht zur deutschen Frage. Beobachtungen und Empfehlungen vom Herbst 1947." *Vierteljahrshefte für Zeitgeschichte* 35 (1987), 135-166.

Hammond, Paul Y. "Directives for the Occupation of Germany: The Washington Controversy," in Harold Stein, ed., *American Civil-Military Decisions* (Birmingham: University of Alabama Press, 1963), 311-464.

Koessler, Maximilian. "American War Crimes Trials in Europe." *Georgetown Law Journal* 9 (1950), 18-112.

Krieger, Wolfgang. "Was General Clay a Revisionist? Strategic Aspects of the United States Occupation of Germany." *Journal of Contemporary History* 18 (1983), 165-184.

Marshall, Barbara. "German Attitudes to British Military Government 1945-1947." *Journal of Contemporary History* 15 (1980), 655-684.

Mendelsohn, John. "War Crimes Trials and Clemency in Germany and Japan," in Robert Wolfe, ed., *Americans as Proconsuls: United States Military Govern-*

ment in Germany and Japan, 1944-1952 (Carbondale: Southern Illinois University Press, 1984), 226-259.

_____. "Trial by Document: The Problem of Due Process for War Criminals at Nuremberg." *Prologue* 8 (1975), 227-234.

Moltmann, Günter. "Zur Formulierung der amerikanischen Besatzungspolitik in Deutschland am Ende des Zweiten Weltkrieges." *Vierteljahrshefte für Zeitgeschichte* 15 (1967), 299-322.

Niethammer, Lutz. "Zum Verhältnis von Reform und Rekonstruktion in der US-Zone am Beispiel der Neuordnung des öffentlichen Dienstes." *Vierteljahrshefte für Zeitgeschichte* 21 (1973), 177-188.

Nobleman, Eli E. "American Military Government Courts in Germany." *The Annals of the American Academy of Political and Social Science* 267 (1950), 87-97.

Plischke, Elmer. "Contractual Agreements and Changing Allied-West German Relations." *Political Science Quarterly* 69 (1954), 241-265.

Prowe, Diethelm. "The New *Nachkriegsgeschichte* (1945-1949): West Germans in Search of their Historical Origins." *Central European History* 10 (1977), 312-328.

Schwartz, Thomas A. "The 'Skeleton Key'—American Foreign Policy, European Unity, and German Rearmament." *Central European History* 19 (1986), 369-385.

Stokes, Lawrence D. "The German People and the Destruction of the European Jews." *Central European History* 6 (1973), 167-191.

Vogel, Walter. "Deutschland, Europa, und die Umgestaltung der amerikanischen Sicherheitspolitik 1945-1949." *Vierteljahrshefte für Zeitgeschichte* 19 (1971), 64-82.

E. PERIODICALS

Abendpost
Bonner Rundschau
Chicago Tribune
The Christian Century
Die Deutsche Zeitung und Wirtschaftszeitung
Neue Zeitung
The New York Times
Presse- und Funkbericht
The Progressive
Volksrecht
Die Welt

Index

About the Author

FRANK M. BUSCHER is an Assistant Professor of History at Christian Brothers College in Memphis, Tennessee.